West Greenlandic

This grammar provides a clear and comprehensive overview of contemporary West Greenlandic. It follows a systematic order of topics beginning with the alphabet and phonology, continuing with nominal and verbal morphology and syntax, and concluding with more advanced topics such as complex sentences and word formation. Grammatical points are illustrated with authentic examples reflecting current life in Greenland. Grammatical terminology is explained fully for the benefit of readers without a background in linguistics.

Features include:

- Full grammatical breakdowns of all examples for ease of identifying individual components of complex words.
- A detailed contents list and index for easy access to information.
- An alphabetical list of the most commonly used West Greenlandic suffixes.
- A glossary of grammatical abbreviations used in the volume.

The book is suitable for a wide range of users, including independent and classroom-based learners of West Greenlandic, as well as linguists and anyone with an interest in Greenland's official language.

Lily Kahn is Professor of Hebrew and Jewish Languages at University College London (UCL). Her research areas include endangered and minority languages, as well as translation studies. She is co-editor with Riitta-Liisa Valijärvi of two UCL Press book series, *Grammars of World and Minority Languages* and *Textbooks of World and Minority Languages*.

Riitta-Liisa Valijärvi is Associate Professor of Finnish and Minority Languages at UCL and Senior Lecturer in Finnish and Finno-Ugric Languages at Uppsala University, Sweden. Her research interests include endangered and minority languages, language pedagogy, and song lyrics. Relevant publications include *Finnish Tutor* (2017) and *North Sámi: An Essential Grammar* (with Lily Kahn; Routledge, 2017).

Routledge Essential Grammars

Essential Grammars describe clearly and succinctly the core rules of each language and are up-to-date and practical reference guides to the most important aspects of languages used by contemporary native speakers. They are designed for elementary to intermediate learners and present an accessible description of the language, focusing on the real patterns of use today.

Essential Grammars are a reference source for the learner and user of the language, irrespective of level, setting out the complexities of the language in short, readable sections that are clear and free from jargon.

Essential Grammars are ideal either for independent study or for students in schools, colleges, universities and adult classes of all types.

Essential Grammars are available for the following languages:

Bosnian, Croatian, Montenegrin and Serbian
Catalan
Chinese
Czech
Danish
Dutch
English
Finnish
German
Greek
Hindi
Hungarian
Korean
Latvian
Modern Hebrew
North Sámi
Norwegian
Polish
Portuguese
Romanian
Serbian
Spanish
Swedish
Thai
Turkish
Urdu
Vietnamese
West Greenlandic

For more information about this series, please visit: www.routledge.com/Routledge-Essential-Grammars/book-series/SE0549

West Greenlandic

An Essential Grammar

 Lily Kahn and Riitta-Liisa Valijärvi

LONDON AND NEW YORK

First published 2022
by Routledge
2 Park Square, Milton Park, Abingdon, Oxon OX14 4RN

and by Routledge
605 Third Avenue, New York, NY 10158

Routledge is an imprint of the Taylor & Francis Group, an informa business

© 2022 Lily Kahn and Riitta-Liisa Valijärvi

The right of Lily Kahn and Riitta-Liisa Valijärvi to be identified as authors of this work has been asserted by them in accordance with sections 77 and 78 of the Copyright, Designs and Patents Act 1988.

All rights reserved. No part of this book may be reprinted or reproduced or utilised in any form or by any electronic, mechanical, or other means, now known or hereafter invented, including photocopying and recording, or in any information storage or retrieval system, without permission in writing from the publishers.

Trademark notice: Product or corporate names may be trademarks or registered trademarks, and are used only for identification and explanation without intent to infringe.

British Library Cataloguing-in-Publication Data
A catalogue record for this book is available from the British Library

Library of Congress Cataloging-in-Publication Data
Names: Kahn, Lily, author. | Valijärvi, Riitta-Liisa, author.
Title: West Greenlandic : an essential grammar / Lily Kahn and Riitta-Liisa Valijärvi.
Description: Abingdon, Oxon ; New York, NY : Routledge, 2022. | Series: Routledge essential grammars | Includes bibliographical references and index.
Identifiers: LCCN 2021014501 (print) | LCCN 2021014502 (ebook) | ISBN 9781138063693 (hardback) | ISBN 9781138063709 (paperback) | ISBN 9781315160863 (ebook)
Subjects: LCSH: Kalâtdlisut dialect—Grammar.
Classification: LCC PM62 .K26 2022 (print) | LCC PM62 (ebook) | DDC 497/.12—dc23
LC record available at https://lccn.loc.gov/2021014501
LC ebook record available at https://lccn.loc.gov/2021014502

ISBN: 978-1-138-06369-3 (hbk)
ISBN: 978-1-138-06370-9 (pbk)
ISBN: 978-1-315-16086-3 (ebk)

DOI: 10.4324/9781315160863

Typeset in Sabon
by Apex CoVantage, LLC

Ataatama inuunermik tunivaanga
Ataatama oqaatsikka pinngortippai
Ataatama Henrik Motzfeldtip eqqaaneqarnera ataqqinartuuli

My father gave me my life
My father gave me my language
Honoured be my father Henrik Motzfeldt's memory

—Naja Motzfeldt

This book is dedicated to the loving memory of Henrik Motzfeldt.

—Riitta-Liisa Valijärvi and Lily Kahn

Contents

Acknowledgements xii
List of abbreviations xiii

Chapter 1 Introduction   1

1.1 Greenlandic within the Eskimo-Aleut language family   1
1.2 Greenlandic language varieties   3
1.3 Historical and sociolinguistic introduction to West Greenlandic   4
    1.3.1 Early history of Greenlandic   4
    1.3.2 History of written West Greenlandic   4
    1.3.3 Contemporary West Greenlandic   5
    1.3.4 Aspects of Greenlandic culture   8
1.4 Characteristic features of West Greenlandic   9
1.5 How to use this grammar   12
    1.5.1 Overall approach   12
    1.5.2 Dictionary forms of words   12
    1.5.3 Additive and truncative suffixes   12
    1.5.4 Examples of grammatical points   13
    1.5.5 Glossing   13

Chapter 2 Phonology and orthography   17

2.1 The alphabet   17
2.2 Vowels   17
2.3 Consonants   19
2.4 Syllables, stress, and intonation   22
2.5 Morphophonological variation   23
    2.5.1 Consonant changes   23
    2.5.2 Vowel changes   25

	2.5.3	Helping vowel -i-	26
	2.5.4	Loss of glides (j and **v**)	27
	2.5.5	Stem types	27
	2.5.6	Sound alternation in the beginning of suffixes	28
2.6	Kleinschmidt's orthography		30

Chapter 3 Nouns   31

3.1	Case and number		31
3.2	Noun stem types		32
	3.2.1	Weak stems	33
	3.2.2	Weak stems with gemination	34
	3.2.3	Additional weak-stem patterns	36
	3.2.4	Weak t-stems	38
	3.2.5	Strong stems	40
	3.2.6	Extra-strong q-stems: word-final q > r	40
	3.2.7	Strong q-stems: word-final -q disappears or becomes -r	41
	3.2.8	Strong stems in -aq > -ap and -at	41
	3.2.9	Strong stems with nasalisation	42
	3.2.10	Strong stems with metathesis	43
	3.2.11	Strong k-stems	46
	3.2.12	Strong k-stems with extra -a- in the grammatical cases	47
3.3	Function of cases		48
	3.3.1	Absolutive	48
	3.3.2	Relative	49
	3.3.3	Allative	50
	3.3.4	Locative	51
	3.3.5	Ablative	52
	3.3.6	Instrumental	54
	3.3.7	Prolative	60
	3.3.8	Equative	63
3.4	Possessive inflection		64
	3.4.1	Possessive absolutive	64
	3.4.2	Possessive relative	68
	3.4.3	Possessive allative	71
	3.4.4	Possessive locative	73
	3.4.5	Possessive ablative	76
	3.4.6	Possessive instrumental	78
	3.4.7	Possessive prolative	81
	3.4.8	Possessive equative	83
3.5	Collective suffixes		85

Chapter 4   Pronouns   87

    4.1   Personal   87
    4.2   Demonstrative   90
    4.3   Interrogative   93
    4.4   Reflexive   96
    4.5   Reciprocal   98
    4.6   Other   100

Chapter 5   Numerals   105

    5.1   Cardinal   105
    5.2   Ordinal   114

Chapter 6   Noun modification (= adjectives)   119

    6.1   Attributive modifiers   119
    6.2   Predicative modifiers   129
    6.3   Comparison   132
        6.3.1   Comparative   132
        6.3.2   Superlative   135

Chapter 7   Verbs   142

    7.1   Person and number   142
        7.1.1   Subject suffixes   142
        7.1.2   Object suffixes   143
    7.2   Mood   144
        7.2.1   Independent/main moods   145
        7.2.2   Subordinate moods   165
    7.3   Tense   190
        7.3.1   Present tense   190
        7.3.2   Past tense   191
        7.3.3   Future tense   195
    7.4   Aspect   201
        7.4.1   Completed   201
        7.4.2   Habitual   201
        7.4.3   Inchoative   204
    7.5   Modality   205
    7.6   Evidentiality   207
    7.7   Causativity   210
    7.8   Reflexivity and reciprocity   213

7.8.1	Reflexivity	213
7.8.2	Reciprocity	214
7.9	Passivity	215
7.10	Valency	219
7.11	Negation	224
7.11.1	Basic negative suffixes	224
7.11.2	Negative suffixes with more specific meanings	240
7.11.3	Negative intransitive participle	243
7.11.4	Negative indefinite pronouns and adverbs	244
7.11.5	Periphrastic negative constructions	245

Chapter 8   Participles   248

8.1	Intransitive participle	248
8.2	Passive participle	252
8.3	Abstract participle	257

Chapter 9   Adverbs   262

9.1	Manner	262
9.2	Time	266
9.3	Place and direction	270
9.4	Degree, measure, and quantity	272
9.5	Modal	278
9.6	Interrogative	279

Chapter 10   Postpositions   281

10.1	Place and direction	281
10.2	Time	285
10.3	Other	288

Chapter 11   Conjunctions   291

11.1	Coordinating	291
11.2	Subordinating	292

Chapter 12   Particles   293

12.1	Discourse particles and interjections	293
12.2	Enclitic particles	294

Chapter 13 Suffixes 297

13.1 Suffix types 297
13.2 Order of suffixes 298

Chapter 14 Phrases, clauses, and sentences 301

14.1 Basic word order 301
14.2 Incorporation 303
    14.2.1 Incorporated predicative 303
    14.2.2 Incorporated direct object 305
    14.2.3 Incorporated noun in oblique cases 308
14.3 Definiteness 311
14.4 Clause types 312
    14.4.1 Copular 312
    14.4.2 Intransitive 313
    14.4.3 Transitive 315
    14.4.4 Half-transitive 316
    14.4.5 Double transitive 316
    14.4.6 Existential 317
    14.4.7 Possessive 319
    14.4.8 Impersonal 323
    14.4.9 Interrogative 324
14.5 Complex sentences 325
    14.5.1 Adverbial 325
    14.5.2 Relative 330
    14.5.3 Complement 332

List of essential suffixes 333
Suggested resources 337
Index 339

Acknowledgements

We would like to thank our editor at Routledge, Andrea Hartill, for her unwavering enthusiasm and guidance throughout this project. Our fieldwork trip was generously supported by the UCL Grand Challenges and Global Engagement funds, and Otavan Kirjasäätiö in Finland. The publication of the volume was also supported by the Department of Modern Languages at Uppsala University in Sweden. Our warmest thanks go to our teacher Marie Møller Udvang and to our fantastic language consultant, Naja Motzfeldt. We owe a special debt of gratitude to Naja Blytmann Trondhjem of the University of Copenhagen and to Sofie Kruse of Tech College Greenland for their exceptional linguistic expertise and invaluable comments on the manuscript. We are also very grateful to the wonderful James Holz for the maps and cheerful support, to the amazing Chris Ward for the encouragement, driving, and takeaways, and to both for the outstanding animal husbandry.

Abbreviations

The following chart lists the abbreviations used in the glossing of West Greenlandic examples appearing throughout this grammar. (See section 1.5.5 for discussion of glossing.)

1	first person
2	second person
3	third person
4	fourth person
ABL	ablative case
ABS	absolutive case
ALL	allative case
AP	abstract participle (verbal noun, gerund)
CAUS	causative mood
COLL	collective suffix
COMP	comparative
CONT	contemporative mood
EQU	equative case
FUT	future
HAB	habitual (progressive)
HV	helping vowel
INS	instrumental case
IMP	imperative mood
IP	intransitive participle
INT	interrogative mood
LOC	locative case
NEG	negative
OPT	optative mood
PART	participial mood
PASS	passive
PAST	past tense
PERF	perfect tense

Abbreviations

PL	plural
PP	passive participle
PRO	prolative case
REC	reciprocal suffix
REL	relative case
SG	singular
SUP	superlative
VAL	valency-changing suffix
>	subject to object

Chapter 1

Introduction

1.1 Greenlandic within the Eskimo-Aleut language family

The Eskimo-Aleut languages are spoken in the Arctic regions of Alaska and Canada, in Greenland, and in the Chukchi Peninsula in Eastern Siberia, as illustrated in Map 1.1.

Eskimo-Aleut languages are not related to the other Indigenous languages of the Americas. They are believed to be relatively late arrivals from Siberia, sharing a similar grammatical structure and vocabulary. The Eskimo-Aleut family is divided into two branches, Eskimo and Aleut, which diverged around 2000 BCE. The Aleut branch has a single representative, Aleut, which is spoken only by around 100 people on the Aleut islands in Alaska and Russia. The Eskimo languages are divided into two branches, Yupik and Inuit, which are thought have diverged around 1,000 years ago. Central Alaskan Yupik has the second largest number of speakers of any Native American language in the United States (after Diné/Navajo): Yupik has around 14,000 speakers and Diné/Navajo around 150,000 speakers. There are a few hundred speakers of Yupik varieties in Russia. These include Central Siberian Yupik (which also has speakers in Alaska) and Naukan Yupik. Sirenik, another Siberian variety, is now extinct.

Inuit languages are spoken in Greenland, Canada, and Alaska, with the majority in Greenland and Canada. The Inuit languages are closely related to each other and generally mutually intelligible. The resemblance between them is similar to the one between the Romance languages or the Scandinavian languages. There are three main Inuit languages: Iñupiaq (2,000 speakers in Alaska), Inuktut (an umbrella term for related Inuit dialects spoken the territory of Nunavut in Canada, of which the biggest is Inuktitut, with around 35,000 speakers), and West Greenlandic (around 50,000 speakers). Another Canadian Inuit variety is Inuvialuktun (Western Canadian Inuit or Western Canadian Inuktitut), which is highly endangered, has

DOI: 10.4324/9781315160863-1

1
Introduction

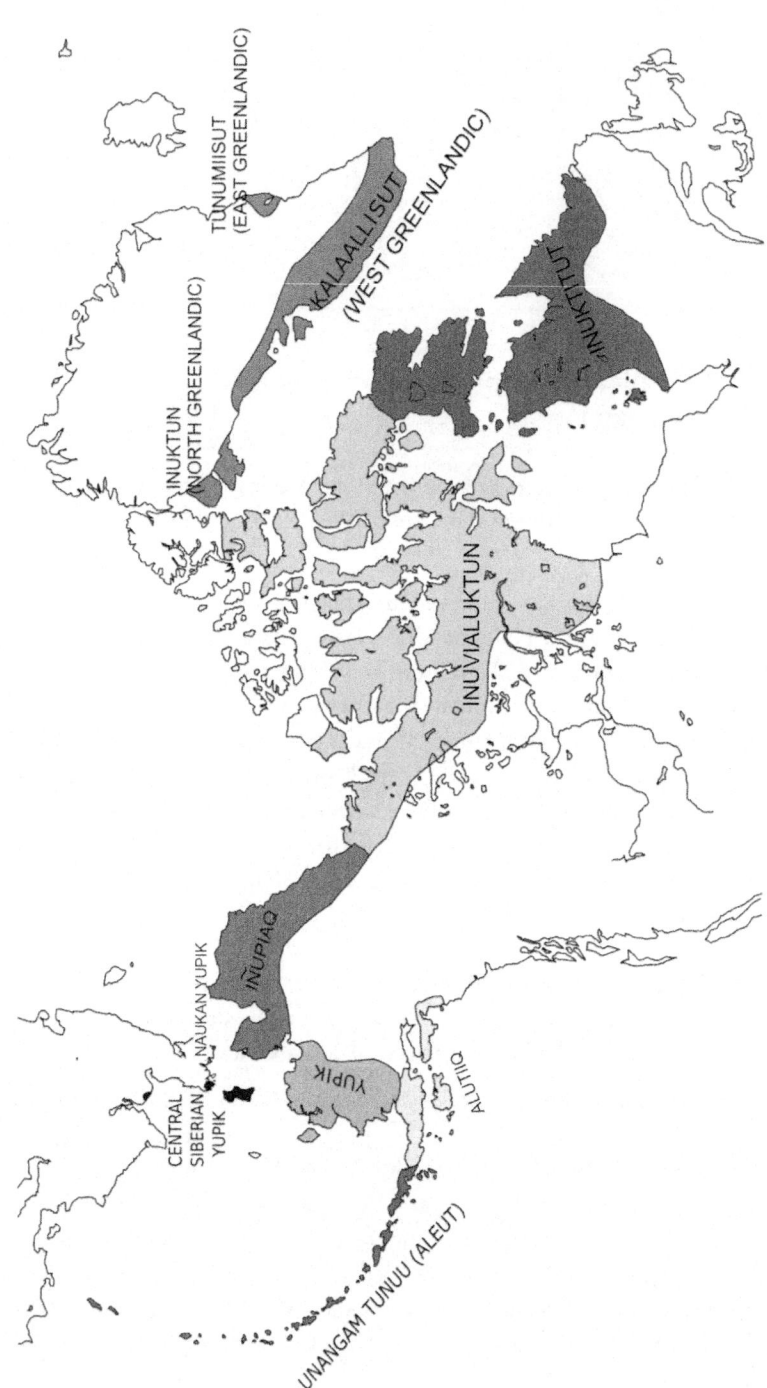

Map 1.1 Eskimo-Aleut languages

a number of different dialects, and is spoken by around 600–1,000 people. Inuktut is written with a syllabic script that was first invented by Protestant missionaries in the mid-1800s to write the Cree language and was adapted for Inuktitut shortly thereafter. The others are written using forms of the Latin alphabet. For a comparative dictionary of Eskimo-Aleut vocabulary, see Fortescue, Jacobson, and Kaplan (2010), listed in the 'Suggested Resources' section at the end of this book.

1.2 Greenlandic language varieties

There are three varieties of Greenlandic: North Greenlandic (also known as Inuktun, Thule Inuit, or Polar Eskimo), which has around 800 speakers, West Greenlandic (also known as Kalaallisut), which has around 50,000 speakers and is the official variety of the language, and East Greenlandic (also known as Tunumiisut), which has around 3,000 speakers. There are differences in pronunciation, grammar, and vocabulary between the three

Table 1.1 Words from the different varieties of Greenlandic

North Greenlandic	West Greenlandic	East Greenlandic	English
nivirhiaq	**niviarsiaraq**	**niiarsiaq**	girl, unmarried woman
ataata	**ataata**	**alaala**	father
irniq	**erneq**	**irniq**	son
inuk	**inuk**	**iik**	person
uanga	**uanga**	**uara**	I
ihhit	**illit**	**ittit**	you (SG)
humi	**sumi**	**sumi**	where
auk	**aak**	**aak**	blood
ihi	**isi**	**ili**	eye
aghak	**assak**	**attak**	hand
arvik	**arfeq**	**arpiq**	whale
tuktu	**tuttu**	**tuttu**	reindeer
qughuk	**qussuk**	**qutsuk**	swan
hiqiniq	**seqineq**	**siirliq**	sun
ulluriaq	**ulloriaq**	**utturiaq**	star
atauhiq	**ataaseq**	**alaasiq**	one

varieties, to such an extent that speakers of one can struggle to understand speakers of another. Table 1.1 illustrates some of the differences between the different varieties of Greenlandic.

1.3 Historical and sociolinguistic introduction to West Greenlandic

1.3.1 Early history of Greenlandic

There is evidence of human settlement in Greenland dating back as far as 2500 BCE. The Saqqaq people migrated to Greenland from Canada around this time and lived there until 800 BCE. The next wave of migration was the Dorset people, a pre-Inuit Eskimo culture, who settled on the island around 1000 BCE. The Thule population, the ancestors of the modern Inuit, arrived in Greenland by the 13th century CE. They first settled in the north of Greenland and then migrated along the coast to the south and east. Their language was the ancestor of the modern Greenlandic varieties. In addition, in the late 10th century CE Viking colonies were established in southwestern Greenland, led by Eric the Red, who came from Iceland around 985. Eric the Red is believed to have given Greenland its name, and the Vikings introduced Christianity to the country. The Vikings spoke a variety of Old Norse (closely related to present-day Icelandic). The Viking settlements in Greenland are estimated to have comprised around 5,000 people at their largest but dwindled and disappeared around the 14th century. There was most likely interaction between the Inuit and Viking populations in southern Greenland, though the extent of this, and of any linguistic contact between the two groups, is unclear. In addition to the Vikings, whale hunters from all over Europe had contact with the Inuit population of Greenland.

1.3.2 History of written West Greenlandic

In the early 1700s, Greenland came under Danish control; the first written records of Greenlandic date to this period, when Danish and Norwegian missionaries and colonisers arrived in the country and began to document the language. Poul Hansen Egede (1708–1789) played a key role in the early development of written Greenlandic. He moved to Greenland from Denmark in 1721 at the age of 12 with his father, the Norwegian missionary Hans Egede, who dreamed of converting the Norsemen of Greenland from Catholicism to Lutheranism. Upon arrival,

Hans Egede discovered that there were no longer any Norsemen on the island, but the family stayed and founded a Christian mission among the local Inuit population in the area of the modern-day capital city of Nuuk. Hans Egede later returned to Denmark, and Poul took over the mission, where he taught theology. Poul later became the Bishop of Greenland. Poul Egede's contribution to the development of written Greenlandic consists of a Greenlandic–Danish–Latin dictionary (1750), a Greenlandic catechism (1756), and a Greenlandic grammar (1760). He also co-produced the first Greenlandic translation of the New Testament (1766) together with Arnarsaq (ca. 1716–1778), a female missionary, interpreter, and translator from northern Greenland, and Hans Punngujooq, one of Egede's students.

Another central figure in the development of written Greenlandic was Samuel Kleinschmidt (1814–1886). Kleinschmidt was the son of Moravian missionaries but was born and bred in Greenland. His father was German and his mother was Danish, and he grew up trilingual in Greenlandic, German, and Danish. He studied Latin, Greek, Hebrew, French, Dutch, and English and worked as a pharmacist's apprentice in Holland. He wrote a grammar of West Greenlandic called *Grammatik der grönländischen Sprache* (1851) and a West Greenlandic-Danish dictionary called *Den grønlandske ordbog* (1871), as well as revising and finalising the first complete West Greenlandic translation of the entire Bible (1893), which his father had begun. In addition, Kleinschmidt devised an orthography for West Greenlandic which remained in use until 1973, when it was replaced by the current orthography. Because Kleinschmidt's orthography was used to write West Greenlandic for much of the 20th century, it is still helpful for learners of the language to familiarise themselves with it because they may need to access texts printed in it. See section 2.6 for a conversion chart between Kleinschmidt's orthography and the current one.

1.3.3 Contemporary West Greenlandic

West Greenlandic, also known as Kalaallisut, has around 50,000 speakers. The vast majority of these are based in Greenland, but there are also a few thousand speakers in Denmark. Until 2009 West Greenlandic and Danish were both official languages in Greenland, but since 2009 (when Greenland achieved self-rule) West Greenlandic has been the only official language in the country. West Greenlandic has a number of dialects, which correspond to different geographical areas in the west of

1
Introduction

Map 1.2 Map of Greenland

Greenland. There is a southwestern dialect and a northwestern dialect, as well as a central dialect which is spoken in the area including the capital Nuuk (see Map 1.2). The central dialect is the basis for the standardised form of West Greenlandic, which is the variety used in the media and official settings (as well as in this book). Most Greenlanders live in towns and rural areas close to the southern, western, and eastern coasts; the inner parts of the country are perpetually covered in ice and thus uninhabitable. Note that there are no roads between the different towns and settlements within Greenland, so internal travel is generally done by plane or helicopter with Air Greenland or by boat with, for example, the ferry company Disko Line.

From the 17th century onwards, West Greenlandic speakers have been in constant contact with Danish, which functioned as the language of colonial rule for several centuries. For the first half of the 20th century, West Greenlandic and Danish were both widely used in educational settings, but from 1959 onwards, West Greenlandic-medium education was eclipsed by Danish. This situation changed in 1979, when Greenland ceased to be a Danish colony and achieved Home Rule. The Home Rule Act granted official status to West Greenlandic, though alongside Danish. Greenland achieved a greater level of political autonomy in 2009, when Home Rule was replaced with Self Rule. Under Self Rule, Greenland now has control over some policy areas, such as education, environment, climate, health, and fisheries. Moreover, in 2009 West Greenlandic became the sole official language in Greenland, and Danish lost its official status. However, Danish has retained a prominent position in the country, and many Greenlanders are bilingual, as are most publications and other media in Greenland. Greenland remains a part of Denmark, and Greenlandic people have Danish citizenship, though unlike Denmark, Greenland is not part of the European Union.

West Greenlandic is the main language of primary education in Greenland, with Danish taught as a second language. However, in practice Danish is also often used as a language of instruction, as it is not uncommon for teachers to be recruited from Denmark. Conversely, high school (or sixth-form college) education is conducted largely in Danish, though West Greenlandic is taught both as a mother tongue and as a foreign language at this level. There is, however, Greenlandic-medium tertiary education, including Ilisimatusarfik (the University of Greenland) and Perorsaanermik Ilinniarfik (the Social Pedagogical College of Greenland). These offer academic and practical training in a range of fields, including Greenlandic language, translation, and pedagogy. In addition, outside of Greenland, the University of Copenhagen offers the world's only MA in Greenlandic and Arctic Studies. There is a range of media available in West Greenlandic, including press, radio, and TV. Some of the most prominent of these are the national newspaper *Sermitsiaq*, which is available online and is bilingual in West Greenlandic and Danish, and Kalaallit Nunaata Radioa (the Greenlandic National Radio), which broadcasts radio programmes mainly in Greenlandic. Greenland also has a national language academy called Oqaasileriffik (the Language Secretariat of Greenland), which develops new West Greenlandic terminology and makes recommendations about grammatical usage via their website and social media.

1.3.4 Aspects of Greenlandic culture

In this section we will highlight some aspects of Greenlandic culture that are relevant to the vocabulary in the examples of grammatical features appearing throughout the volume. Greenland, like the rest of the Nordic region, is almost exclusively Lutheran, and **juulli** 'Christmas' and **poorski** 'Easter' are both big holidays, as is the annual confirmation of 13- to 15-year-olds known as **apersortinneq** in the midwestern and southwestern regions of Greenland or **qeqarneq** in the northwestern region of Greenland. Another significant date on the Greenlandic calendar is **Ullortuneq** 'National Day' (literally 'longest day'), which takes place on 21 June. **Ullortuneq** celebrations feature the Greenlandic flag, which consists of a red sun symbol reflected on an ice-covered sea.

Piniarneq 'hunting' and **aalisarneq** 'fishing' have traditionally been both a common occupation and a popular pastime in Greenland. Greenlandic cuisine is characterised by meat and fish. The staples are **puisip neqaa** 'seal meat', **mattak** 'whale skin', **tuttup neqaa** 'reindeer meat', **aqisseq** 'ptarmigan', **umimmak** 'musk ox', **eqaluk** 'trout', and **kapisilik** 'salmon'. **Kalaaliaraq** is a market in central Nuuk next to the shopping centre where fish, seal, and reindeer meat and other traditional foods are sold.

One important part of Greenlandic culture is the **kaffimik**, a traditional open-house coffee drinking session where people come over for two cups of coffee and then leave, making room for new guests. The **kaffimik** is a way to celebrate christenings, birthdays, and other milestones.

The West Greenlandic word for art is **eqqumiitsuliorneq**, literally 'the making of strange things'. One type of popular Greenlandic craft consists of soapstone, wood, and reindeer antler carvings, often in the shape of a **tupilak**, a small monster figure with staring eyes, wide set of teeth and a crooked body. **Kakiorneq** 'tattooing' is another traditional Inuit artform which is now enjoying a revival, especially among women. **Sapangaaqqiat** 'beadwork' is also a very prominent Greenlandic craft which remains popular to the present day. Traditional Greenlandic clothes were made from animal skin; the outfit consisted of **kamik** 'boot', trousers, and an **anoraq** 'anorak'. These national outfits are nowadays mostly reserved for holidays, weddings, and other special occasions.

1.4 Characteristic features of West Greenlandic

The West Greenlandic sound system is relatively simple. There are three basic vowels, **a**, **i**, and **u**, and a fairly small number of consonants. Nouns do not have gender, and there is no definite or indefinite article. However, nouns have different singular and plural forms and are inflected in eight cases. Possession is indicated by a suffix attached to the noun. Verbs have two basic tenses, non-future and future. Non-future verbs can indicate either present or past tense, so, for example, the verb **sinippunga** can mean either 'I sleep' or 'I slept' depending on the context. The basic word order is subject-object-verb (SOV). A characteristic feature of West Greenlandic transitive verbs (i.e. verbs that take a direct object) is that they take suffixes which indicate both the subject and the direct object; for example, the verb form **atuarpara** 'I read it' encodes both the subject 'I' and the direct object 'it'.

A prominent feature of West Greenlandic is its large number of suffixes. These can be attached to nouns, verbs, or both and can be stacked to form long chains which make up a single word. Even words corresponding to English conjunctions such as 'and' or 'but' can be expressed by means of a suffix at the very end of the word, called an enclitic particle. The phenomenon of stacking suffixes is known as agglutination or concatenation. Note that in many cases the last consonant of stems and suffixes either disappears or is assimilated into the following consonant when another suffix is added, which lends the language a fusional element more similar to Indo-European languages such as German or Latin. This phenomenon is explained and exemplified in section 2.5. It is also worth noting that nouns commonly have stem-internal changes, e.g. the word **meeraq** 'child' becomes **meeqqat** 'children' in the plural, which is also a hallmark of fusional languages. This phenomenon is explained and illustrated in section 3.2. The following table illustrates some of the different types of suffixes that you can expect to see in West Greenlandic.

Table 1.2

Morpheme	Function	English translation	Example
mi	case suffix	in (locative)	**Nuummi** in Nuuk
punga	person suffix	1SG (intransitive)	**atuarpunga** I'm reading
t	possessive suffix	your (SG)	**illut** your house
lu	enclitic particle	and	**anaanalu** and mother
fik	verb to noun suffix	place	**siniffik** bed
qarpoq	noun to verb suffix	has	**meeraqarpoq** has a child/children
suaq	noun to noun suffix	big	**qimmersuaq** a big dog
ssavoq	verb to verb suffix	future	**sulissavoq** he will work

West Greenlandic, like other Eskimo-Aleut languages, is known for noun incorporation. This means that a noun functioning as a subject or an object can melt into one with the verb in the clause. English has simple object incorporation with verbs and nouns that come from verbs: 'babysit' (sit a baby), 'dogwalker' (walks a dog) and 'mind-blowing' (blows your mind). One could also analyse 'you're', 'I'll' and 'she'd' as instances of subject incorporation, as the subject has become one with the verb and they are written and pronounced as one. West Greenlandic takes this principle further. An example of object incorporation is: **kaffisorpoq** 'drinks coffee', that is coffee-consume-3SG, literally 'coffee-consumes'. An example of subject incorporation is: **nakorsaavoq** 's/he is a doctor', that is doctor-is-3SG, literally 'doctor-is'. An example of the incorporation of an adverbial phrase: **Nuummiippoq** 'is in Nuuk', that is Nuuk-in-is-3SG, literally 'Nuuk-in-is'.

Noun incorporation is a typical feature of so-called polysynthetic languages, which means that one word can express the equivalent of a whole sentence in a language such as English. For example, the West Greenlandic word **kaffiliussanngilanga** means 'I'm not going to make coffee'; it can be divided into a number of components, mostly affixes, namely: **kaffi-** 'coffee' **-lior-** 'make' **-ssa-** 'future' **-nngilanga** 'I'm not'.

West Greenlandic vocabulary contains a large number of Danish loanwords, reflecting the many centuries of Danish rule. Many of these loanwords, particularly the more recent ones, are spelt as in Danish, including Danish letters such as **æ** and **ø**, which are not part of the native Greenlandic alphabet. For example, the word for 'sausage' in Greenlandic is **pølsi**, from Danish **pølse**, and the word for 'president' is **præsidenti**, from Danish **præsident**. Danish loanwords that entered the language at an earlier stage, by contrast, have typically been adapted to the Greenlandic sound system, so for example the Greenlandic word **palasi** 'priest' is derived from the Danish word **præst** but has been domesticated. Further examples of Danish loanwords in West Greenlandic can be seen in the following table. Moreover, Danish numerals are used in West Greenlandic from 13 onwards (see section 5). Danish first names and surnames are also very commonly used in Greenland (e.g. **Karen, Lise, Birgitte, Ole, Jensen**), in some cases with phonological adaptation (e.g. West Greenlandic **Kaasipat** from Danish **Casper**).

Characteristic features of West Greenlandic

Table 1.3 Danish loanwords in West Greenlandic with their English translations

West Greenlandic	Danish	English
aggusti	**august**	August
cykeli	**cykel**	bicycle
juulli	**jul**	Christmas (cf. Yule)
kammalaat	**kammerat**	friend (cf. comrade)
kutaa	**god dag**	hello (cf. good day)

West Greenlandic has an extremely rich system of word derivation, that is, the creation of new words by means of a combination of stems and suffixes. The following table gives you an illustration of the principle of word derivation by showing a number of different West Greenlandic words that can be formed from a single stem, all relating to fishing:

Table 1.4 West Greenlandic word derivation

West Greenlandic	English translation
aalisagaq	fish
aalisarpoq	fishes
aalisartoq	fisherman
aalisarneq	fishing, fishery
aalisariut	fishing vessel
aalisarfik	fishing spot
aalisaat	fishing line
aalisakkerivik	fish-processing plant

1.5 How to use this grammar

1.5.1 Overall approach

This grammar aims to provide a simple, user-friendly overview of West Greenlandic suitable for non-specialists. Our approach differs from the previous English-medium grammars of West Greenlandic in that we have focused on everyday language explained in terms accessible to a general audience without extensive training in linguistics. In our presentation of West Greenlandic grammar, we tend to follow the established tradition and terminology used in the most widely used Danish-language grammars of Greenlandic (see 'Suggested Resources' at the end of the book for a list). However, we have also aimed to describe the language from a cross-linguistic perspective where appropriate, so as to make it easily relatable for readers with a background in more commonly taught languages. For example, we have divided the rich array of West Greenlandic suffixes up by semantic and functional categories (as well as listing them alphabetically at the end of the volume). This means that readers can easily find those suffixes with a meaning corresponding to English adverbs in the Adverbs section and those with a meaning corresponding to English tense markers in the Tense section, even though in grammatical terms they are all suffixes.

1.5.2 Dictionary forms of words

The basic, or dictionary, form of West Greenlandic nouns is the absolutive case (see section 3.1 and 3.3.1 for details). Note that the dictionary form of some nouns is plural; for example, **biilit** 'car', **tarajuaqqat** 'table salt', and **ilaqutariit** 'family' are all plural even when their meaning corresponds to English singular forms. (In many cases, these basic nouns are plural because they denote concepts or objects composed of more than one element; for example, a car has four wheels, while a family is made up of several members, and salt is comprised of many granules.)

The dictionary form of West Greenlandic verbs is the third-person singular, e.g. **sinippoq**, which literally means 's/he sleeps'. However, when citing the dictionary form of West Greenlandic verbs in this book, we have translated them with the English infinitive, e.g. **sinippoq** 'to sleep'.

1.5.3 Additive and truncative suffixes

West Greenlandic suffixes fall into two categories, called additive and truncative. When an additive suffix is added to a word, the last consonant of the word assimilates with the first consonant of the suffix. When a truncative ending is added to a word, the last consonant of the word is deleted. In this grammar (as in the widely used Danish-language grammars of West Greenlandic), additive suffixes are marked with a plus sign and truncative suffixes are marked with a hyphen, e.g. **+niarpoq** 'to be going to; to try to; to want to (also: to go hunting)', **-ssavoq** 'will'. Note that some suffixes can be either additive or truncative. These are marked with both a plus sign and a hyphen, e.g. **+/-tooq** 'in the manner of'. See also section 2.5 for an explanation and illustration of the changes that occur when additive and truncative suffixes are added to stems.

1.5.4 Examples of grammatical points

The grammatical explanations are accompanied by example phrases and sentences illustrating the points under examination. Most examples have been provided by native speakers of West Greenlandic and illustrate common spoken usage. Some examples are adapted from authentic West Greenlandic sources such as the online newspaper *Sermitsiaq*, magazines, signs, notices, and other realia and illustrate constructions more typical of written genres. The simpler examples appear first, followed by more complex examples. In the examples, the West Greenlandic words, phrases, and sentences appear in bold font and the grammatical element being illustrated is underlined. Thus, in an example illustrating the use of the future tense suffix **-ssa-**, the suffix would be underlined, e.g. **nalussaanga** 'I am going to swim'.

1.5.5 Glossing

Because West Greenlandic has such a complex morphology, it can be difficult for learners to identify the internal structure of longer words. Therefore, in the examples, we have provided a line with a segmented version of the example sentence (with hyphens between each meaningful element of a word) so that you can see what each component of the complex West Greenlandic word looks like. Underneath that we have provided a line of glossing, that is, a literal English translation of each word or component of a word combined with grammatical abbreviations in small caps (e.g. FUT for 'future', NEG for 'negative', etc.) The glossing appears in a smaller font than the examples themselves, so if you would prefer not to look at it, you can skip it and focus on the West Greenlandic and English translations. A full list of abbreviations used in the glossing can be found at the beginning of the volume after the Contents and Acknowledgements. The system of examples and glossing is illustrated here.

1 Introduction

West Greenlandic example →	**Kaffiliussanngilanga.**
Segmented West Greenlandic example →	kaffi-liu-ssa-nngi-langa
Literal English translation and glossing →	coffee-make-FUT-NEG-1SG
English translation of West Greenlandic →	I'm not going to make coffee.

We have tried to make the glossing as user-friendly as possible, so we have kept grammatical abbreviations to a relative minimum, using them only when the element in question is a frequent feature of West Greenlandic and has a regular grammatical meaning which cannot easily be rendered with English words. For example, the future tense marker **-ssa-** is glossed as FUT for 'future', the habitual marker **-tar-** is glossed as HAB for 'habitual', the various past tense forms, such as **-sima-** and **-nikuu-**, are glossed as PAST, etc.). However, where possible and appropriate, we have tended to use English words rather than grammatical abbreviations in order to make the glossing more easily understandable to readers. For example, the modal suffix **-sinnaa-** means 'be able' and is glossed as such, while the suffix **-suaq** means 'big' and is glossed as such.

Similarly, when a given word can be broken into multiple smaller elements but is an established form that has its own set meaning, we have chosen not to segment each individual component so as not to overwhelm the reader and possibly obscure its meaning. For example, the word **atuarfik** 'school' is composed of the verbal stem **atuar-**, meaning 'read', plus the suffix **-fik** 'place, location', with a literal meaning of 'read-place'. When this word appears in the examples we have simply glossed it as **atuarfik** 'school' rather than breaking it down into its components. The only exception to this is when we are actually presenting the specific component in question and need to highlight it in the examples.

In many cases, a single West Greenlandic form encodes multiple or complex meanings. For example, the single West Greenlandic suffix **-galuar-** means 'would have done, but ...', while the single noun **naja** means 'little sister' (to an older brother) and the single suffix **-nut** encodes both the allative case (meaning 'to' or 'for') and plural number (i.e. many). In such cases, a dot is used in the glossing to separate the different English words or grammatical abbreviations that correspond to the single West Greenlandic element. This convention is illustrated here.

sulissagaluarput	naja	illunut
suli-ssa-galuar-put	naja	illu-nut
work-FUT-would.but-3PL	little.sister	house-ALL.PL
They would work, but ...	little sister	to the houses

In many cases, a West Greenlandic word or suffix can have more than one meaning. For example, the suffix **+niarpoq** can mean 'to intend to; to try to; to want to', in addition to 'to hunt'. In such instances, we gloss the word or suffix according to its meaning in the particular context in which it appears, so you may see **+niarpoq** glossed as intend.to in one case but try.to in another.

You may see glossing abbreviations such as 1SG, 2SG, 3SG, etc. These indicate possessive suffixes (e.g. 'my', 'your', 'his/her', etc.), which are discussed in detail in section 3.4. The following examples illustrate this convention:

paniga	**qimmerput**	**illua**
pani-ga	qimmer-put	illu-a
daughter-1SG	dog-1PL	house-3SG
my daughter	our dog	his/her house

If the possessum (i.e. the possessed noun) is plural, the possessive suffix takes a different form that marks both the person and number of the possessor and the person and number of the possessum. This is indicated in the glossing by means of the abbreviation PL before the person and number of the possessor, as follows:

panikka	**qimmivut**	**illui**
pani-kka	qimmi-vut	illu-i
daughter- PL.1SG	qimmi- PL.1PL	house- PL.3SG
my daughters	our dogs	his/her houses

The same glossing abbreviations can be used to denote subject and object suffixes on verbs. Because a single suffix can encode both a subject and direct object, we have used a right-pointing arrow symbol > to separate subject and object suffix abbreviations in the glossing. When you see the symbol > in one of the glosses, you will find the subject in a verbal suffix to the left of the symbol, and the direct object to its right. The following examples illustrate this convention:

asavakka	**ornippatsigut**	**atuarpai**
asa-vakka	ornip-patsigut	atuar-pai
love-1SG>2SG	approach-1SG>1PL	read-3SG>3PL
I love you	You approach us	S/he read them

Note that the glossing does not show the absolutive noun case, as this is the basic or default form of nouns. It does not show singular noun number for

How to use this grammar

Introduction

the same reason. In the plural, the relative case is not shown because it is the same as the absolutive case.

Similarly, the glossing does not label indicative verbs as such because the indicative is their basic form. Likewise, it does not show the intransitive/transitive distinction in verbs because this is made clear by the fact that transitive verbs are glossed with their subject and object, whereas intransitive verbs are glossed with their subject only.

These points are illustrated in the following examples. In the example on the left, the subject **meeraq** 'child' is in the absolutive singular, which is not labelled in the glossing, while the verb **atuarpoq** 'reads' is an intransitive indicative, which is also not indicated explicitly but is clear from the subject abbreviation 3SG. In the example on the right, the subject **meeqqat** 'children' is in the relative plural, but this is not indicated in the glossing as it is the same form as the absolutive. The object **atuagaq** 'book' is in the absolutive, but this is not labelled. Finally, the verb **atuarpaat** 'they read it' is transitive, but this is not labelled because it is clear from the subject and object abbreviation 3PL>3SG.

Meeraq atuarpoq.	**Meeqqat atuagaq atuarpaat.**
meeraq atuar-poq	meeqa-t atuagaq atuar-paat
child read-3SG	child-PL book read-3PL>3SG
The child reads.	The children read the book.

Chapter 2
Phonology and orthography

2.1 The alphabet

The West Greenlandic alphabet is as follows:

Aa, Bb, Cc, Dd, Ee, Ff, Gg, Hh, Ii, Jj, Kk, Ll, Mm, Nn, Oo, Pp, Qq, Rr, Ss, Tt, Uu, Vv, Ww, Xx, Yy, Zz, Ææ, Øø, Åå

Note that the letters **b, c, d, h, w, x, y, z, æ, ø,** and **å** are found only in words borrowed from Danish or other languages and in proper names of Danish and other origins.

2.2 Vowels

There are three vowels in West Greenlandic which have a number of allophones (variant pronunciations) depending on the context. The vowels are **a, i,** and **u**. Some of the variants are specified in the writing system: the vowel **i** has the variant **e** and the vowel **u** has the variant **o** (these variants appear only before **r** and **q**).

Orthography	Phoneme	Allophone	Context	Example
a	/a/	[a] or [æ]	generally	**aki** price
a	/a/	[ɑ]	before **r** and **q**	**arnaq** woman
i	/i/	[i]	generally	**ini** room
i	/i/	[y]	before labial consonants **p, v,** and **m**	**imaarpoq** to be empty
e	/i/	[e]	variant of **i** appearing before **r** and **q**	**tupeq** tent

DOI: 10.4324/9781315160863-2

2 Phonology and orthography

Orthography	Phoneme	Allophone	Context	Example
u	/u/	[u]	generally	**sumi** where
u	/u/	[ʉ]	before **s, n,** and **t**	**-rusuppoq** to want to
o	/u/	[ɔ]	variant of **u** appearing before **r** and **q**	**orsoq** fat

The Danish letters **y, æ, å,** and **ø** appear in loanwords from Danish and are generally pronounced as follows:

Orthography	Allophone	Example
y	[y]	**Lynge** (a surname)
æ	[ɛ] or [æ]	**præsidenti** president
ø	[ø] or [œ]	**pølse** sausage
å	[ɔ]	**nå** um, well

West Greenlandic also has a series of long vowels, illustrated as follows:

Orthography	Phoneme	Allophone	Context	Example
aa	/aː/	[aː] or [æː]	generally	**maanna** now
aa	/aː/	[ɑː]	before **r** and **q**	**ullaaq** this morning
ii	/iː/	[iː]	generally	**tii** tea
ii	/iː/	[ɛː]	before **r** and **q**	**qeeq** white hair
ee	/iː/	[eː]	variant of **i** appearing before **r** and **q**	**meeraq** child
uu	/uː/	[uː]	generally	**Nuuk**[1]
oo	/uː/	[ɔː]	variant of **u** appearing before **r** and **q**	**sooq** why

1 The capital of Greenland.

There is only one diphthong in West Greenlandic. It is generally found only at the end of words.

Orthography	Phoneme	Allophone	Context	Example
ai	/ai/	[ai]	at the end of words	**ornippai** s/he approaches them

Other combinations of vowels, for example, **ui**, are not considered to be diphthongs, but rather the two vowels are in different syllables.

2.3 Consonants

The following table contains the West Greenlandic single consonants.

Orthography	IPA	Notes	Example
f	/f/	voiceless labiodental fricative; appears only as a variant of /v/ after another consonant (except in loanwords, where it can appear in any position)	**atuarfik** school **februaari** February
g	/ɣ/	voiced velar fricative; does not appear at the beginning of words except in loanwords	**uagut** we **Guuti** God
j	/j/	voiced palatal glide; does not typically appear at the beginning of words except for loanwords	**qujanaq** thank you **journalisti** journalist

2 Phonology and orthography

Orthography	IPA	Notes	Example
k	/k/	voiceless velar stop	**kamik** boot
l	/l/	voiced alveolar approximant	**ilinniartoq** student
m	/m/	voiced bilabial nasal	**matu** door
n	/n/	voiced alveolar nasal	**neqi** meat
ng	/ŋ/	voiced velar nasal	**angut** man
p	/p/	voiceless bilabial stop	**panik** daughter
q	/q/	voiceless uvular stop	**qanoq** how **qajaq** kayak
r	/ʁ/	voiced uvular fricative	**naluara** I don't know
s	/s/	voiceless alveolar fricative	**sila** weather
t	/t/; has allophones [tʰ] and [tˢ]	voiceless alveolar stop; pronounced as [tʰ] at the end of words; pronounced as [tˢ] before **i** and **e**	**tallimat** five
v	/v/	voiced labiodental fricative	**anivoq** to go out

Point to note:

- Native West Greenlandic words can only begin in a vowel or one of the consonants **k, m, n, p, q, s,** and **t**. They can only end a vowel or in **k, p, q, t,** or, rarely, **n**.

Most of the consonants can appear as double consonants, as shown here.

Orthography	IPA	Notes	Example
ff	/vv/ > [fː]	voiceless labiodental fricative	**siniffik** bed
gg	/ɣɣ/ > [çː]	realised as a palatal voiceless fricative	**aggerpoq** to come

jj	/jj/	only in the exclamation	**ajja!** that was close!
kk	/kk/	voiceless velar stop	**atuakkat** books
ll	/ɬ/	voiceless lateral fricative	**illu** house
mm	/mm/	voiced bilabial nasal	**aamma** and
nn	/nn/	voiced alveolar nasal	**kisianni** but
nng	/ŋŋ/	voiced velar nasal	**ajunngilaq** well, fine, no problems
pp	/pp/	voiceless bilabial stop	**allappoq** to write
qq	/qq/	voiceless uvular stop	**qaqqaq** mountain
rr	/ʁʁ/ > [χ:]	realised as a voiceless uvular fricative	**nerrivik** table
ss	/ss/	voiceless alveolar fricative	**assak** hand
tt	/tt/	voiceless alveolar stop	**tuttu** reindeer

Point to note:

- The combination **rl** is pronounced as /rɬ/, for example, **marluk** 'two'.

The consonants **b**, **c**, **d**, **h**, **w**, **x**, **y**, and **z** appear only in loanwords from Danish and other languages, as illustrated in the following examples. (Note that **y** is more typically used as a vowel – also in loanwords, as discussed earlier.)

Orthography	IPA	Notes	Example
b	/b/		**banani** banana
c	/s/ or /k/	pronunciation depends on the word	/s/: **cykeli** bicycle /k/: **cola**

2 Phonology and orthography

Orthography	IPA	Notes	Example
d	/d/		**Danmarki** Denmark
h	/h/		**hesti** horse
w	/v/		**whisky**
x	/ks/		**taxa** taxi
y	/j/	pronounced as a consonant only at the beginning of a word	**yoga**
z	/s/		**zebra**

2.4 Syllables, stress, and intonation

Words are divided into syllables as follows.

- Between double consonants: **il-lu** 'house', **kaf-fi** 'coffee', **as-sak** 'hand'.
- Between an r and a consonant: **ar-naq** 'woman', **or-pik** 'tree', **ar-fi-neq** 'five'.
- Before a single consonant: **a-taa-ta** 'father', **naa-mik** 'no', **nu-na** 'land'.
- Between two different vowels: **a-tu-a-gaq** 'book', **nu-i-aq** 'cloud'.

West Greenlandic has no stress; that is, each syllable is given the same weight in pronunciation. However, the language has a number of different intonation patterns. In statements (as opposed to questions) the intonation goes up on the antepenultimate syllable, down on the penultimate syllable, and up on the last syllable.

If-fi-ar-si-vu-nga

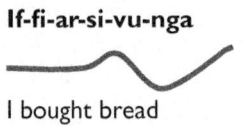

I bought bread

In questions the intonation goes up on the penultimate syllable and down on the last syllable.

Qa-su-i-naa-siit?

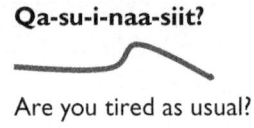

Are you tired as usual?

Note that if a question word is used on its own it has question intonation. But if a question word is used in conjunction with a verb the whole sentence has statement intonation.

Su-mi?

Where?

Su-mi na-ju-ga-qar-pit?

Where do you live?

2.5 Morphophonological variation

2.5.1 Consonant changes

In West Greenlandic, consonant assimilation is very common when suffixes are attached to stems or to each other. All word-final consonants, apart from q and r, assimilate when an additive ending is attached. Additive suffixes are indicated in this book with a plus sign. The suffixes could be case endings (e.g. +mi 'in, at'), verbalising suffixes (e.g. +sivoq 'to buy'), nominalising suffixes (e.g. +fik '(place)'), or enclitic particles (+lu 'and').

Base word	Additive suffix	Resulting word
panik daughter	**+mit** from	**panimmit** from the daughter
Najap Naja's	**+lu** and	**Najallu** and Naja's
angut man	**+mut** to	**angummut** to the man

The q at the end of a noun changes into r before an additive suffix.

Base word	Additive suffix	Resulting word
qimmeq dog	**+suaq** big	**qimmersuaq** a big dog
tupeq tent	**+mi** in	**tupermi** in the tent
qanoq how	**+ippit** you are	**qanorippit?** how are you?

2 Phonology and orthography

When an enclitic particle beginning with a vowel is attached to a word that ends in one of the stops **p**, **t**, or **k**, nasalisation of the stop takes place. In other words, p > m, t > n, and k > ng, e.g.:

Base word	Enclitic particle	Resulting word
palasip the priest's	**+una** it is	**palasimuna** it is the priest's
kaffisorpugut we're drinking coffee	**+aasiit** as usual	**kaffisorvugunaasiit** we're drinking coffee as usual
oqaluffik church	**+una** it is	**oqaluffinguna** it is a church

When **-i-** is added to word-final **t**, the **t** sometimes becomes an **s**. This is not predictable from the shape of the word, and each instance has to be learnt individually (see section 3.1 for further information).

Base word	Suffix starting in -i-	Resulting word
aallaat gun, rifle	**+it** (plural suffix)	**aallaasit** guns, rifles
ikitsit toothpick	**+it** (plural suffix)	**ikitsisit** toothpicks

A similar phenomenon can be seen in the verbal system as well. For example, the intransitive participle suffix (discussed in section 8.1) is usually **-toq**, but in some cases it appears as **-soq**, as in the following example. Such cases need to be learnt individually.

Base word	Suffix	Resulting word
aggerpoq to approach	**-toq/-soq** (intransitive participle)	**aggersoq** the one who approaches

Another change concerns the consonant **r**. An **r** may appear following a vowel-stem noun or weak t-stem noun (see section 2.2.5 for an introduction to noun stem types) when a suffix beginning with **+pa**, **+pi**, **+put**, **+si**, **+su**, or **+tik** is attached. This so-called 'recessive r' is illustrated in the following examples.

Base word	Suffix	Resulting word
illu house	**+paat** lots of	**illorpaat** lots of houses
ini room	**+suaq** big	**inersuaq** a big room
nuna land	**+put** our	**nunarput** our land
ikinngut friend	**+put** our	**ikinnguterput** our friend

2.5.2 Vowel changes

The vowels **e** and **o** in West Greenlandic are variants of **i** and **u** which appear only before **q** and **r**. If a noun ending in **q** or **r** loses its final consonant (e.g. when a truncative suffix is added), the **e** or **o** invariably change to **i** or **u** respectively. This phenomenon is illustrated in the following examples:

Base word	Suffix	Resulting word
qimmeq dog	**-t** (plural suffix)	**qimmit** dogs
nanoq polar bear	**-p** (relative suffix)	**nannup** a polar bear's

An **a** always assimilates the following vowel, e.g.:

Base word	Suffix	Resulting word
qaaqqusaq invited guest	**-uvoq** to be	**qaaqqusaavoq** to be an invited guest

A word-final **+i** (marking a 3SG possessor with a 3PL possessum) is an exception to this rule, as it is not assimilated, e.g.:

Base word	Suffix	Resulting word
nuka (a girl's) younger sister/(a boy's) younger brother	**+i** his/her/its (PL)	**nukai** her younger sisters/his younger brothers
atisat clothes (PL)	**+i** his/her/its (PL)	**atisai** his/her clothes

Likewise, **i** typically changes to **a** when followed by a vowel, e.g.:

Base word	Suffix	Resulting word
neqi meat	**+a** his/her/its (SG)	**neqaa** his/her/its meat

There are some exceptions to this rule whereby **i** does not change to **a**, e.g.:

Base word	Suffix	Resulting word
bussi bus	**+i** his/her/its (PL)	**Nuup bussii** Nuuk's buses'

Enclitic particles which begin with a vowel (**+una** 'it is', **+aasiit** 'as usual, again') can be written as one word with the preceding word or with a hyphen. When written as one word the assimilation is indicated in writing but pronounced either way.

Base word	Suffix	Resulting hyphenated words	Resulting word
suna what	**+una** it is	**suna-una** [sunaana] what is it?	**sunaana** what is it?
qasuvunga I am tired	**+aasiit** as usual, again	**qasuvunga-aasiit** I'm tired as usual	**qasuvungaasiit** I'm tired as usual

2.5.3 | Helping vowel -i-

When a foreign word or name ending in a consonant is used in West Greenlandic, a helping vowel -i- is usually attached to the end of it before any suffix is added. For example, the West Greenlandic equivalent of the phrase 'in London' is **Londonimi**, which consists of the foreign name **London**, the helping vowel -i-, and the locative suffix -mi, meaning 'in'. In order to make it easier for readers to be able to tell when a helping vowel -i- is present in a given West Greenlandic word, we have segmented it and indicated it in the glossing by means of the abbreviation HV for 'helping vowel'. Note that in some cases this helping vowel has become such an integral part of the West Greenlandic version of the word that it appears in all contexts, not just when a suffix is added. This is often the case with established borrowings from Danish, e.g. **banani** 'banana', **banki** 'bank', **cykeli** 'bicycle', **Brugseni** 'Brugsen'.[1] In such cases, we have not indicated the helping vowel in the glossing because it is considered to be an inseparable element of the word and appears in dictionaries.

Morphophonological variation

2.5.4 Loss of glides (j and v)

The letter j cannot appear after the vowel i in West Greenlandic. Therefore, j is dropped from the beginning of a suffix when attached to a stem ending in -i. Comparison of the two verbal stems here illustrates this: the first ends in -a and takes a suffix beginning in -j, while the second one ends in -i, and therefore the -j does not appear at the beginning of the suffix.

Verbal stem	Suffix	Suffixed verb
igav- to cook	**-juaannarpoq** all the time	**igajuaannarpoq** to cook all the time
suli- to work	**-juaannarpoq** all the time	**suliuaannarpoq** to work all the time

Similarly, the letter **v** cannot appear after the vowel **u**. Therefore, **v** is dropped from the beginning of a suffix when attached to a stem ending in -**u**. Comparison of the following two verbal stems illustrates this phenomenon. The first ends in -**a** and takes the suffix -**vaa**, meaning 'he or she does something to him/her/it', while the second ends in -**u**, and therefore the -**v** does not appear at the beginning of the suffix.

Verbal stem	Suffix	Suffixed verb
asa- to love	**-vaa** 3SG>3SG	**asavaa** s/he loves him/her/it
taku- to see	**-vaa** 3SG>3SG	**takuaa** s/he sees him/her/it

2.5.5 Stem types

West Greenlandic nouns and verbs can be divided into different categories depending on the sound they end in. These categories are important to be

1 The Greenlandic name of a well-known Danish and Greenlandic supermarket chain.

aware of because they can cause sound changes when suffixes are added. Nominal stems can be divided into the following broad categories (see section 3.1 for a detailed discussion of the different nominal stem types).

- vowel-stem, e.g. **ini** 'room'
- weak k-stem, e.g. **ujarak** 'stone'
- strong k-stem, e.g. **inuk** 'person'
- weak q-stem, e.g. **qimmeq** 'dog'
- strong q-stem, e.g. **arnaq** 'woman'
- t-stem, e.g. **suit** 'ear'

Verbal stems can be divided into the following categories (see section 7 for more detailed discussion of the different verbal stem types).

- vowel-stem, e.g. **sulivoq** 'to work'
- consonant-stem, e.g. **sinippoq** 'to sleep'
- r-stem, e.g. **piniarpoq** 'to hunt'

2.5.6 Sound alternation in the beginning of suffixes

Sound alternations can occur at the beginning of suffixes depending on which stem type they are attached to. Some of the more common sound variations that occur when suffixes are added to the different nominal and verbal stem types are listed here. See section 13 for a detailed discussion of West Greenlandic suffixes.

Sound alternation		Example suffix	Example word
Two variants: **-g, -r**	**-g** is used with: • vowel-stems • k-stems • t-stems **-r** is used with: • q-stems	-giit -riit each other, mutually, reciprocally	**ikinngutigiit** (mutual) friends **ateeriit** (two or more) people with the same name
Three variants: **+g, -r, +k**	**+g** is used with: • vowel-stems **-r** is used with: • r-stems **+k** is used with: • consonant-stems	+galuarpoq -raluarpoq +kaluarpoq to do something, but...	**atuaraluarpoq** studied, but ... **suligaluarpoq** worked, but ... **tikikkaluarpoq** arrived home, but...

Morphophonological variation

Three variants: -i, -a, -g	-i is used with: • i- • u- -a is used with: • a- -g is used with: • e- • ii- • aa-	-innarpoq -annarpoq -ginnarpoq only, just	**neriinnarpoq** just to eat **ikaannarpoq** just to play **ilaaginnarpoq** just to follow along
Four variants: +j, -r, +k, +vowel	+j is used with: • a- • u- -r is used with: • r-stems +k is used with: • consonant-stems +vowel is used with: • i-	+junnaarpoq +unnaarpoq -runnaarpoq +kunnaarpoq no longer	**ikumajunnaarpoq** to be no longer burning **pinnerunnaarpoq** to be no longer beautiful **atuukkunnaarpoq** to be no longer valid **neriunnaarpoq** to be done eating
Three variants: +j, +t, +vowel	-j is used with: • a- and u- +t is used with: • consonant-stems • r-stems +vowel is used with: • i-	-juaannarpoq +tuaannarpoq +uaannarpoq always, continually	**qiajuaannarpoq** to cry continually **sinittuaannarpoq** to sleep all the time **apiuaannarpoq** to snow continually
Two variants: +t and +s	+t is used with: • consonant-stems • r-stems +s is used with: • vowel-stems	+tarpoq/ +sarpoq to do something usually, habitually	**naluttarpoq** to swim regularly **sulisarpoq** to work regularly
Three variants: +v, +p, +vowel	+v is used with: • a- • i- +p is used with: • consonant-stems • r-stems +vowel is used with: • u-	+vallaarpoq +allaarpoq +pallaarpoq too much	**sulivallaarpoq** to work too much **ittoorpallaarpoq** to be too shy **kukkuallaarpoq** to make too many mistakes

2.6 Kleinschmidt's orthography

The following table lists some of the biggest differences between Kleinschmidt's orthography and the current one.

Description	Kleinschmidt	Current	Example
voiceless uvular stop /q/	ĸ	q	ĸajaĸ > qajaq kayak
long vowel	^ on the vowel	two vowels	anâna > anaana mother
double consonant	' on the preceding vowel	two consonants	támarpâ > tammarpaa to lose (something)
double consonant	consonant combinations	two consonants	ĸingmeĸ > qimmeq dog sinigput > sinipput they sleep mêrĸat > meeqqat child
double vowel + double consonant	~ on the vowel	two vowels + two consonants	mãna > maanna now
word-final /i/ and /u/	e, o	i, u	Ivalo > Ivalu[1]
voiceless lateral fricative /ɬ/	gdl, tdl, vdl	ll	igdlo > illu house Kalâtdlit Nunât > Kalaallit Nunaat Greenland

[1] Greenlandic woman's name.

See https://tech.oqaasileriffik.gl/tools/kleinschmidt/ for an automatic converter between Kleinschmidt's orthography and the current one.

Chapter 3

Nouns

3.1 Case and number

West Greenlandic nouns are not marked for gender, but they have different singular and plural forms. In addition, nouns can take different case suffixes to indicate the role that they play in the sentence in question (e.g. whether they are the subject or object of the verb, etc.). West Greenlandic has eight different noun cases.

The absolutive case is the basic form of the noun that you find in a dictionary. It is used for the subject of an intransitive clause (i.e. a clause with no direct object) or the object of a transitive clause (i.e. a clause with a direct object). The relative case is used for marking possession and for the subject of a transitive clause. (If this explanation seems daunting right now, there is no need to worry, as the concepts of absolutive and relative with respect to subjects and objects will be explained in detail in section 3.3) The allative case means 'to' or 'for', the locative case means 'in' or 'at', the ablative case means 'from', the instrumental case means 'with' or 'by', the prolative case means 'via', and the equative case means 'as' or 'similar to'. The absolutive and relative cases are sometimes grouped together and referred to as 'grammatical cases', while the remaining cases are termed 'oblique cases'. The functions of each case will be discussed more fully and exemplified in 3.3.

The case endings are shown in the following table.

Greenlandic cases		
	SG	PL
ABSOLUTIVE	no ending	-t
RELATIVE	-p	
ALLATIVE	-mut	-nut
LOCATIVE	-mi	-ni
ABLATIVE	-mit, -miit	-nit, -niit
INSTRUMENTAL	-mik	-nik
PROLATIVE	-kkut	-tigut, -sigut
EQUATIVE	-tut, -sut	

DOI: 10.4324/9781315160863-3

Points to note:

- These suffixes can be truncative or additive depending on the stem of the noun to which they are attached. See section 1.5.3 for explanation of truncative and additive suffixes.
- See section 3.2 for explanation of the ways in which the different noun stem types combine with the case suffixes shown here.
- When a case suffix starts with -m in the singular, its plural counterpart starts with -n.
- The variants of the prolative and equative starting with -s typically appear after a vowel.

In most respects, West Greenlandic noun number (i.e. singular vs. plural) works like in English. However, there are several categories where West Greenlandic uses a plural when English would use a singular. These categories are listed here. As the West Greenlandic nouns in these categories invariably appear in the plural form, only context can tell you whether the sense is singular or plural in any given instance.

- Objects with wheels generally appear in the plural, even when the English equivalent would be singular, e.g. **biilit** 'car', **bussit** 'bus'.
- Collective nouns consisting of many small components, such as powder, granules, etc., appear in the plural, e.g. **kaffit** 'ground coffee', **ivikkat** 'grass', **katitertakkat** 'puzzle', **sukkut** 'sugar'.
- Nouns referring to groups of people, institutions, or teams often appear in the plural, e.g. **ilagisat** 'family', **eqqartuussisut** 'court', **naalakkersuisut** 'government'.
- A number of other everyday items and concepts appear in the plural, e.g. **allakkat** 'letter', **oqaatsit** 'language'.

When such nouns appear in conjunction with a modifier, the modifier also appears in the plural, even if the sense of the noun is singular. See section 6 for discussion of noun modification. Similarly, when such nouns appear in conjunction with a verb, the verb also takes a plural ending. See section 7 for discussion of verbal endings.

3.2 Noun stem types

West Greenlandic nouns are divided into weak stems and strong stems. Weak stems end in a vowel, **k**, **q**, or **t**. Weak **k** and **q** are dropped when a suffix is added. Weak stems have -p in the relative singular and -t in the absolutive/relative plural.

Strong stems end in -k, -eq, or -aq. Strong stems are generally more irregular than weak stems. They have -up or -ap in the relative singular and -it and -at in the absolutive/relative plural. Strong stems have a double t in the equative.

The main characteristics of the different stem types and subtypes are explained in the following sections. The explanations list the basic (absolutive) form of the nouns as well as their inflectional stem, which is the form to which the various case endings are attached.

Noun stem types

3.2.1 Weak stems

Weak stems end in a vowel or a so-called weak q or k. Weak q and k are dropped when the case suffixes are added. Endings can be attached to weak vowel-stems and q-stems without any other changes, as illustrated in the following table. Additional changes take place in the weak k-stem nouns, so they are not shown in the following table but are instead discussed in 3.2.2.

Stem type	Absolutive singular	Inflectional stem
vowel-stem	**illu** house	**illu-**
q-stem	**qimmeq** dog	**qimmi-**
	piniartoq hunter	**piniartu-**

Points to note:

- If a weak-stem noun ends in -eq, the -e changes to -i in the inflectional stem. Similarly, if a weak-stem noun ends in -oq, the -o changes to -u. (This is in accordance with the predictable vowel changes relating to q and r discussed in section 2.5.2.)
- The word **piniartoq** 'hunter, one who hunts' is an example of an intransitive participle, a very common West Greenlandic construction which ends in -toq or -soq and is used in the sense of 'one who does X'. All intransitive participles inflect like this type of weak-stem noun. (See sections 6.1 and 8.1 for discussion of the formation and use of intransitive participles.)

The following table illustrates the complete inflection of a weak vowel-stem noun:

	illu house	
	SG	PL
ABSOLUTIVE	**illu**	**illut**
RELATIVE	**illup**	
ALLATIVE	**illumut**	**illunut**
LOCATIVE	**illumi**	**illuni**
ABLATIVE	**illumit**	**illunit**
INSTRUMENTAL	**illumik**	**illunik**
PROLATIVE	**illukkut**	**illutigut**
EQUATIVE	**illutut**	

The following table illustrates the complete inflection of a weak q-stem noun.

	qimmeq dog	
	SG	PL
ABSOLUTIVE	**qimmeq**	**qimmit**
RELATIVE	**qimmip**	
ALLATIVE	**qimmimut**	**qimminut**
LOCATIVE	**qimmimi**	**qimmini**
ABLATIVE	**qimmimit**	**qimminit**
INSTRUMENTAL	**qimmimik**	**qimminik**
PROLATIVE	**qimmikkut**	**qimmitigut**
EQUATIVE	**qimmitut**	

3.2.2 Weak stems with gemination

Weak q-stems can have gemination (consonant doubling) in the stem, and all weak k-stems geminate. Vowel-stems can occasionally have gemination as well. In some cases, gemination is accompanied by additional consonant and, occasionally, vowel changes. Some of the main gemination patterns for weak stems are listed in the following table.

Noun stem types

Single consonant	Geminated version	Absolutive singular	Inflectional stem
g	kk	**iigaq** wall	**iikka-**
j	ts	**tarajoq** salt	**taratsu-**
aj	aann	**qajaq** kayak	**qaanna-**
l	ll	**kalaaleq** Greenlander	**kalaalli-**
m	mm	**isuma** opinion	**isumma-**
n	nn	**nanoq** polar bear	**nannu-**
ng	nng	**qingaq** nose	**qinnga-**
q	qq	**niaqoq** head	**niaqqu-**
r	qq	**ujarak** stone	**ujaqqa-**
s	ts	**qarasaq** brain	**qaratsa-**
t	tt	**iperaataq** whip	**iperaatta-**

Point to note:

- There are some other patterns, e.g. j > ss, t > ts, -iu/-ioq > -issu-, -uaq > -ukka-, which you may sometimes encounter.

The following table illustrates the complete inflection of a weak vowel-stem noun with gemination.

isuma opinion		
	SG	PL
ABSOLUTIVE	**isuma**	**isummat**
RELATIVE	**isummap**	
ALLATIVE	**isummamut**	**isummanut**
LOCATIVE	**isummami**	**isummani**
ABLATIVE	**isummamit**	**isummanit**
INSTRUMENTAL	**isummamik**	**isummanik**
PROLATIVE	**isummakkut**	**isummatigut**
EQUATIVE	**isummatut**	

The following table illustrates the complete inflection of a weak q-stem noun with gemination.

3 Nouns

nanoq polar bear		
	SG	PL
ABSOLUTIVE	nanoq	nannut
RELATIVE	nannup	
ALLATIVE	nannumut	nannunut
LOCATIVE	nannumi	nannuni
ABLATIVE	nannumit	nannunit
INSTRUMENTAL	nannumik	nannunik
PROLATIVE	nannukkut	nannutigut
EQUATIVE	nannutut ||

The following table illustrates the complete inflection of a weak k-stem noun with germination.

ujarak stone		
	SG	PL
ABSOLUTIVE	ujarak	ujaqqat
RELATIVE	ujaqqap	
ALLATIVE	ujaqqamut	ujaqqanut
LOCATIVE	ujaqqami	ujaqqani
ABLATIVE	ujaqqamit	ujaqqanit
INSTRUMENTAL	ujaqqamik	ujaqqanik
PROLATIVE	ujaqqakkut	ujaqqatigut
EQUATIVE	ujaqqatut ||

3.2.3 Additional weak-stem patterns

There are additional weak-stem patterns which feature gemination plus a further consonant change. In many cases these involve the loss of a final q. The following examples illustrate some of the more common of these patterns.

Noun stem types

Absolutive ending	Inflectional variation	Absolutive singular	Inflectional stem
-gaq	**-kka-**	**atuagaq** book	**atuakka-**
-raq	**-qqa-**	**meeraq** child	**meeqqa-**
-utaq	**-utta-**	**ernutaq** grandchild	**ernutta-**
-seq	**-tsi-**	**oqaaseq** word	**oqaatsi-**

The following table illustrates the complete inflection of a weak-stem noun with gemination and a further change.

	meeraq child	
	SG	PL
ABSOLUTIVE	meeraq	meeqqat
RELATIVE	meeqqap	
ALLATIVE	meeqqamut	meeqqanut
LOCATIVE	meeqqami	meeqqani
ABLATIVE	meeqqamit	meeqqanit
INSTRUMENTAL	meeqqamik	meeqqanik
PROLATIVE	meeqqakkut	meeqqatigut
EQUATIVE	meeqqatut	

Some weak-stem nouns feature -ss- in the inflectional stem, e.g.:

Absolutive ending	Inflectional variation	Absolutive singular	Inflectional stem
-aaq	**-assa-**	**naaq** stomach	**nassa- (naa-)**
-iaq	**-issa-**	**timmiaq** bird	**timmissa-**
-ioq	**-issu-**	**pamioq** tail	**pamissu-**
-uaq	**-ussa-**	**sikuaq** newly formed ice	**sikussa-**
-iak	**-issa-**	**kikiak** seam	**kikissa-**
-iu	**-ssu-**	**niu** leg, bone	**niussu-**
-uak	**-ussa-**	**soraluaq** nephew, niece	**soralussa-**

3 Nouns

The following table illustrates the complete inflection of a weak-stem noun with -ss- in the inflectional stem.

	timmiaq bird	
	SG	PL
Absolutive	timmiaq	timmissat
Relative	timmissap	
Allative	timmissamut	timmissanut
Locative	timmissami	timmissani
Ablative	timmissamit	timmissanit
Instrumental	timmissamik	timmissanik
Prolative	timmissakkut	timmissatigut
Equative	timmissatut	

3.2.4 Weak t-stems

A special weak-stem type is comprised of certain words ending in -t. These historically ended in a vowel, which does not appear in the absolutive form in the modern language. Thus, the absolutive singular ends in -t. However, the historical -i- reappears in the relative, prolative, and equative singular, and in all the plural forms. When appearing with possessive suffixes (see section 3.4), the historical -i- appears in all the forms apart from the third-person singular.

There are two subcategories of this type of noun. These rules apply to both, but in one of the subcategories the t becomes an s when suffixes are added. Both subcategories are illustrated in the following table. We have included the grammatical cases for illustration of the forms taking -i- and the allative singular form for comparison, as an example of a case that does not include the -i-.

The following table illustrates the first subcategory of weak t-stem nouns.

Absolutive SG	Relative SG	Absolutive/relative PL	Allative SG
angut man	angutip	angutit	angummut
siut ear	siutip	siutit	siummut
ikinngut friend	ikinngutip	ikinngutit	ikinngummut

The following table illustrates the second subcategory of weak t-stem nouns.

Noun stem types

Absolutive SG	Relative SG	Absolutive/relative PL	Allative SG
aallaat rifle	**aallaasip**	**aallaasit**	**aallaammut**
ikitsit toothpick	**ikitsisip**	**ikitsisit**	**ikitsimmut**

The following table illustrates the complete inflection of a weak t-stem noun from the second subcategory.

	angut man	
	SG	PL
ABSOLUTIVE	**angut**	**angutit**
RELATIVE	**angutip**	
ALLATIVE	**angummut**	**angutinut**
LOCATIVE	**angummi**	**angutini**
ABLATIVE	**angummit**	**angutinit**
INSTRUMENTAL	**angummik**	**angutinik**
PROLATIVE	**angutikkut**	**angutigut**
EQUATIVE	**angutitut**	

The following table illustrates the complete inflection of a weak t-stem noun from the second subcategory.

	aallaat rifle	
	SG	PL
ABSOLUTIVE	**aallaat**	**aallaasit**
RELATIVE	**aallaasip**	
ALLATIVE	**aallaammut**	**aallaasinut**
LOCATIVE	**aallaammi**	**aallaasini**
ABLATIVE	**aallaammit**	**aallaasinit**
INSTRUMENTAL	**aallaammik**	**aallaasinik**
PROLATIVE	**aallaasikkut**	**aallaasitigut**
EQUATIVE	**aallaasitut**	

3.2.5 Strong stems

Strong stems end in -k, -eq, or -aq. Because some weak-stem nouns also end in these same consonants, it is impossible to tell from the absolutive (dictionary) form of a noun with one of these endings whether it is weak or strong. Instead, strong-stem nouns can be identified based on their relative singular and absolutive/relative plural form. Most strong-stem nouns take **up** in the relative singular, with a smaller subsection taking **-ap** (which will be indicated where relevant). All strong-stem nouns take **-it** in the absolutive/relative plural. This means that the strong stems typically have a slightly different form in the grammatical cases (i.e. relative singular and absolutive/relative plural) than in the oblique cases. For this reason, in the tables of strong-stem nouns discussed in the following sections, we have included examples in the allative singular for illustration of how the strong stems look in an oblique case. Strong-stem nouns can be divided into a number of subcategories, which are discussed in turn in the following sections.

3.2.6 Extra-strong q-stems: word-final q > r

In this subcategory, word-final -q turns into -r before all case suffixes.

Absolutive SG	Relative SG	Absolutive/relative PL	Allative SG
erneq son	**ernerup**	**ernerit**	**ernermut**
arfeq whale	**arferup**	**arferit**	**arfermut**
kalleq thunder	**kallerup**	**kallerit**	**kallermut**

The following table illustrates the complete inflection of an extra-strong q-stem noun.

	arfeq whale	
	SG	PL
ABSOLUTIVE	**arfeq**	**arferit**
RELATIVE	**arferup**	
ALLATIVE	**arfermut**	**arfernut**
LOCATIVE	**arfermi**	**arferni**
ABLATIVE	**arfermit**	**arfernit**
INSTRUMENTAL	**arfermik**	**afternik**
PROLATIVE	**arfikkut**	**arfertigut**
EQUATIVE	**arfertut**	

3.2.7 Strong q-stems: word-final -q disappears or becomes -r

Noun stem types

In this subcategory, word-final -q disappears in the relative singular and absolutive/relative plural (that is, endings beginning with a vowel) but turns into -r before other case suffixes. This subcategory is very commonly seen, as it applies to the superlative form of modifiers (see section 6).

Absolutive singular	Relative singular	Absolutive/ relative plural	Allative singular
qulleq lamp	**qulliup**	**qulliit**	**qullermut**
tulleq the nearest	**tulliup**	**tulliit**	**tullermut**

The following table illustrates the complete inflection of a strong q-stem noun of this category.

	qulleq lamp	
	SG	PL
ABSOLUTIVE	qulleq	qulliit
RELATIVE	qulliup	
ALLATIVE	qullermut	qullernut
LOCATIVE	qullermi	qullerni
ABLATIVE	qullermit	qullernit
INSTRUMENTAL	qullermik	qullernik
PROLATIVE	qullikkut	qullertigut
EQUATIVE	qullermut	

3.2.8 Strong stems in -aq > -ap and -at

For some strong nouns ending in -aq, the final -q is replaced with -a in the relative singular and absolutive/relative plural, resulting in the endings -ap and -at in these forms. (Note that the suffix meaning 'only' listed in the table here is nominal in form.)

Absolutive SG	Relative SG	Absolutive/ relative PL	Allative SG
utoqqaq old man, old woman	**utoqqaap**	**utoqqaat**	**utoqqarmut**
marraq mud	**marraap**	**marraat**	**marrarmik**
-innaq only	**-innaap**	**-innaat**	**-innarmut**

The following table illustrates the complete inflection of a strong q-stem noun with -a- in the grammatical cases.

utoqqaq old man		
	SG	PL
ABSOLUTIVE	**utoqqaq**	**utoqqaat**
RELATIVE	**utoqqaap**	
ALLATIVE	**utoqqarmut**	**utoqqarnut**
LOCATIVE	**utoqqarmi**	**utoqqarni**
ABLATIVE	**utoqqarmit**	**utoqqarnit**
INSTRUMENTAL	**utoqqarmik**	**utoqqarnik**
PROLATIVE	**utoqqakkut**	**utoqqartigut**
EQUATIVE	**utoqqartut**	

3.2.9 Strong stems with nasalisation

Some strong-stem nouns take a nasalised element -ng- before endings beginning with a vowel. These nouns can end in -k or -q. In some cases, they end in a vowel, as there was historically a -k or -q which is no longer present in the modern language. Nasalisation is illustrated in the following examples. Contrast the nasalised forms with the allative singular, which does not contain the nasalised element because the suffix starts with a consonant.

Absolutive SG	Relative SG	Absolutive/ relative PL	Allative SG
killeq border	**killingup**	**killingit**	**killermut**
assi picture	**assingup**	**assingit**	**assimut**
mumik reverse side, back side	**mumingup**	**mumingit**	**mumimmut**

The following table illustrates the complete inflection of a strong q-stem noun with nasalisation.

Noun stem types

	killeq border	
	SG	PL
ABSOLUTIVE	**killeq**	**killingit**
RELATIVE	**killingup**	
ALLATIVE	**killermut**	**killernut**
LOCATIVE	**killermi**	**killerni**
ABLATIVE	**killermit**	**killernit**
INSTRUMENTAL	**killermik**	**killernik**
PROLATIVE	**killekkut**	**killertigut**
EQUATIVE	**killertut**	

3.2.10 Strong stems with metathesis

Metathesis refers to a sound change that alters the order of consonants in a word. This reordering can take place in the grammatical cases of words with strong q-stems that end in -meq, -neq, or -veq. In such cases, the q is moved to the beginning of the syllable. When this metathesis takes place, the q is no longer in final position and becomes r. In the case of nouns with an n before the final q, a g can appear when the metathesis takes place, resulting in the cluster **rn(g)**. The process of metathesis is illustrated in the following table. Note that the v in the -veq forms changes to f in the metathesised version.

Absolutive SG ending	Metathesis (intermediary forms)	Resulting metathesised inflectional stem for the grammatical cases
-meq	**-mq- > -qm-**	**-rm-**
-neq	**-nq- > -qn-**	**-rn(g)-**
-veq	**-vq- > -qv-**	**-rf-**

These types of metathesis are illustrated here. Remember that the metathesised forms only occur in the grammatical cases (i.e. the relative singular and the absolutive and relative plural).

3 Nouns

Absolutive SG	Relative SG	Absolutive/relative PL	Allative SG
imeq water	**erngup, ermup**	**erngit, ermit**	**imermut**
seqineq sun	**seqern(g)up**	**seqern(g)it**	**seqinermut**
sianeq clock	**siarngup**	**siarngit**	**sianermut**
qaneq mouth	**qarn(g)up**	**qarn(g)it**	**qanermut**
aqqusineq road	**aqqusern(g)up**	**aqqusern(g)it**	**aqqusinermut**
aaveq walrus	**aarfup, aarfip**	**aarfit**	**aavermut**

Points to note:

- Some of these forms have parallel variants which are regular, e.g. **aqqusineq** can have the relative singular form **aqqusinerup** as well as **aqqusern(g)it**.
- Sometimes a form ending in -**meq** may have two variants, one with -**rng**- and another with -**m**-; that is, **imeq** 'water' may take the form **erngup** or **ermup** in the relative singular.
- Sometimes a form ending in -**veq** may have an alternative variant with assimilation as well as metathesis (see the table that follows).
- It is sometimes very difficult to predict when a given noun may have a metathesised form in the grammatical cases. It is therefore necessary to learn the absolute and relative singular forms of such words by heart (much like English irregular plural forms such as 'men', 'geese', 'mice').

The following table illustrates the complete inflection of a strong-stem noun with metathesis.

	sianeq clock	
	SG	PL
ABSOLUTIVE	**sianeq**	**siarngit**
RELATIVE	**siarngup**	
ALLATIVE	**sianermut**	**sianernut**
LOCATIVE	**sianermi**	**sianerni**
ABLATIVE	**sianermit**	**sianernit**
INSTRUMENTAL	**sianermik**	**sianernik**
PROLATIVE	**sianikkut**	**sianertigut**
EQUATIVE	**sianertut**	

A slightly different type of metathesis occurs with stems ending in **-peq**, **-teq**, and **-veq**. In these stems, the **p** and **t** are replaced by **qq**, while **v** is replaced by **rr**. There are actually two phenomena at work here: first metathesis, followed by assimilation of the second consonant (and in the case of **-veq** forms, an additional change from **qq** to **rr**). The following chart illustrates the progression of these sound changes (metathesis, followed by assimilation).

Absolutive SG ending	Metathesis (intermediary forms)	Resulting metathesised and assimilated inflectional stem for the grammatical cases
-peq	**-pq- > -qp-**	**-qq-**
-teq	**-tq- > -qt-**	**-qq-**
-veq	**-vq- > -qv-**	**-rr-**

These types of metathesis are shown in the following examples.

Absolutive SG	Relative SG	Absolutive/relative PL	Allative SG
tupeq tent	**toqqup**	**toqqit**	**tupermut**
ateq name	**aqqup, aqqip, atip**	**aqqit, atit**	**atermut**
nateq floor	**naqqup, natip**	**naqqit, natit**	**natermut**
aaveq walrus	**aarrup**	**aarrit**	**aavermik**

Point to note:

- Some of these forms have regular variants; e.g. **ateq** 'name' has the variant relative singular form **atip**.

The following table illustrates the complete inflection of a strong-stem noun ending in **-peq** with metathesis and variant forms.

	tupeq tent	
	SG	PL
ABSOLUTIVE	**tupeq**	**toqqit, tupit**
RELATIVE	**toqqup, tupip**	
ALLATIVE	**tupermut**	**tupernut**
LOCATIVE	**tupermi**	**tuperni**
ABLATIVE	**tupermit**	**tupernit**
INSTRUMENTAL	**tupermik**	**tupernik**
PROLATIVE	**tupikkut**	**tupertigut**
EQUATIVE	**tupertut**	

3.2.11 Strong k-stems

Most of the strong k-stems are regular: the k is dropped in the grammatical cases and assimilates in the other cases.

Absolutive SG	Relative SG	Absolutive/relative PL	Allative SG
inuk person	**inuup**	**inuit**	**inummut**
panik daughter	**paniup**	**paniit**	**panimmut**
kamik boot	**kamiup, kammip**	**kamiit, kammit, kanngit**	**kamimmut**
malik wave	**maliup, mallip**	**maliit**	**malimmut**
saarullik cod	**saarulliup**	**saarulliit**	**saarullimmut**
aappalik (romantic) partner	**aappaliup, aappallip, aappallup**	**aappalliit**	**aappalimmut**

Points to note:

- Some have variant forms in the grammatical cases, e.g. **kamiup, kammip**.
- This category contains many words ending in -**lik**, which is a suffix meaning 'having' that can be attached to nouns.

The following table illustrates the complete inflection of a strong k-stem noun.

	inuk person	
	SG	PL
ABSOLUTIVE	**inuk**	**inuit**
RELATIVE	**inuup**	
ALLATIVE	**inummut**	**inunnut**
LOCATIVE	**inummi**	**inunni**
ABLATIVE	**inummit**	**inunnit**
INSTRUMENTAL	**inummik**	**inunnik**
PROLATIVE	**inukkut**	**inutsigut**
EQUATIVE	**inuttut**	

3.2.12 Strong k-stems with extra -a- in the grammatical cases

Some strong k-stems gain an extra -a- before the grammatical case suffixes, as illustrated here.

Absolutive SG	Relative SG	Absolutive/relative PL	Allative SG
akkak uncle	**akkaap**	**akkaat**	**akkamut**
assak hand	**assaap**	**assaat**	**assamut**

Point to note:

- With this type of noun, the k at the end of the stem is dropped before the oblique case suffixes as well as before the grammatical case suffixes.

The following table illustrates the complete inflection of a strong k-stem noun with -a- in the grammatical cases.

	akkak uncle	
	SG	PL
ABSOLUTIVE	akkak	akkaat
RELATIVE	akkaap	
ALLATIVE	akkamut	akkanut
LOCATIVE	akkami	akkani
ABLATIVE	akkamit	akkanit
INSTRUMENTAL	akkamik	akkanik
PROLATIVE	akkakkut	akkatsigut
EQUATIVE	akkatut	

Noun stem types

3 Nouns

3.3 Function of cases

As mentioned in 3.1, West Greenlandic has eight noun cases, i.e. eight different forms that nouns can appear in depending on the function that they have in the sentence (subject, direct object, indirect object, etc.). The functions of the different cases are explained and illustrated in the following sections.

3.3.1 Absolutive

The absolutive case does not have one specific ending in the singular; however, absolutive nouns can only end in -k, -q, -t, or a vowel depending on the stem type (see section 3.2). In the plural, the absolutive ending is -t (or -it or -at for some strong-stem nouns; see 3.2.5–11). The most basic function of the absolutive is to denote the subject of an intransitive clause (that is, a clause without a direct object), as in the following example. Note that as the absolutive is the default case, it is not marked in the glossing.

> **Meeraq qiavoq.**
> meeraq qia-voq
> child cry-3SG
> The child is crying.

The absolutive is also the case of the object in a transitive clause (that is, a clause with a direct object). Note that this differs from languages with case systems based on a nominative and accusative (e.g. German, Russian, Finnish, Arabic), in which the subject in both transitive and intransitive clauses is marked by the nominative, whereas the object in a transitive clause is marked by the accusative. Absolutive nouns functioning as direct objects are illustrated in the following examples.

> **Mariep atuagaq atuarpaa.**
> marie-p atuagaq atuar-paa
> marie-REL book read-3SG>3SG
> Marie read the book.

> **Arnap ilaqutariit pilersugarai.**
> arna-p ilaqutari-it pilersugar-ai.
> arna-REL family-PL supply.food-3SG>3PL
> Arnaq supplied the family with food.

3.3.2 Relative

The relative case (singular -**p**, plural -**t**, -**it**, or -**at**) is the case used to denote the subject in a transitive clause. This type of system, where the subject of an intransitive clause appears in the same case as the object of a transitive clause while the subject of a transitive clause appears in a different case, is called an absolutive/ergative system. Other languages with an absolutive/ergative system include Basque and Georgian. This differs from the case system of languages such as German, Russian, and Latin, where the subject of both intransitive and transitive clauses appears in the same case (i.e. the nominative case), while the object of transitive clauses appears in a different case (i.e. the accusative).

The following examples illustrate the use of the relative case in West Greenlandic as the subject of a transitive sentence. You can also see that the direct object of the sentence appears in the absolutive case, as discussed in 3.3.1. Note that the relative is marked by the abbreviation REL in the glossing.

Meeqqap atuagaq atuarpaa.
meeqqa-p atuagaq atuar-paa
child-REL book read-3SG>3SG
The child read the book.

The relative is also the case used to mark the possessor in a possessive phrase. In this function it resembles the genitive case in German and Russian or the English 's, as in the following example. Note that the word following the relative, which indicates the possessed noun, appears with a third-person possessive ending, literally meaning 'his/hers/its', so that the phrase literally means 'the child's dog-its'. See section 3.4 for an explanation of how possession works in West Greenlandic.

meeqqap qimmia
meeqqa-p qimmi-a
child-REL dog-3SG
the child's dog

Note that in the plural, there is no way to tell the difference between the absolutive and the relative cases. Only context can distinguish between the two. This is illustrated in the following two examples. Each contains an identical-looking plural noun, but the first is absolutive (as it is the subject of an intransitive sentence), while the second is relative (as it is the possessor in a possessive phrase). Because the absolutive form and the relative form are the same in the plural, the glossing does not distinguish between the two, simply marking them as PL.

Qitsuit pinnguarput.
qitsu-it pinnguar-put
cat-PL play-3PL
The cats are playing.

qitsuit arsai
qitsu-it arsa-i
cat-PL ball-PL.3PL
the cats' balls

3.3.3 Allative

The allative case (singular **-mut**, plural **-nut**) has the basic meaning 'to, into, for', as illustrated in the following examples. Note that the allative case is marked by the abbreviation ALL in the glossing.

Hans Maniitsumut aallarpoq.
hans maniitsu-mut aallar-poq
hans maniitsoq-ALL go-3SG
Hans goes to Maniitsoq.

Nakorsaq napparsimmavimmut iserpoq.
nakorsaq napparsimmavim-mut iser-poq
doctor hospital-ALL enter-3SG
The doctor goes into the hospital.

Arnap taskimut seqinersiutit ilavai.
arna-p taski-mut seqinersiut-it ila-vai
woman-REL bag-ALL sunglass-PL put-3SG>3PL
The woman put the sunglasses into the bag.

The allative can also sometimes be used to indicate the indirect object of a verb (e.g. to give something to someone, to tell something to someone, etc.). However, it is only used in such contexts when there is no direct object explicitly appearing in the sentence (i.e. 'I wrote to a friend', as in the example that follows). When there is also a direct object (e.g. 'I wrote a letter to a friend'), a different construction is typically used (see section 3.3.6 and 7.10.1 for discussion).

Ikinngum<u>mut</u> allappunga.
ikinngum-mut allap-punga
friend-ALL write-1SG
I wrote to a friend.

The allative is used to indicate the time when something happens. In such contexts the allative form appears in the plural (though, particularly among older speakers, the singular can also be used with the numbers **ataaseq** 'one', **arfineq** 'six', and **aqqaneq** 'eleven', e.g. **ataatsimut** 'at one', **arfinermut** 'at six', and **aqqanermut** 'at eleven'). This use of the allative is illustrated in the following example. (See section 5 for discussion of West Greenlandic numerals.)

Qassi<u>nut</u> ataatsimiinneq aallaartissava? – Quli<u>nut</u>.
qassi-nut ataatsimiinneq aallaarti-ssa-va? – quli-nut.
how.much-ALL.PL meeting start-FUT-INT.3SG – ten-ALL.PL
What time will the meeting start? – At 10 o'clock.

The allative is also used to indicate 'per' for weights and measures, e.g.:

Kiilu<u>mut</u> 20 kroneqarpoq.
kiilu-mut 20 krone-qar-poq
kilo-ALL 20 kroner-have-3SG
It costs 20 kroner per kilo.

3.3.4 Locative

The locative case (singular **-mi**, plural **-ni**) is used to describe where something is, much like the English 'in, on, at'. These uses are illustrated in the following examples respectively. Note that the locative case is marked by the abbreviation LOC in the glossing.

Nuum<u>mi</u> najugaqarpugut.
nuum-mi najugar-qar-pugut
Nuuk-LOC home-have-1PL
We live in Nuuk.

Siku<u>mi</u> angallanneq inerteqqutaavoq.
siku-mi angallan-neq inerteqqutaa-voq
ice-LOC go-VN be.forbidden-3SG
Going on the ice is forbidden.

> Function of cases

Jensenikkun<u>ni</u> viinisorpugut.
jensen-i-kkun-ni viini-sor-pugut
Jensen-HV-COLL-LOC wine-consume-1PL
We are drinking wine at the Jensens'.

Illoqarfin<u>ni</u> atuarfeqarpoq.
illoqarfin-ni atuarfe-qar-poq
town-LOC.PL school-have-3SG
There are schools in the towns.

It can also be used in a temporal sense, as in the following examples:

Februari<u>mi</u> Kalaallit Illuutaat pulaarparput.
februari-mi kalaallit illu-uta-at pulaarpar-put
february-LOC greenlander-PL house-belonging.to-3PL visit-3PL
In February we visited the Greenlandic House.

Ullu<u>mi</u> Naja naapipparput.
ullu-mi naja naapip-parput
day-LOC naja meet-1PL>3SG
Today we met Naja.

Aasa<u>mi</u> nasartaartarput.
aasa-mi nasartaar-tar-put
summer-LOC hat-HAB-3PL
In the summer they graduate high school.[1]

3.3.5 Ablative

The ablative case (singular -mit, -miit, -minngaaniit, plural -nit, -niit, -ninngaaniit) is used in the sense of 'from, out of'. The different variants listed here are used interchangeably. Note that the ablative case is marked by the abbreviation ABL in the glossing.

Atuarfim<u>mit</u> anipput.
atuarfim-mit ani-pput
school-ABL come-3PL
They came out of the school.

Kalaaleq inuusuttoq Mexico<u>miit</u> aallartariaqarpoq.
kalaaleq inuusut-toq mexico-miit aallar-tariaqar-poq

---

1 Literally: get hats.

greenlander be.young-IP Mexico-ABL leave-must-3SG
The young Greenlander has to leave (from) Mexico.

Juuni<u>miit</u> aggustip tungaanut Nunatsinniittarpunga.
juuni-miit aggusti-p tungaanut Nunatsi-nni-it-tar-punga
june-ABL august-REL until greenland-LOC.3PL-be-HAB-1SG
I'm usually in Greenland from June until August.

Ullaakkorsiorneq arfiner<u>niit</u> qulit tungaanut pissaaq.
ullaakkorsior-neq arfiner-niit qulit tungaanut pi-ssaaq
have.breakfast-AP six-ABL.PL ten until happen-FUT.3SG
Breakfast will be served[2] from six until ten.

The ablative case has the meaning 'than' when used in conjunction with the comparative (see section 6.3.1), e.g.:

Qimmeq qitsum<u>miit</u> anneruvoq.
qimmeq qitsum-miit anner-u-voq
dog cat-ABL bigger-be-3SG
The dog is bigger than the cat.

Platini kuulti<u>miit</u> qaqutigoorneruvoq kuulti<u>millu</u> akisunerulluni.
platini kuulti-mit qaqutigoor-ner-u-voq kuulti-mil-lu akisu-ner-u-lluni
platinum gold-ABL rare-COMP-be-3SG gold-ABL-and expensive-COMP-be-CONT.4SG
Platinum is rarer than gold and more expensive than gold.

The ablative can also be used in the sense of 'because of'. In this type of context, only the short version of the ablative ending is used. The following example illustrates this usage.

Napparsimaner<u>mit</u> atuarfimmiinngilanga.
napparsima-ner-mit atuarfim-mi-i-nngi-langa
be.sick-AP-ABL school-LOC-be-NEG-1SG
I wasn't in school because of illness.[3]

---

2 Literally: will happen.
3 I.e. because I was sick.

The ablative can also be used in the sense of 'out of', 'from' to indicate the type of material that something is made of, e.g.:

Annoraat siullermik amer<u>mit</u> mersorneqarput.
annoraa-t siullermik amer-mit mersor-neqar-put
anorak-PL originally skin-ABL sew-PASS-3PL
Anoraks were originally made of skin.

The ablative can also be used to denote the agent in a passive clause, as in the following examples. See section 7.9 for discussion of the passive.

Biilit angum<u>mit</u> suliarineqarput
biili-t angum-mit suliari-neqar-put
car-PL man-ABL repair-PASS-3PL
The car was repaired by the man.

Atuagaq Robert Peterseni<u>miit</u> allanneqarpoq.
atuagaq robert peterseni-miit allan-neqar-poq
book robert peterseni-ABL write-PASS-3SG
The book was written by Robert Petersen.

Attaveerunneq teknikeri<u>nit</u> iluarsineqarpoq.
attaveerunneq teknikeri-nit iluarsi-neqar-poq
server.fault technician-ABL.PL repair-PASS-3SG
The server fault was fixed by the technicians.

3.3.6 Instrumental

The instrumental case (singular -**mik**, plural -**nik**) has a wide range of meanings in West Greenlandic. Its most basic function is to indicate the means by which something is done. It often corresponds to the English prepositions 'with' or 'by', as in the following examples. Note that the instrumental case is marked by the abbreviation INS in the glossing.

Allaam<u>mik</u> allappara.
allaam-mik allap-para
pen-INS write-1SG>3SG
I wrote it with a pen.

Alussaam<u>mik</u> nerivaa.
alussaam-mik neri-vaa
spoon-INS eat-3SG>3SG
S/he is eating it with a spoon.

The instrumental is also used in the sense of 'about', e.g.:

Rasmusseni<u>mik</u> atuagaq
rasmusseni-mik atuagaq
rasmussen-INS book
a book about Rasmussen

arna<u>mik</u> oqaluttuaq
arna-mik oqaluttuaq
woman-INS story
a story about a woman

The instrumental can also denote 'for' in the sense of going somewhere for an item, e.g.:

Igaffimmut immum<u>mik</u> aallerpoq.
igaffim-mut immum-mik aaller-poq
kitchen-ALL milk-INS go-3SG
S/he goes to the kitchen for milk.

Requests for something can be made by adding the instrumental suffix to a noun, e.g.:

Sukkulaa<u>mik</u>.
sukkulaa-mik
chocolate-INS
Some chocolate, please. / Can I have some chocolate?

The instrumental can also be used to indicate that an object is indefinite, for example, 'a book', as opposed to definite, as in 'the book'. (West Greenlandic does not have words corresponding to the English indefinite article 'a' and definite article 'the'.) By contrast, putting the object in the absolutive typically indicates that it is definite. Compare the following two examples: the first contains an absolutive object, which is translated into English with a definite noun, while the second contains an instrumental object, which is translated into English as an indefinite noun. (See also section 14.3 for further discussion of the ways in which West Greenlandic can indicate definiteness.)

<u>Nanoq</u> takuara.
nanoq taku-ara
polar.bear see-1SG>3SG
I saw the polar bear.

Nanumik takuvunga.
nanu-mik taku-vunga
polar.bear-INS see-1SG
I saw a polar bear.

Note that if the direct object is indefinite and thus in the instrumental case, the subject will appear in the absolutive case rather than in the relative case, as in the first example here. This can be contrasted with a clause with a definite direct object, where the direct object is in the absolutive case and the subject is in the relative case, as in the second example.

Naja nanumik takuvoq.
naja nanu-mik taku-voq
naja polar.bear-INS see-3SG
Naja saw a polar bear.

Najap nanoq takuaa.
naja-p nanoq taku-aa
naja-REL polar.bear see-3SG>3SG
Naja saw the polar bear.

Another example of the instrumental functioning as the marker of an indefinite direct object is shown here.

Akunnittarfinnik sanaartorluta aallartikkusuppugut.
akunnittarfin-nik sanaartor-luta aallarti-kkusup-pugut
hotel-INS.PL build-CONT.1PL begin-want-1PL
We want to start building hotels.

The instrumental can also be used in the sense of 'some' when referring to indefinite amounts, e.g.:

Iffiamik nerivunga.
iffia-mik neri-vunga
bread-INS eat-1SG
I ate some (rye) bread.

Atuakkanik pisivunga.
atuakka-nik pisi-vunga
book-INS.PL buy-1SG
I bought some books.

In a transitive clause containing an indirect object in addition to a direct object which is indefinite or a mass (collective) noun, the direct object appears in the instrumental case and the indirect object appears in the absolutive case. In such cases the verb gains a special suffix, **-up-** (glossed here as VAL for 'valency'), which indicates that there is more than one object in the clause. This type of construction is discussed in more detail in section 7.10.

Function of cases

> **Hans kaffi<u>mik</u> aalliuppara.**
> hans kaffi-mik aalli-up-para
> hans coffee-INS fetch-VAL-1SG>3SG
> I fetched coffee for Hans.

> **Meeqqat tunissuti<u>nik</u> pisiniuppakka.**
> meeqqa-t tunissut-inik pisini-up-pakka
> child-PL present-INS.PL buy-VAL-1SG>3PL
> I bought presents for the children.

When an object is incorporated into a verb (see section 14.2 for discussion of noun incorporation), its modifier appears in the instrumental case before the incorporated construction. (See section 6 for discussion of noun modifiers.) The following examples illustrate this type of usage. Note that in such contexts it is not possible to tell whether the incorporated noun is singular or plural in meaning, as it always appears in singular form. If it is plural in meaning, this is only marked on the independent modifier, which will have an instrumental plural ending.

> **Mamartu<u>mik</u> kaffisorpugut.**
> mamartu-mik kaffi-sor-pugut
> tasty-INS coffee-consume-1PL
> We drink good coffee.

> **Nutaa<u>nik</u> kamissivoq.**
> nutaa-nik kamis-si-voq
> new-INS.PL boot-buy-3SG
> He's bought new boots.

The instrumental is also used in constructions indicating names and ages. In such instances, the instrumental is suffixed to the name or age. This is followed by the noun **ateq** 'name' or **ukioq** 'year' incorporated into the verb **-qarpoq** 'to have', as in the following two examples respectively.

Aki<u>mik</u> ateqarpunga.
aki-mik ate-qar-punga
aki-INS name-have-1SG
My name is Aki.

Ulloriaq quli<u>nik</u> ukioqarpoq.
ulloriaq quli-nik ukio-qar-poq
ulloriaq ten-INS.PL year-have-3SG
Ulloriaq is ten years old.

Similarly, the instrumental is used for other numbers, amounts, degrees, and prices. In such contexts, the instrumental suffix (in the singular or plural, as relevant) is attached to the quantity word (e.g. 'ten', 'many', 'metre', etc.). This usage is illustrated in the following examples.

Quli<u>nik</u> issippoq.
quli-nik issip-poq
ten-INS.PL freeze-3SG
It's minus ten degrees.[4]

Inissiat nuanneq! Qassi<u>nik</u> initaqarpa?
inissia-t nuanneq! qassi-nik inita-qar-pa
flat-2SG nice many-INS.PL room-have-INT.3SG
Your flat is nice. How many rooms does it have?

Ippassaq Nuummi 1 meteri<u>mik</u> apisimavoq.
ippassaq nuum-mi 1 meteri-mik api-sima-voq
yesterday nuuk-LOC 1 metre-INS snow-PAST-3SG
Yesterday it snowed 1 metre in Nuuk.

Arnaaluk neqimik pisivoq 75 kr-<u>nik</u> akilerlugu.
arnaaluk neqi-mik pisi-voq 75 kr-nik akiler-lugu
arnaaluk seal.meat-INS buy-3SG 75 krone-INS.PL pay-CONT.4SG
Arnaaluk bought some seal meat and paid 75 kroner for it.

The instrumental is also the case used to indicate adverbs, much like the English -ly. See section 9 for discussion of West Greenlandic adverbs.

---

4 Literally: it's freezing by ten degrees.

Sukkasuumik ingerlavoq.
sukkasuu-mik ingerla-voq
fast-INS go-3SG
S/he/it went quickly.

Nipituumik erinarsorpoq.
nipituu-mik erinarsor-poq
loud-INS sing-3SG
S/he sings loudly.

Ilaasut sukkasuumik aamma isumannaatsumik angalareerlutik tikipput.
ilaasu-t sukkasuu-mik aamma isumannaatsu-mik angala-reer-lutik tikip-put
passenger-PL fast-INS and safe-INS travel-PERF-CONT.4PL arrive-3PL
The passengers arrived quickly and safely after their journey.

The instrumental is also used in the formation of constructions equivalent to English compound nouns such as 'electronics store', 'sealskin'. The first noun in such constructions, which modifies the head noun, appears in the instrumental. This is illustrated in the following examples.

matumik paarsisoq
matu-mik paarsisoq
door-INS guard
doorman, concierge

imigassamik ajornartorsiut
imigassa-mik ajornartorsiut
alcohol-INS problem
alcohol problem

aalisarnermik siunnersorti
aalisarner-mik siunnersorti
fishery-INS consultant
fishery consultant

atomimik nukissiorfik
atomi-mik nukissiorfik
atom-INS power.plant
atomic power plant

Much like the ablative, the instrumental can be used to indicate the material that something is made out of. For example:

Tujuuloq qiviunik sanaajuvoq.
tujuuloq qiviu-nik sanaa-ju-voq
jumper wool-INS.PL product-be-3SG
The jumper is made out of (musk ox) wool.

Illut qisummik sanaajupput.
illu-t qisum-mik sanaa-jup-put
house-PL wood-INS product-be-3PL
The houses are made out of wood.

3.3.7 Prolative

The prolative case (singular -**kkut**, plural -**tigut** or -**sigut**) has the sense of 'via, through, along'. It is also known by a number of other terms, including 'vialis', 'prosecutive', and 'perlative'. The following examples illustrate its usage. Note that the prolative case is marked by the abbreviation PRO in the glossing.

Nuummut Kangerlussuakkut aallarpugut.
nuum-mut kangerlussua-kkut aallar-pugut
nuuk-ALL kangerlussuaq-PRO go-1PL
We went to Nuuk via Kangerlussuaq.

Arnaq putukkut nakkarpoq.
arnaq putu-kkut nakkar-poq
woman hole-PRO fall-3SG
The woman fell through the hole.

Tuttu aqqusinikkut pangalippoq.
tuttu aqqusini-kkut pangalip-poq
reindeer road-PRO run-3SG
The reindeer ran along the road.

Anaanap talikkut tiguaanga
anaana-p tali-kkut tiguaanga
mother-REL arm-PRO take-3SG>1SG
Mother took me by the arm.

Eqqumiitsuliat umiarsuakkut Nuummut tikipput.
eqqumiitsulia-t umiarsua-kkut nuum-mut tikip-put
art-PL boat-PRO nuuk-ALL arrive-3PL
The artwork arrived in Nuuk by boat.

>Function of cases

The prolative is often found in conjunction with nouns denoting different types of media, in the meaning of 'by phone, on TV, on Facebook, online', etc., as in the following examples:

tv-kkut aallakaatitassat
tv-kkut aallakaatissa-t
tv-PRO programme-PL
TV programmes

radiukkut naalagiarneq
radiu-kkut naalagiarneq
radio-PRO church.service
a radio church service

facebookikkut oqallinneq
facebook-i-kkut oqallinneq
Facebook-HV-PRO debate
a debate on Facebook

Telefonikkut ataatsimiinnerit pillugit apeqqutissaqarpit?
telefoni-kkut ataatsimiinneri-t pillugit apeqquti-ssa-qar-pit
telephone-PRO meeting-PL regarding question-FUT-have-INT.2SG
Do you have questions regarding telephone meetings?

Internettikkut niuerneq siuariartoqaaq.
internetti-kkut niuerneq siuariarto-qaaq
internet-PRO trade make.progress-be.a.lot.3SG
There is a lot of progress in online trade.

Internettikkut atuarpara.
internetti-kkut atuar-para
internet-PRO read-1SG>3SG
I read it online.

Snapchatikkut assimik nassiussivoq.
snapchat-i-kkut assi-mik nassiussi-voq
snapchat-HV-PRO photo-INS send-3SG
S/he sent a photo via Snapchat.

With writing, signing, logging in, and related activities, the place where the activity occurs is indicated with the prolative, e.g.:

Su<u>kkut</u> isissaanga? – Matu<u>kkut</u>.
su-kkut isi-ssa-anga? – matu-kkut
where-PRO enter-FUT-1SG – door-PRO
Where shall I enter? – Through the door.

Su<u>kkut</u> log in-issaanga? – Facebooki<u>kkut</u>.
su-kkut log in-i-ssa-anga? – facebook-i-kkut
what-PRO log in-HV-FUT-1SG facebook-H-VPRO
Where shall I log in?

It is also used to indicate a place on the body where pain is felt or where on the body someone has been hit.

Tali<u>kkut</u> annerpoq.
tali-kkut anner-poq
arm-PRO hurt-3SG
The arm hurts.

When something happens regularly, the temporal expression has the prolative ending, e.g. **sapaatikkut** 'on Sundays'. The verb will often have the habitual suffix **+tarpoq/+sarpoq** in these cases. The following examples illustrate this usage.

Sapaati<u>kkut</u> naalagiartarpugut.
sapaati-kkut naalagar-tar-pugut
sunday-PRO attend.church-HAB-1PL
We attend church on Sundays.

Nuummi politiit unnua<u>kkut</u> nakkutilliinerulerput.
nuum-mi politi-it unnua-kkut nakkutillii-neru-ler-put
nuuk-LOC police-PL night-PRO patrol-be.more-begin-3PL
The police will start patrolling more at night.

Arfininngorni<u>kkut</u> uali<u>kkut</u> Erik timersortarfimmi arsartarpoq.
arfininngorni-kkut uali-kkut erik timersortarfim-mi arsar-tar-poq
saturday-PRO afternoon-PRO erik sportshall-LOC play.football-HAB-3SG
On Saturday afternoons Erik plays football in the sportshall.

3.3.8 Equative

Function of cases

The equative case does not have separate singular and plural forms; it is always -**tut**/-**sut**. It has the meaning of 'as, like', as illustrated in the following examples. Note that the equative case is marked by the abbreviation EQU in the glossing.

Ilinniartitsisutut sulisarpunga.
ilinniartitsisu-tut suli-sar-punga
teacher-EQU work-HAB-1SG
I work as a teacher.

Nuummi inuusuttunut guidetut sulisarput.
nuum-mi inuusuttu-nut guide-tut suli-sar-put
nuuk-LOC young-PL guide-EQU work-HAB-3PL
In Nuuk, young people tend to work as guides.

Issiavik ilisivittut atortarpara.
issiavik ilisivit-tut ator-tar-para
chair shelf-EQU use-HAB-1SG>3SG
I use the chair as a shelf.

Ilinniartitsisuulluartutut isigaara.
ilinniartitsisu-u-lluar-tu-tut isi-gaara
teacher-be-good-IP-PRO regard-1SG>3SG
I regard him/her as a good teacher.

It is also used when indicating 'a certain language', 'in a certain language', 'like a certain nationality', e.g.:

Atuagaq kalaallisut saqqummernikuuvoq.
atuagaq kalaalli-sut saqqummer-nikuu-voq
book greenlander-EQU come.out-PAST-3SG
The book came out in Greenlandic.

Tuluttut ilinniarpoq.
tulut-tut ilinniar-poq
english.person-EQU study-3SG
S/he studies English.

Thailandimiu<u>sut</u> oqaluppoq.
thailandimiu-sut oqalup-poq
thailander-EQU speak-3SG
S/he speaks Thai.

Pukkitsormiu<u>sut</u> atisaqarpoq
pukkitsormiu-sut atisa-qar-poq
dutch.person-EQU clothes-have-3SG
S/he is dressed like a Dutch person.

3.4 Possessive inflection

Noun possession in West Greenlandic is expressed by means of possessive suffixes attached to the possessum (i.e. the possessed noun). The suffix changes depending on the case of the possessum; for example, the form of the suffix for 'your' will be different depending on which case the noun to which it is attached is in. The following sections explain and illustrate the possessive suffixes and their uses in the various cases.

3.4.1 Possessive absolutive

The possessive suffixes as attached to absolutive nouns are shown next. Note that the labels 4SG and 4PL in the table refer to the 'fourth person', which is a common feature of West Greenlandic and means 'one's own', referring back to the subject of the clause. The difference between the third person and the fourth person can be seen by comparing the following two examples: 3SG **qimmi<u>a</u> takuaa** 's/he saw his/her (i.e. someone else's) dog' vs. 4SG **qimmi<u>ni</u> takuaa** 's/he saw his/her (own) dog'.

Possessive absolutive suffixes		
Possessor	Possessum	
	SG	PL
1SG	-ga, -ra	-kka
2SG	-t	-tit
3SG	-a	-i
4SG	-ni	
1PL	-(r)put	-vut
2PL	-(r)si	-si
3PL	-at	-at, -i
4PL	-(r)tik, -tsik	-tik

Points to note:

- In the first-person singular, the variant **-ga** is used with vowel-stem, weak t-stem, and all k-stem nouns (both weak and strong). The variant **-ra** is used with all q-stem nouns (both weak and strong).
- With weak t-stem nouns, the historical vowel **-i** appears before the possessive suffix, e.g. **-ga**, e.g. **siut** 'ear' > **siutiga** 'my ear'; **siutit** 'your ear'.
- The possessive variant with **-r** appears with some of the singular suffixes following a vowel-stem or weak t-stem noun, e.g. **illu** 'house' > **illorput** 'our house'. This is an example of the so-called 'recessive r' discussed in section 2.5.1.
- When the third-person singular suffix is attached to some nouns ending in **-i**, this **-i** will become **-a**, e.g. **ini** 'room' > **inaa** 'his/her room'. (See section 2.5.2 for discussion of this type of vowel change.)
- For extra-strong-stem nouns in the plural, the final consonant disappears before all possessive absolutive suffixes except the 3SG and 3PL, e.g. **erneq** 'son' > **ernikka** 'my sons' vs. **erneri** 'his sons'.
- The third-person plural suffix on plural nouns is usually **-at**. However, weak-stem nouns ending in **-u**, most weak- and strong-stem nouns ending in **-q**, and strong-stem nouns ending in **-k** take **-i**, e.g. **illu** 'house' > **illui** 'their houses'; **qimmeq** 'dog' > **qimmii** 'their dogs'; **ateq** 'name' > **atii** 'their names' (note that this also has the variant form **aqqi**); **panik** 'daughter' > **panii** 'their daughters'.
- In the case of q-stem nouns whose inflectional stem ends in a double vowel, a **v** may be inserted before the third-person plural suffix on the plural form of the noun, e.g. **igalaaq** 'window', inflectional stem **igalaa-** > **igalaavi** 'their windows'.
- In some cases the fourth-person plural suffix on singular nouns appears as **-tsik**. This includes strong-stem nouns ending in **-k**, e.g. **panik** 'daughter' > **panitsik** 'their (own) daughter'.
- Some nouns may have more than one variant when certain possessive suffixes are added, e.g. **asseq** 'picture' > **assia** or **assinga** 'his/her picture'; **tupeq** 'tent' > **tupia** or **toqqa** 'his/her tent'; **umik** 'beard' > **umia** or **umma** 'his beard'.

Here we have listed the possessive absolutive forms for three different common noun types: **illu** 'house', a weak vowel-stem noun; **meeraq** 'child', a weak-stem noun with gemination and a further change; and erneq 'son', a strong-stem noun. See https://oqaasileriffik.gl/sprogteknologi/lookdown/ for an automatic word generator which can produce the correct form of all different types of nouns with possessive suffixes.

Possessive absolutive – **illu** house		
Possessor	Possessum SG	Possessum PL
1SG	**illuga** my house	**illukka** my houses
2SG	**illut** your house	**illutit** your houses
3SG	**illua** his/her house	**illui** his/her houses
4SG	**illuni** his/her (own) house/houses	
1PL	**illorput** our house	**illuvut** our houses
2PL	**illorsi** your house	**illusi** your houses
3PL	**illuat** their house	**illui** their houses
4PL	**illortik** their (own) house	**illutik** their (own) houses

Possessive absolutive – **meeraq** child		
Possessor	Possessum SG	Possessum PL
1SG	**meerara** my child	**meeqqakka** my children
2SG	**meeqqat** your child	**meeqqatit** your children
3SG	**meeraa** his/her child	**meerai** his/her children
4SG	**meeqqani** his/her (own) child/children	
1PL	**meerarput** our child	**meeqqavut** our children
2PL	**meerarsi** your child	**meeqqasi** your children
3PL	**meeraat** their child/children	
4PL	**meerartik** their (own) child	**meeqqatik** their (own) children

Possessive inflection

Possessor	Possessive absolute – **erneq** son	
	Possessum SG	Possessum PL
1SG	**ernera** my son	**ernikka** my sons
2SG	**ernerit** your son	**ernitit** your sons
3SG	**ernera** his/her son	**erneri** his/her sons
4SG	**ernini** his/her (own) son/sons	
1PL	**ernerput** our son	**ernivut** our sons
2PL	**ernersi** your son	**ernisi** your sons
3PL	**ernarat** their son	**erneri** their sons
4PL	**ernertik** their (own) son	**ernitik** their (own) sons

The use of the possessive absolutive suffixes are illustrated in the following examples.

Anaanaga Nuummiippoq.
anaana-ga nuum-mi-ip-poq
mother-1SG nuuk-LOC-be-3SG
My mother is in Nuuk.

Mobiilit sumiippa?
mobiili-t sumi-ip-pa
mobile-2SG where-be-INT.3SG
Where is your mobile?

Nunarput Great Nordic Feastimut peqataavoq.
nuna-rput great nordic feasti-mut peqataa-voq
country-1PL great nordic feast-ALL take.part-3SG
Our country is taking part in the Great Nordic Feast.

Sebastianip nalaasaarfini siniffittut atorpaa.
sebastiani-p nalaasaarfi-ni siniffit-tut ator-paa
sebastian-REL sofa-4SG bed-EQU use-3SG>3SG
Sebastian uses his sofa as a bed.

3.4.2 Possessive relative

The possessive suffixes as attached to relative nouns are shown next.

Possessive relative suffixes		
Possessor	Possessum	
	SG	PL
1SG	-ma	
2SG	-(r)pit, -vit	-vit
3SG	-ata	-isa
4SG	-mi	
1PL	-tta	
2PL	-ssi	
3PL	-ata	-isa
4PL	-mik	

Points to note:

- For the 2SG suffix, the bracketed **r** appears following vowel-stem nouns not ending in -a, e.g. **illu** 'house' > **illorpit** 'your house's'. This can also happen with weak t-stem nouns, e.g. **ikinngut** 'friend' > **ikinnguterpit** 'your friend's' (but see the following point).
- Weak t-stem nouns may have three different variants of the 2SG suffix, e.g. **ikinngut** 'friend' has the possessive relative variants **ikinngutivit** and **ikunnguppit** 'your friend's' as well as **ikinnguterpit**.
- The 2SG variant -**vit** is used with weak-stem nouns ending in -a and -i, e.g. **nuna** 'land' > **nunavit** 'your land's', **ini** 'room' > **inivit** 'your room's'; and weak-stem nouns with gemination, e.g. **meeraq** > **meeqqavit** 'your child's'.
- Weak consonant-stem nouns lose their final consonant before suffixes starting with a single consonant, e.g. **qimmeq** 'dog' > **qimmima** 'my dog's'.
- Extra-strong-stem singular nouns (see section 3.2.6) lose their final consonant before possessive suffixes beginning with a double consonant, e.g. **erneq** 'son' > **ernitta** 'our son's'.
- Extra-strong-stem plural nouns lose their final consonant before all suffixes except the 3PL, e.g. **ernerit** 'sons' > **ernima** 'my sons' vs. **ernerisa** 'their sons'.

- The final consonant of other strong-stem singular nouns typically assimilates before a possessive relative suffix beginning with a consonant, e.g. **panik** 'daughter' > **panimma** 'my daughter's'.
- The final consonant of such strong-stem singular nouns typically disappears before a possessive relative suffix beginning with a vowel, e.g. **panik** 'daughter' > **paniata** 'his/her daughter's'.
- When the 2PL possessive suffix **-vit** is attached to nouns ending in **-u**, the **v** of the suffix disappears (in accordance with the rule discussed in section 2.5.4), e.g. **illu** 'house' > **illuit** 'of your houses'.

Here we have listed the possessive relative forms for **illu** 'house', **meeraq** 'child', and **erneq** 'son'.

	Possessive relative – **illu** house	
Possessor	Possessum SG	Possessum PL
1SG	**illuma** of my house/houses	
2SG	**illorpit** of your house	**illuit** of your houses
3SG	**illuata** of his/her house	**illuisa** of his/her houses
4SG	**illumi** of his/her (own) house/houses	
1SG	**illutta** of our house/houses	
2SG	**illussi** of your house/houses	
3SG	**illuata** of their house	**illuisa** of their houses
4PL	**illumik** of their (own) house/houses	

	Possessive relative – **meeraq** child	
Possessor	Possessum SG	Possessum PL
1SG	**meeqqama** of my child/children	
2SG	**meeqqavit** of your child/children	
3SG	**meeraata** of his/her child	**meeraasa** of his/her children
4SG	**meeqqami** of his/her (own) child/children	
1PL	**meeqqatta** of our child/children	
2PL	**meeqqassi** of your child/children	
3PL	**meeraata** of their child	**meeraasa** of their children
4PL	**meeqqamik** of their (own) child/children	

Possessive inflection

3 Nouns

Possessive relative – **erneq** son		
Possessor	Possessum SG	Possessum PL
1SG	**ernerma** of my son	**ernima** of my sons
2SG	**ernerpit** of your son	**ernivit** of your sons
3SG	**ernerata** of his/her son	**ernerisa** of his/her sons
4SG	**ernermi** of his/her (own) son	**ernimi** of his/her (own) sons
1PL	**ernitta** of our son/sons	
2PL	**ernissi** of your son/sons	
3PL	**ernerata** of their son	**ernerisa** of their sons
4PL	**ernermik** of their (own) sons	**ernimik** of their own sons

The use of the possessive relative suffixes is shown here. Note that nouns with the possessive relative suffix can function either to indicate possession (like the English 'my father's' and 'of the house', as in the first two examples), or as the subject of a transitive clause, as in the final two examples. This is in keeping with the two main functions of the relative case in general (see section 3.3.2 for discussion).

ataata̲m̲a̲ biilii
ataata-ma biili-i
father-REL.1SG car-3SG>3PL
my father's car

illu̲s̲s̲i̲ qalipaataa
illu-ssi qalipaata-a
house-REL.2PL colour-3SG>3SG
the colour of your (PL) house

Anaana̲m̲a̲ nammattakkani qimappaa.
anaana-ma nammattakka-ni qimap-paa
mother-REL.1SG backpack-4SG forget-3SG>3SG
My mother forgot her backpack.

Ilinniartitsisu̲t̲t̲a̲ atuagaq atuarpaa.
ilinniartitsisu-tta atuagaq atuar-paa
teacher-REL.1PL book read-3SG>3SG
Our teacher is reading the book.

3.4.3 Possessive allative

Possessive inflection

The possessive suffixes as attached to allative nouns are shown next.

Possessive allative suffixes		
Possessor	Possessum	
	SG	PL
1SG	-nnut	
2SG		
3SG	-anut	-inut, -annut
4SG	-minut	
1PL	-tsinnut	
2PL	-ssinnut	
3PL	-annut	-inut, -annut
4PL	-minnut	

Points to note:

- Most of the forms are the same for both singular and plural possessums, e.g. **illutsinnut** can mean either 'to our house' or 'to our houses'.
- The suffix for the 1SG and 2SG possessor is the same, so **illunnut** can mean 'to my house/houses' as well as 'to your (SG) house/houses'.
- The usual form of the 3SG and 3PL possessive allative suffix on plural nouns is -**inut**.
- The -**anut** variant of the 3SG possessive allative suffix on plural nouns can sometimes appear with weak t-stem nouns, e.g. **siut** 'ear' > **siutaanut** 'to his/her ears', as well as any type of noun ending in **a** plus a consonant, e.g. 'child' > **meeraanut** 'to his/her children'.
- The -**annut** variant of the 3PL possessive allative suffix on plural nouns can sometimes appear with weak t-stem nouns, e.g. **siut** 'ear' > **siutaannut** 'to their ears', as well as any type of noun ending in **a** plus a consonant, e.g. 'child' > **meeraannut** 'to their children'.

Next we have listed the possessive allative forms for **illu** 'house', **meeraq** 'child', and **erneq** 'son'.

3
Nouns

Possessive allative – **illu** house		
Possessor	Possessum SG	Possessum PL
1SG / 2SG	**illunnut** to my house/houses, to your house/houses	
3SG	**illuanut** to his/her house	**illuinut** to his/her houses
4SG	**illuminut** to his/her own house/houses	
1PL	**illutsinnut** to our house/houses	
2PL	**illussinnut** to your house/houses	
3PL	**illuannut** to their house	**illuinut** to their houses
4PL	**illuminnut** to their own house/houses	

Possessive allative – **meeraq** child	
Possessor	Possessum SG/PL
1SG / 2SG	**meeqqannut** to my/your child/children
3SG	**meeraanut** to his/her child/children
4SG	**meeqqaminut** to his/her (own) child/children
1PL	**meeqqatsinnut** to our child/children
2PL	**meeqqassinnut** to your child/children
3PL	**meeraannut** to their child/children
4PL	**meeqqaminnut** to their (own) child/children

Possessive allative – **erneq** son		
Possessor	Possessum SG	Possessum PL
1SG / 2SG	**erninnut** to my/your son/sons	
3SG	**erneranut** to his/her son	**ernerinut** to his/her sons
4SG	**ernerminut** to his/her (own) son/sons	
1PL	**ernitsinnut** to our son/sons	
2PL	**ernissinnut** to your son	**ernissinnut** to your sons
3PL	**ernerannut** to their son	**ernerinut** to their sons
4PL	**ernerminnut** to their (own) son(s)	

The use of the possessive allative suffixes is shown here.

Angut illumi<u>nut</u> iserpoq.
angut illuminut iserpoq
man house-ALL.4SG go.in-3SG
The man enters his house.

Issiavik ineeqqa<u>nnut</u> iliartoruk!
issiavik ineeqqa-nnut iliartor-uk
chair room-ALL.2SG put-IMP.2SG>3SG
Put the chair in your room!

Kammalaati<u>tsinnut</u> allakkanik nassiussivugut.
kammalaati-tsinnut allakka-nik nassiussi-vugut
friend-ALL.1PL letter-INS.PL send-1PL
We send letters to our friends.

Illu<u>minnut</u> maanna angerlarsinnaanngorput.
illu-minnut maanna angerlar-sinnaa-nngor-put
house-PL.ALL.4PL now return-be.able-become-3PL
Now they have become able to return to their homes.

Tuppiarsi ujarannguamik Kaasipap illuata qali<u>anut</u> miloriussivoq.
tuppiarsi ujaranngua-mik kassipa-p illu-ata qali-anut miloriussi-voq
tuppiarsi stone-INS kaasipat-REL house-REL.3SG roof-ALL.3SG throw-3SG
Tuppiarsi threw a stone onto the roof of Kaasipat's house.

3.4.4 Possessive locative

The possessive suffixes as attached to locative nouns are shown next.

Possessor	Possessive locative suffixes	
	Possessum	
	SG	PL
1SG	-nni	
2SG		
3SG	-ani	-ini, -ani

Possessive inflection

3 Nouns

Possessive locative suffixes		
Possessor	Possessum	
	SG	PL
4SG	-mini	
1PL	-tsinni	
2PL	-ssinni	
3PL	-anni	-ini, -anni
4PL	-minni	

Points to note:

- Like the possessive allative suffixes discussed in 3.4.3, in most instances the possessive locative suffixes have the same form in the singular and plural.
- The two variants of the 3SG (-**ini** and -**ani**) and the 3PL (-**ini** and -**anni**) possessive locative suffixes on the plural form of nouns are subject to the same patterns as those discussed in the 'points to note' for the possessive allative suffixes discussed in 3.4.3.

Next we have listed the possessive locative forms for **illu** 'house', **meeraq** 'child', and **erneq** 'son'.

Possessive locative – **illu** house		
Possessor	Possessum SG	Possessum PL
1SG / 2SG	**illunni** in my/your house/houses	
3SG	**illuani** in his/her house	**illuini** in his/her houses
4SG	**illumini** in his/her (own) house/houses	
1PL	**illutsinni** in our house/houses	
2PL	**illussinni** in your house/houses	
3PL	**illuanni** in their house	**illuini** in their houses
4PL	**illuminni** in their own house/houses	

Possessive inflection

Possessive locative – **meeraq** child	
Possessor	Possessum SG/PL
1SG	**meeqqanni** in my/your child/children
2SG	
3SG	**meeraani** in his/her child/children
4SG	**meeqqamini** in his/her (own) child/children
1PL	**meeqqatsinni** in our child/children
2PL	**meeqqassinni** in your child/children
3PL	**meeraanni** in their child/children
4PL	**meeqqaminni** in their (own) child/children

Possessive locative – **erneq** son		
Possessor	Possessum SG	Possessum PL
1SG	**erninni** in my/your son/sons	
2SG		
3SG	**ernerani** in his/her son	**ernerini** in his/her sons
4SG	**ernermini** in his/her (own) son/sons	
1PL	**ernitsinni** in our son/sons	
2PL	**ernissinni** in your son/sons	
3PL	**erneranni** in their son/sons	**ernerini** in their sons
4PL	**ernerminni** in their (own) son/sons	

The use of the possessive locative suffixes is shown here:

Nukappiaraq siniffimmini sinippoq.
nukappiaraq siniffim-mini sinip-poq
boy bed-LOC.4SG sleep-3SG
The boy is sleeping in his bed.

E-mail-inni imak allapputit:"Ataasinngornermi naapilerpugut!"
e-mail-inni imak allap-putit ataasinngorner-mi naapi-ler-pugut
e-mail-LOC.2SG in.this.way write-2SG monday-LOC meet-FUT-1PL
You wrote this in your email: 'We'll meet on Monday!'

Atuakkatsinni assersuuteqaqaaq.
atuakka-tsinni assut assersu-uteqa-qaaq
book-LOC.1PL many example-have-a.lot.3SG
In our book there are many examples.

3.4.5 Possessive ablative

The possessive suffixes as attached to ablative nouns are shown here.

Possessor	Possessive ablative suffixes	
	Possessum	
	SG	PL
1SG	-nnit	
2SG		
3SG	-anit	-init, -anit
4SG	-minit	
1PL	-tsinnit	
2PL	-ssinnit	
3PL	-annit	-init, -annit
4PL	-minnit	

Points to note:

- Like the possessive allative and locative suffixes discussed in 3.4.3 and 3.4.4, in most cases the possessive ablative suffixes have the same form in the singular and plural.
- The two variants of the 3SG (-init and -anit) and the 3PL (-init and -annit) possessive ablative suffixes on the plural form of nouns are subject to the same patterns as those discussed in the 'points to note'

for the possessive allative and locative suffixes discussed in 3.4.3 and 3.4.4.

Possessive inflection

Here we have listed the possessive ablative forms for **illu** 'house', **meeraq** 'child', and **erneq** 'son'.

	Possessive ablative – **illu** house	
Possessor	Possessum SG	Possessum PL
1SG / 2SG	**illunnit** from my/your house/houses	
3SG	**illuanit** from his/her house	**illuinit** from his/her houses
4SG	**illuminit** from his/her (own) house/houses	
1PL	**illutsinnit** from our house/houses	
2PL	**illussinnit** from your house/houses	
3PL	**illuannit** from their house	**illuinit** from their houses
4PL	**illuminnit** from their own house/houses	

	Possessive ablative – **meeraq** child	
Possessor	Possessum SG	Possessum PL
1SG / 2SG	**meeqqannit** from my/your child/children	
3SG	**meeraanit** from his/her child/children	
4SG	**meeqqaminit** from his/her (own) child/children	
1PL	**meeqqatsinnit** from our child/children	
2PL	**meeqqassinnit** from your child/children	
3PL	**meeraannit** from their child/children	
4PL	**meeqqaminnit** from their (own) child/children	

3 Nouns

Possessive ablative – **erneq** son		
Possessor	Possessum SG	Possessum PL
1SG		
2SG	**erninnit** from my/your son/sons	
3SG	**erneranit** from his/her son	**ernerinit** from his/her sons
4SG	**ernerminit** from his/her (own) son/sons	
1PL	**ernitsinnit** from our son/sons	
2PL	**ernissinnit** from your son/sons	
3PL	**ernerannit** from their son	**ernerinit** from their sons
4PL	**ernerminnit** from their (own) son/sons	

The use of the possessive ablative suffixes is shown here.

Illoqarfitsinnit tikip-poq.
illoqarfi-tsinnit tikip-poq
town-ABL.1PL arrive-3SG
S/he arrived from our town.

Tujuuloq anaanannit piviuk?
tujuuloq anaana-nnit piv-iuk
jumper mother-ABL.2SG get-INT.2SG>3SG
Did you get the jumper from your mother?

Illooqqaminnit angerlamut pisuppoq.
illooqqa-minnit angerla-mut pisup-poq
cousin-ABL.4SG home-ALL walk-3SG
S/he is walking home from his/her cousins.

3.4.6 Possessive instrumental

The possessive suffixes as attached to instrumental nouns are shown here.

Possessive inflection

Possessive instrumental suffixes		
Possessor	Possessum	
	SG	PL
1SG	-nnik	
2SG	-nnik	
3SG	-anik	-inik, -anik
4SG	-minik	
1PL	-tsinnik	
2PL	-ssinnik	
3PL	-annik	-inik, -annik
4PL	-minnik	

Points to note:

- Like the other possessive oblique suffixes discussed in 3.4.5–3.4.3, in most cases the possessive instrumental suffixes have the same form in the singular and plural.
- The two variants of the 3SG (-**inik** and -**anik**) and the 3PL (-**inik** and -**annik**) possessive instrumental suffixes on the plural form of nouns are subject to the same patterns as those discussed in the 'points to note' for the other possessive oblique suffixes discussed in 3.4.5–3.4.3.

Here we have listed the possessive instrumental forms for **illu** 'house', **meeraq** 'child', and **erneq** 'son'.

Possessive instrumental – **illu** house		
Possessor	Possessum SG	Possessum PL
1SG	**illunnik** about my/your house/houses	
2SG		
3SG	**illuanik** about his/her house	**illuinik** about his/her houses
4SG	**illuminik** about his/her (own) house/houses	
1PL	**illutsinnik** about our house/houses	
2PL	**illussinnik** about your house/houses	
3PL	**illuannik** about his/her house	**illuinik** about his/her houses
4PL	**illuminnik** about his/her (own) house/houses	

3 Nouns

Possessive instrumental – **meeraq** child	
Possessor	Possessum SG/PL
1SG 2SG	**meeqqannik** about my/your child/children
3SG	**meeraanik** about his/her child/children
4SG	**meeqqaminik** about his/her (own) child/children
1PL	**meeqqatsinnik** about our child/children
2PL	**meeqqassinnik** about your child/children
3PL	**meeraannik** about their child/children
4PL	**meeqqaminnik** about their (own) child/children

Possessive instrumental – **erneq** son		
Possessor	Possessum SG	Possessum PL
1SG 2SG	**erninnik** about my son/sons, your son/sons	
3SG	**erneranik** about his/her son	**ernerinik** about his/her sons
4SG	**erherminik** about his/her (own) son/sons	
1PL	**ernitsinnik** about our son/sons	
2PL	**ernissinnik** about your son/sons	
3PL	**ernerannik** about their son	**ernerinik** about their sons
4PL	**ernerminnik** about their (own) son/sons	

The use of the possessive instrumental suffixes is shown here:

Biili<u>nnik</u> niuerniarta?
biili-nnik niuerniar-ta
car-INS.2SG go.shopping-IMP.1PL
Shall we go shopping with your car?

Tom kaffisukka<u>ssinik</u> najorsivoq.
tom kaffisukka-ssinik najorsi-voq
tom coffee-INS.2PL drink-3SG
Tom took a sip of your coffee.

Aqerluusannik allappoq.
aqerluusa-nnik allap-poq
pencil-INS.1SG write-3SG
S/he is writing with my pencil.

3.4.7 Possessive prolative

The possessive suffixes as attached to prolative nouns are shown here.

Possessor	Possessum	
	SG	PL
1SG		-kkut
2SG		
3SG	-a(ti)gut	-isigut, -asigut
4SG		-migut
1PL		-tsigut
2PL		-ssigut
3PL	-atigut	-isigut, -asigut
4PL		-mikkut

Points to note:

- Like the other possessive oblique suffixes discussed in 3.4.6–3.4.3, in most cases the possessive prolative suffixes have the same form in the singular and plural.
- The two variants of the 3SG and the 3PL possessive prolative suffixes on the plural form of nouns (-**isigut** and -**asigut**) are subject to the same patterns as those discussed in the 'points to note' for the other possessive oblique suffixes discussed in 3.4.6–3.4.3.
- The 3SG possessive prolative suffix on singular nouns has two variant forms, -**agut** and -**atigut**, e.g. **illu** 'house' > **illuagut** or **illuatigut** 'via his/her house'.

Next we have listed the possessive prolative forms for **illu** 'house', **meeraq** 'child', and **erneq** 'son'.

3 Nouns

Possessive prolative – **illu** house

Possessor	Possessum SG	Possessum PL
1SG	**illukkut** via my/your house/houses	
2SG		
3SG	**illua(ti)gut** via his/her house	**illuisigut** via his/her houses
4SG	**illumigut** via his/her (own) house/houses	
1PL	**illutsigut** via our house/houses	
2PL	**illussigut** via their house/houses	
3PL	**illuatigut** via their house	**illuisigut** via their houses
4PL	**illumikkut** via their own house/houses	

Possessive prolative – **meeraq** child

Possessor	Possessum SG	Possessum PL
1SG	**meeqqakkut** via my/your child/children	
2SG		
3SG	**meeraa(ti)gut** via his/her child	**meerasigut** via his/her children
4SG	**meeqqamigut** via his/her (own) child/children	
1PL	**meeqqatsigut** via our child/children	
2PL	**meeqqassigut** via your child/children	
3PL	**meeraatigut** via their child	**meeraasigut** via their children
4PL	**meeqqamikkut** via their (own) child/children	

Possessive prolative – **erneq** son

Possessor	Possessum SG	Possessum PL
1SG	**ernikkut** via my/your son/sons	
2SG		
3SG	**ernera(ti)gut** via his/her son	**ernerisigut** via his/her sons
4SG	**ernermigut** via his/her own son/sons	
1PL	**ernitsigut** via our son/sons	
2PL	**ernissigut** via your son/sons	
3PL	**erneratigut** via their son	**ernerisigut** via their sons
4PL	**ernermikkut** via their (own) son/sons	

The use of the possessive prolative suffixes is shown in the following examples.

Possessive inflection

Tillinniaq igalaatigut iserpoq.
tillinniaq igalaa-tigut iser-poq
thief window-PRO.1PL go.in-3SG
The thief went in through our window.

Anaanap Naja taliatigut tiguaa.
anaana-p naja tali-atigut tigu-aa
mother-REL naja arm-PRO.3SG take-3SG>3SG
Mother took Naja by her arm.

Nivip Facebookimigut assamiortaarnini saqqummiuppaa.
Nivi-p facebook-i-migut assamiortaarni-ni saqqummiup-paa
nivi-REL facebook-HV-PRO.4SG engagement-4SG announce-3SG>3SG
Nivi announced her engagement on her Facebook (page).

3.4.8 Possessive equative

The possessive suffixes as attached to equative nouns are shown here.

Possessive equative suffixes		
Possessor	Possessum	
	SG	PL
1SG	-ttut	
2SG	-ttut	
3SG	-atut	-isut, -asut
4SG	-misut	
1PL	-tsitut	
2PL	-ssisut	
3PL	-attut	-isut, -asut
4PL	-missut	

Points to note:

- Like the other possessive oblique suffixes discussed in 3.4.7–3.4.3, in most cases the possessive equative suffixes have the same form in the singular and plural.
- The two variants of the 3SG and 3PL possessive equative suffixes on the plural form of nouns (-**isut** and -**asut**) are subject to the same patterns as those discussed in the 'points to note' for the other possessive oblique suffixes discussed in 3.4.7–3.4.3.

Here we have listed the possessive equative forms for **illu** 'house', **meeraq** 'child', and **erneq** 'son'.

Possessive equative – **illu** house		
Possessor	Possessum SG	Possessum PL
1SG 2SG	**illuttut** as my/your house/houses	
3SG	**illuatut** as his/her house	**illuisut** as his/her houses
4SG	**illumisut** as his/her (own) house/houses	
1PL	**illutsitut** as our house/houses	
2PL	**illussisut** as your house/houses	
3PL	**illuattut** as their house	**illuisut** as their houses
4PL	**illumissut** as their own house/houses	

Possessive equative – **meeraq** child		
Possessor	Possessum SG	Possessum PL
1SG 2SG	**meeqqattut** as my/your child/children	
3SG	**meeraatut** as his/her child	**meeraasut** as his/her children
4PL	**meeqqamisut** as his/her (own) child/children	
1PL	**meeqqatsitut** as our child/children	
2PL	**meeqqassisut** as your child/children	
3PL	**meeraattut** as their child	**meeraasut** as their children
4PL	**meeqqamissut** as their (own) child/children	

Collective suffixes

Possessive equative – **erneq** son		
Possessor	Possessum SG	Possessum PL
1SG	**ernittut** as my/your son/sons	
2SG		
3SG	**erneratut** as his/her son	**ernerisut** as his/her sons
4SG	**ernermisut** as his/her (own) son/sons	
1PL	**ernitsitut** as our son/sons	
2PL	**ernissisut** as your son/sons	
3PL	**ernerattut** as their son	**ernerisut** as their sons
4PL	**ernermissut** as their sons/sons	

The use of the possessive equative suffixes is illustrated in the following.

Rusland Kinap nuka<u>atut</u> iliuuseqarpoq.
rusland kina-p nuka-atut iliuuse-qar-poq
russia china-REL younger.sibling-EQU.3SG behaviour-have-3SG
Russia is behaving like China's younger sibling.

3.5 Collective suffixes

West Greenlandic has several suffixes that can be attached to nouns and convey the meaning of 'a group of'. These suffixes are listed in the table that follows. They are all marked by the abbreviation COLL in the glossing.

Suffix	English translation
-kkut	a group of, a family of (typically with proper nouns)
-kkormiut	a group of people living together or associating with each other
+(r)paat	a group of
-aluit, +(r)paaluit, -(r)passuit	a group of, many

The use of these suffixes is illustrated here.

Base word	Suffix	Suffixed form
Hansen Hansen	-kkut	**Hansenikkut** the Hansens
Anna Anna	-kkut	**Annakkut** Anna and her family, Anna and the others
ilinniartitsisoq teacher	-kkut	**ilinniartitsisukkut** the teacher and others
utoqqaq elder, old man, old woman	-kkut	**utoqqakkut** the elders
Per Per	-kkormiut	**Perikkormiut** Per and the people who live with him
Siumut Siumut[1]	-kkormiut	**Siumukkormiut** the members of the Siumut party
inuk person	+(r)paat	**inuppaat** a group of people
arnaq woman	+paaluit	**arnarpaaluit** a group of women
qimmeq dog	+passuit	**qimmerpassuit** a pack of dogs
tuttu reindeer	+passuit	**tuttorpassuit** a herd of reindeer
ussuk bearded seal	+paaluit	**ussuppaaluit** a herd of bearded seal
tiitorfik cup	+paaluit	**tiitorfippaaluit** a bunch of cups

1 Greenlandic political party.

Chapter 4
Pronouns

4.1 Personal

The personal pronouns in West Greenlandic are listed here. Note that only first- and second-person pronouns appear in this list. West Greenlandic does not have any true third-person pronouns (corresponding to 'he', 'she', 'it', and 'they'); instead, demonstrative pronouns are used in this sense (see section 4.2).

	SG	PL
FIRST PERSON	**uanga** I, me	**uagut** we, us
SECOND PERSON	**illit** you	**ilissi** you

The pronouns are not used as often in West Greenlandic as in English because they are indicated in the verbal suffixes (see section 7.1). However, pronouns can be used to add emphasis to another element in the clause. The following exchange illustrates this usage: the independent pronouns serve to draw added attention to the possessive suffixes, much like the italics in the English translation.

– **Allaffiit assut nuannerpoq.**
allaffi-it assut nuanner-poq
office-2SG very be.nice-3SG
– Your office is very nice.

– **Kisianni illit allaffinnit inikinneruvoq.**
kisianni illit allaffi-nnit ini-kin-ner-u-voq
but you office-ABL.2SG room-little-COMP-be-3SG
– But it has less room than *your* office.

DOI: 10.4324/9781315160863-4

4 Pronouns

– Aap, <u>uanga</u> allaffiga <u>illit</u> allaffinnit inituneruvoq.
aap, uanga allaffi-ga illit allaffi-nnit ini-tu-ner-u-voq
yes, i office-1SG you office-ABL.2SG room-be.big-COMP-be-3SG
– Yes, *my* office has more room than your room.

The personal pronouns decline for case. The absolutive and the relative cases share the same form (listed earlier). The forms of the personal pronouns in the remaining cases are shown in the following table.

	1SG	2SG	1PL	2PL
ABSOLUTIVE/ RELATIVE	**uanga** I	**illit** you	**uagut** we	**ilissi** you
ALLATIVE	**uannut** to me	**ilinnut** to you	**uatsinnut,** **uagutsinnut** to us	**ilissinnut** to you
LOCATIVE	**uanni** at my place	**ilinni** at your place	**uatsinni,** **uagutsinni** at our place	**ilissinni** at your place
ABLATIVE	**uanni(i)t** from me	**ilinni(i)t** from you	**uatsinni(i)t,** **uagutsinni(i)t** from us	**ilissinni(i)t** from you
INSTRUMENTAL	**uannik** about me	**ilinnik** about you	**uatsinnik,** **uagutsinnik** about us	**ilissinnik** about you
PROLATIVE	**uakkut** via me	**il(l)ikkut** via you	**uatsigut,** **uagutsigut** via us	**ilissigut** via you
EQUATIVE	**uattut** as me	**ilittut** as you	**uatsitut,** **uagutsitut** as us	**ilissisut** as you

Points to note:

- The meaning of the locative personal pronouns is similar to that of the French *chez*, that is, 'at someone's place' or 'in someone's immediate possession', 'on someone's person'.

- The instrumental forms of the personal pronouns are not used often and are mostly seen in Bible translations.
- There are two variants of the stem of the 1PL pronoun in all of the oblique cases, **uagu-** and **ua-**. Both of these forms are widely used.
- There are two variants of the ablative suffix, one ending in -it and the other ending in -iit. Both of these forms are widely used.

The use of the personal pronouns in the various cases is illustrated in the following examples.

Asanninnera <u>uanniit ilinnut</u> tunniuppara.
asanninner-a uanniit ilinnut tunniup-para
love-1SG from.me to.you give-1SG>3SG
I give my love from me to you.

Ilinniagaq suna <u>uannut</u> naleqquppa?
ilinniagaq suna uannut naleqqu-ppa
educational.training what to.me suit-INT.3SG
Which kind of educational training suits me?

<u>Uanni</u> kaffillilerpugut.
uanni kaffilli-ler-pugut
at.me have.kaffimik-going.to-1PL
We're going to have a kaffimik at mine.

Jiisusi <u>ilikkut</u> uumaguni eqqissisissavaatit.
jiisusi ilikkut uuma-guni eqqissi-si-ssa-vaatit
jesus through.you live-COND.4SG find.peace-let-FUT-3SG>2SG
If Jesus lives through you he will let you find peace.

<u>Ilittut</u> timersornermut pikkorikkusuppunga.
ilittut timersorner-mut pikkorik-kusup-punga
like.you sport-ALL be.good-want-1SG
I would like to be good at sport like you.

4 Pronouns

4.2 Demonstrative

The West Greenlandic demonstrative pronouns (words equivalent to the English 'this' and 'that') are as follows.

Demonstrative pronoun		Anaphoric demonstrative pronoun	
SG	PL	SG	PL
una s/he/it; that	**uku** they; those	**taanna** that	**taakku** those
manna this	**makku** these	**tamanna** this	**tamakku** these
innga that over there	**ikku** those over there	**taann(g)a, taajinnga** that over there	**taakku** those over there

Points to note:

- The prefix **ta-** attached to the pronouns, strictly speaking, indicates that the one being spoken about is already known or has already been mentioned. (This is called anaphoric reference.) However, the forms with **ta-** are the most commonly used demonstratives in general in contemporary spoken West Greenlandic.
- The first two demonstrative pronouns on the list, **una** and **uku**, also serve as third-person personal pronouns (corresponding to the English 's/he/it' and 'they' respectively).
- Demonstrative pronouns can be used as adverbs (see section 9.3).

The demonstrative pronouns can be inflected for case. The following table lists the case suffixes that are attached to demonstratives.

	SG	PL
RELATIVE	**-ma**	**-a**
ALLATIVE	**-munnga**	**-nunnga**
LOCATIVE	**-mani**	**-nani**
ABLATIVE	**-mannga**	**-nannga**
INSTRUMENTAL	**-minnga**	**-ninnga**
PROLATIVE	**-muuna**	**-nuuna, -natigut**
EQUATIVE	**-matut**	**-natut**

Note that the singular form of these demonstrative pronouns (both cataphoric and anaphoric) changes slightly when the case endings are attached to them, as listed here:

Cataphoric demonstrative pronoun inflectional stems		
Base form	Inflectional stem	Example cases
una s/he/it; that	**uu-**	uuma, uumunnga, uumani
manna this	**matu-**	matuma, matumunnga, matumani
innga that over there	**issu-**	issuma, issumunnga, issumani

Point to note:

- The plural case suffixes are attached to the absolutive form, e.g. **uku** 'they'; 'those' > relative **ukua**.

Anaphoric demonstrative pronoun inflectional stems		
Base form	Inflectional stem	Example cases
taanna he/she/it; that	**taassu-**	taassuma, taassumunnga, taassumani
manna this	**matu-**	matuma, matumunnga, matumani
innga that over there	**issu-**	issuma, issumunnga, issumani

Point to note:

- The plural case suffixes are attached to the absolutive form, e.g. **taakku** 'they'; 'those' > relative **taakkua**.

There are also several other demonstrative pronouns with more specific directional meaning, as follows:

Demonstrative pronoun		Anaphoric demonstrative pronoun		English translation
SG	PL	SG	PL	
sanna	sakku	tasanna	tasakku	that down there (by the shore, by the sea), that in the west, that out there (on the sea)
kanna	kakku	takanna	takakku	that further down
panna	pakku	tappanna	tappakku	that inland or up, or to the east, that in the sky
pinnga	pikku	tappinnga	tappikku	that higher up
qanna	qakku	taqqanna	taqqakku	that inside/outside the house (other side of the wall), in the other room, other side of the road or opposite the speaker; in the south
anna	akku	taajanna	taajakku	that up towards the north

Points to note:

- In the singular, the inflectional stems of these demonstrative pronouns (both cataphoric and anaphoric) all follow the same pattern: the final -anna or -innga is replaced with -ssu before the case suffixes, e.g. **sanna** 'that down there' > relative **sassuma**, allative **sassumunnga**.
- In the plural, the inflectional stems are the same as the absolutive, e.g. **sakku** 'those further down' > relative **sakkua**, allative **sakkununnga**.

The following examples illustrate the use of the demonstrative pronouns.

Suliaq <u>taanna</u> maanna naammassivoq.
suliaq taanna maanna naammassi-voq

work that now be.done-3SG
That work is now finished.

Kuussuit taakku aalisagaliupput.
kuussu-it taakku aalisaga-li-up-put
river-PL those fish-having-be-3PL
Those rivers contain fish.

Ulluni makkunani mobiilikkut atuartarpunga.
ullu-ni makku-nani mobiili-kkut atuar-tar-punga
day-LOC.PL these-LOC.PL mobile-PRO read-HAB-1SG
These days I usually read on my phone.

Ittoqqortoormiit 21-riarluni nanoqarpoq ukioq manna.
ittoqqortoormiit 21-riar-luni nano-qar-poq ukioq manna
ittoqqortoormiit 21-time-CONT.3SG polar.bear-have-3SG year this
Ittoqqortoormiit has had polar bears 21 times this year.

Tamanna uannut qanoq isumaqarpa?
tamanna uannut qanoq isuma-qar-pa
this for.me how meaning-have-INT.3SG
What[1] does this mean for me?

The use of the demonstrative forms **una** and **uku** as third-person personal pronouns is shown in the following examples. Note that, as in the case of the first- and second-person personal pronouns discussed in section 4.1, the use of the third-person pronouns is less common than in English and usually serves to draw attention to the subject.

Una pinnerpoq.
una pinner-poq
s/he be.beautiful-3SG
S/he is beautiful.

Uku pinnguarput.
uku pinnguar-put
they play-3PL
They are playing.

4.3 Interrogative

The following tables show the inflected forms of the West Greenlandic interrogative pronouns **kina** 'who' and **suna** 'what'.

---
1 Literally: how.

4 Pronouns

	kina who	
	SG	PL
ABSOLUTIVE	**kina** who	**kikkut**
RELATIVE	**kia, kiap** whose	
ALLATIVE	**kimut** to whom	**kikkunnut**
LOCATIVE	**kimi** at whose	**kikkunni**
ABLATIVE	**kimit** from whom	**kikkunnit**
INSTRUMENTAL	**kimik** about whom	**kikkunnik**
PROLATIVE	**kikkut** via whom	**kikkutigut**
EQUATIVE	**kinatut** as whom	**kikkutut**

	suna what	
	SG	PL
ABSOLUTIVE	**suna** what	**suut**
RELATIVE	**suup** what	
INSTRUMENTAL	**sumik** with what	**sunik**
ALLATIVE	**sumut** where to	**sunut**
LOCATIVE	**sumi** where	**suni**
ABLATIVE	**sumit** where from	**sunit**
PROLATIVE	**sukkut** which way	**sutigut**
EQUATIVE	**sutut** as what, in what language	**sutut**

Points to note:

- These pronouns are based on two stems: **ki-** (referring to people) and **su-** (referring to things).
- The form **su-** can be incorporated into a verb (see section 14.2.2).

There are two other interrogative pronouns, shown next:

Pronoun	English translation
qassit	how many
sorleq	which of them

The interrogative pronouns are illustrated in the following examples:

Kinaavit?
kina-a-vit
who-be-INT.2SG
Who are you?

Rosat kimut tunniunniarpigit?
rosa-t ki-mut tunni-un-niar-pigit
rose-PL who-ALL give-to.someone-intend.to-INT.2SG>3PL
Who are you going to give the roses to?

Kikkut nipilersulerpat?
ki-kkut nipilersu-ler-pat
who-PRO play.music-going.to-INT.3SG
Who is going to play music?

Kikkunni nerilerpugut?
ki-kkunni neri-ler-pugut
who-LOC.PL eat-going.to-1PL
Whose house shall we eat at?

Kiap Akamali takuaa?
kia-p akamali taku-aa
who-REL akamali see-3SG>3SG
Who saw Akamali?

Sumi najugaqarpit?
su-mi najugaqar-pit
what-LOC live-INT.2SG
Where do you live?

Sunit sanaajuppat?
su-nit sanaa-ju-ppat
what-ABL.PL product-be-3PL
What are they made of?

Sukkut tikippit?
su-kkut tikip-pit
what-PRO come-INT.2SG
Which way did you arrive by?

Sutut ilinniarpit?
su-tut ilinniar-pit
what-EQU study-INT.2SG
What are you studying to become?[2]

Suup meqqua?
su-up meqqu-a
what-REL feather-3SG
What is that the feather of?[3]

Ukiut qassit Danmarkimiippit?
ukiu-t qassit danmarki-mi-ip-pit
year-PL how.many denmark-LOC-be-INT.2SG
How many years have you been in Denmark?

Sodavandi sorleq mamaraajuk?
sodavandi sorleq mama-raa-juk
soft.drink which tasty-consider-INT.2SG>3SG
Which soft drink do you like the best?

4.4 Reflexive

West Greenlandic has two reflexive pronouns, **imminut** and **nammineq**. Both of these pronouns mean 'oneself', but they differ in form and meaning, as explained here in turn.

	imminut oneself	
	SG	PL
ALLATIVE	**imminut** oneself, to oneself	**imminnut** themselves, to themselves
LOCATIVE	**immini** at oneself	**imminni** at themselves
ABLATIVE	**imminit** from oneself	**imminnit** from themselves
INSTRUMENTAL	**imminik** by oneself	**imminnik** by themselves
PROLATIVE	**immikkut** for themself/themselves	
EQUATIVE	**immisut** as oneself	**immissut** as themselves

2 Literally: as what are you studying?
3 Literally: what's feather?

Points to note:

- **Imminut** 'oneself' appears only in the oblique cases.
- The allative **imminut** is the basic form of this pronoun and can have the meaning of 'oneself' (i.e. functioning as an absolutive or relative form) in addition to 'to oneself'.
- **Imminut** does not explicitly indicate person, i.e. the same form can mean 'myself', 'yourself', 'himself', 'herself', 'ourselves', 'yourselves', etc. In any given context the meaning will be clear because it always refers back to the subject of the sentence.
- In the plural, **imminut** can also have a reciprocal meaning (i.e. 'each other'); see 4.5 for details.
- **Imminut** has the implied meaning that one does the action for one's own benefit.
- A variant, **immineq**, which is modelled on a typical absolutive noun, is sometimes used as the base form of this pronoun instead of **imminut** in the sense of 'oneself' when functioning in the absolutive sense.

The use of **imminut** is illustrated in the following examples.

Imminut innartippunga.
imminut innar-tip-punga
oneself go.to.bed-cause-1SG
I'll force myself to go to bed.

Taamaallaat imminnut eqqarsaatigipput.
taamaallaat imminnut eqqarsaatigip-put
only themselves think-3PL
They only think about themselves.

The other reflexive pronoun, **nammineq**, typically appears in the absolutive. It can take oblique cases and inflects like an extra-strong-stem noun (such as **erneq** 'son') but only appears in the oblique cases relatively rarely. Some of the oblique case forms that you might encounter include the ablative **namminermit** 'from oneself' and the allative **namminermut** 'to oneself'.

Uanga **nammineq kaagiliara.**
uanga nammineq kaagi-li-ara
i oneself cake-make-1SG>3SG
I made the cake myself.

Uagut <u>nammineq</u> hoteli inniminnerparput.
uagut nammineq hoteli inniminner-parput
we oneself hotel book-1PL>3SG
We booked the hotel ourselves.

Panini ilagalugit aavariarpoq <u>nammineq</u> aqulluni.
pani-ni ilaga-lugit aavariar-poq nammineq aqu-lluni
daughter-PL.4PL together.with-3PL hunt.reindeer-3SG oneself steer-CONT.4SG
He went out to hunt reindeer with his daughters, steering by himself.

In addition to **imminut** and **nammineq**, reflexivity can also sometimes be indicated within a particular verb. This can happen when there is a verb that has transitive and intransitive variants (see section 7.2.1.1 and 7.2.1.2 for discussion of transitive and intransitive verbs). In such instances, the intransitive variant may have reflexive meaning. This phenomenon is not always something that can be predicted automatically but rather depends on the meaning of the individual verb and so must be learnt on a case-by-case basis. Some examples of intransitive verbs with reflexive meaning are shown here.

Transitive variant	Intransitive variant
asappaa to wash something	**asappoq** to wash oneself
ammarpaa to open something	**ammarpoq** to open (itself, i.e. of a door)
piareersarpaa to make something ready	**piareersarpoq** to get ready (i.e. to get oneself ready)

Point to note:

- Reflexive verbs can sometimes be formed by placing an intransitive ending on a verb with a causative or valency suffix such as **+tarpaa/+sarpaa** 'to make someone do something; to try and make someone do something', as in the last example in the table. See section 7.7 for discussion of the causative suffixes, 7.8 for discussion of reflexive suffixes, and 7.10 for discussion of valency suffixes.

4.5 Reciprocal

The plural forms of the reflexive pronoun **imminut** 'oneself' (discussed in 4.4) can have reciprocal meaning (i.e. 'each other') in West Greenlandic. The forms of this reciprocal pronoun are listed here.

Reciprocal

	imminnut each other
ALLATIVE	**imminnut** each other
LOCATIVE	**imminni** at each other
ABLATIVE	**imminnit** from each other
INSTRUMENTAL	**imminnik** by each other
PROLATIVE	**immikkut** for each other
EQUATIVE	**immisut** as each other

Points to note:

- These same forms can have plural reflexive meaning (i.e. 'themselves'; see section 4.4), but context will make it clear which meaning is intended.
- As with the reflexive pronoun **imminut** (discussed in 4.4), the reciprocal pronoun **imminnut** only appears in the oblique cases, and the base form is the allative.
- These forms can be used in conjunction with possessive suffixes to make the meaning clearer. For example, **immitsinnut** '(we) ... each other' contains the suffix -tsinnut, which is the 1PL possessive allative suffix, matching the subject of the clause in question.

Angut arnarlu – imminnut tulluartumik pinngortitat.
angut arnar-lu – imminnut tulluartumik pinngortita-t
man woman-and – each.other well.suited creation-PL
Man and woman [are] well suited for each other.[4]

Immitsinnut nuannariunnaarpugut.
immi-tsinnut nuannar-i-unnaar-pugut
each.other-ALL.1PL like-VAL-anymore-1PL
We don't like each other anymore.

The reciprocal suffix -qatigiipput can also be used to mean 'each other'. The use of this reciprocal suffix is illustrated in the following examples. Note that the reciprocal suffix is marked by the abbreviation REC in the glossing.

Asaqatigiipput.
asa-qatigiip-put
love-REC-3PL
They love each other.

---

4 Literally: well-suited creations for each other.

Suleqatigiippisi?
sule-qatigiip-pisi
work-REC-INT.2PL
Do you guys work with each other?

Danmark Kalaallit Nunaallu suleqatigiilluarput.
danmark kalaalli-t nuna-al-lu sule-qatigiil-luar-put
denmark greenlander-PL country-3PL-and work-REC-well-3PL
Denmark and Greenland collaborate well with each other.

The reciprocal suffix -qatigiipput can also be used in conjunction with the independent reciprocal pronoun **imminnut**. In everyday speech (under the influence of Danish), this practice has become more common. It is illustrated in the following examples.

Immitsinnut allaqatigiippugut.
immi-tsinnut alla-qatigiip-pugut
each.other-ALL.1PL write-REC-1PL
We write to each other.

Ukiorpassuarni inooqatigiipput.
ukior-passuar-ni inoo-qatigiip-put
year-many-LOC.PL live-REC-3PL
They lived with each other for many years.

4.6 Other

West Greenlandic has a number of other pronouns (i.e. pronous such as 'many', 'some', 'all', 'the only one', etc.). Two of the most frequently used such pronouns commonly appear in a number of different forms. These are explained in the following tables.

kisi- only	
kisimi (subject); **kisiat** (object and in fixed expressions) (SG)	the only one, the sole one
kisimik (subject); **kisiisa** (object and in fixed expressions) (PL)	the only ones, the sole ones

tama- all, every	
tamarmi (subject); **tamaat** (object and in fixed expressions) (SG)	everyone, everybody, each one
tamarmik (subject); **tamaasa** (object and in fixed expressions) (PL)	all, everyone, everybody

Points to note:

- The forms appearing in basic (subject) contexts, i.e. **kisimi** (SG), **kisimik** (PL) and **tamarmi** (SG), **tamarmik** (PL) 'everyone, everybody, each one', have 3SG and 3PL possessive suffixes.
- The pronouns **kisimi** (SG) and **kisimik** (PL) 'the only, the sole' and **tamarmi** (SG) and **tamarmik** (PL) 'everyone, everybody, all, each one' can take case suffixes when used in conjunction with a noun appearing in a particular case; for example, the locative of **tamarmik** is **tamani** 'in all', e.g. **illoqarfinni tamani** 'in all the towns'. Note that in such cases the pronouns may have a meaning closer to an English adverb.
- The pronouns **kisimi** (SG) and **kisimik** (PL) 'the only, the sole' have separate object forms, **kisiat** (SG)) and **kisiisa** (PL). The object forms are also used adverbially in certain fixed expressions, e.g. **una kisiat** 'only it'.
- Similarly, the pronouns **tamarmi** (SG) 'everyone, everybody, each one' and **tamarmik** (PL) 'all, everyone, everybody' have separate object forms, **tamaat** (SG) and **tamaasa** (PL). The object forms are also adverbially used in fixed expressions, e.g. **ullut tamaasa** 'every day' (literally: all the days).
- The pronouns **kisimi** (SG) and **kisimik** (PL) 'the only, the sole' and **tamarmi** (SG) and **tamarmik** (PL) 'everyone, everybody, all, each one' can also take possessive suffixes to convey meanings such as 'all of us', 'all of you', 'all of them', etc., e.g. **kisimi** 'the only, the sole' > **kisima** 'I alone, only I'; **tamarmi** 'everyone' > **tamatta** 'all of us'.

The following examples illustrate the use of **kisimi**.

Kisima Nuummi najugaqarpunga.
kisi-ma nuum-mi najugar-punga
only-REL.1SG nuuk-LOC live-1SG
Only I live in Nuuk.

Maannakkorpiaq taxat 35-it kisimik ingerlaarput.
maannakkorpiaq taxa-t 35-it kisimik ingerlaar-put
right.now taxi-PL 35-PL only be.out.and.about-3PL
Right now only 35 taxis are in service.

4 Pronouns

The following examples illustrate the use of **tamarmi**.

Tamatta nuannaarpugut.
tamatta nuannaar-pugut
all.of.us happy-1PL
We are all happy.

Tamarmik neripput.
tamarmik neri-pput
everyone eat-3PL
Everyone is eating.

Inuit **tamarmik** illoqarfimmut nuupput.
inu-it tamarmik illoqarfim-mut nuup-put
person-PL all town-ALL move-3PL
All the people are moving to town.

Ulloq **tamaat** silagippoq.
ulloq tamaat silagip-poq
day whole be.good.weather-3SG
The weather has been great all day.

Ullut **tamaasa** kaffisortarpunga.
ullu-t tamaasa kaffisor-tar-punga
day-PL every drink.coffee-HAB-1SG
I drink coffee every day.

Tamaasa ilinniartippakka.
tamaasa ilinniartip-pakka
all teach-1SG>3PL
I'm teaching all of them.

Brugsenip arpatsitsinera illoqarfinni Brugsenilinni tamani ingerlanneqassaaq.
brugseni-p arpatsitsiner-a illoqarfin-ni brugseni-lin-ni tamani ingerlan-neqa-ssaaq
brugseni-REL running-3SG town-LOC.PL brugsen-having-LOC.PL all hold-PASS-FUT.3SG
The Brugseni run will be held in all towns that have a Brugseni shop.

There are several other forms that are used in a similar way to English pronouns, shown here.

West Greenlandic	English
assinga	the same, similar to
kinaluunniit	anyone, anybody, someone, somebody, whoever
sunaluunniit	anything, something, whatever, any

These forms are illustrated in the following examples.

Kinaluunniit ikiuisinnaavoq.
kinaluunniit ikiui-sinnaa-voq
anyone help-be.able-3SG
Anyone can help.

Qarlimma assinganik peqarpoq.
qarlim-ma assinga-nik peqar-poq
trouser-PL.REL.1SG same-INS.PL have-3SG
S/he has the same trousers as me.

There is also a verbal suffix that corresponds in usage to an English pronoun, **+soqarpoq/+toqarpoq**, meaning 'there is/are someone/something'. The **+soq/+toq** part of this suffix is actually the intransitive participle (discussed in 8.1). This suffix is used as follows:

Base verb	Verbal suffix	Resulting construction
igavoq to cook	**+soqarpoq**	**igasoqarpoq** there is someone who cooks
oqarpoq to say something	**+toqarpoq**	**oqartoqarpoq** there is someone who says something

This indefinite suffix can be combined with a noun in the plural instrumental case to convey the meaning of 'some', as in 'some children', 'some dogs', etc., e.g.:

Meeqqanik atuartoqarpoq.
meeqqa-nik atuar-toqar-poq
child-LOC.PL read-be.some-3SG
There are some children reading/Some children are reading.

In intransitive sentences, negative pronominal meanings are expressed by means of the negative verbal suffix **-nngi-** 'not' (indicated by the abbreviation NEG in the glossing). This negative suffix can be attached to any verb in

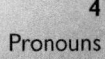

4 Pronouns

any person to form a negative (see section 7.11 for discussion of negation in West Greenlandic). Positive pronouns can be used in conjunction with the negative to convey a negative pronominal sense, e.g.:

Positive construction	Negative construction
Kikkulluunniit tingisinnaapput.	**Kikkulluunniit tingisinnaanngillat.**
kikkulluunniit tingi-sinnaa-pput	kikkulluunniit tingi-sinnaa-nngi-llat
anyone fly-be.able-3PL	anyone fly-be.able-NEG-3PL
Anyone can fly.	No one can fly.[1]
1 Literally: anyone cannot fly.	

The use of the negative suffix in this type of context is illustrated in the following examples:

Nalliuttorsiornermut takkuttoqanngilaq.
nalliuttorsiorner-mut takkut-to-qa-nngi-laq
party-ALL come-IP-be.there-NEG-3SG
No one came to the party.

Allamik nalissaqanngilaq.
alla-mik nali-ssa-qa-nngi-laq
other-INS compare-FUT-be.there-NEG-3SG
Nothing can ever compare to it.

Akornatsinni Japanimiusut oqaluttoqarsinnaanngilaq.
akorna-tsinni japanimiu-sut oqalut-to-qar-sinnaa-nngi-laq
among-LOC.1PL japanese-EQU speak-IP-be.there-be.able-NEG-3SG
There's no one among us that can speak Japanese.

Kikkulluunniit tingisinnaanngillat.
kikkulluunniit tingi-sinnaa-nngi-llat
anyone fly-be.able-NEG-3PL
No one can fly.

Sumilluunniit nassataqanngilaq.
sumilluunniit nassa-ta-qa-nngi-laq
anything carry-HAB-be.there-NEG-3SG
S/he didn't bring anything.

Nerrivik sumiiffissaqanngilaq.
nerrivik sumiiffi-ssa-qa-nngi-laq
table place-FUT-be.there-NEG-3SG
There's no place for the table.

Chapter 5
Numerals

5.1 Cardinal

The cardinal numbers in Greenlandic are as follows.

0	noor'lu
1	ataaseq
2	marluk
3	pingasut
4	sisamat
5	tallimat
6	arfinillit
7	arfineq-marluk
8	arfineq-pingasut
9	qulingiluat
10	qulit
11	aqqaneq, aqqanillit
12	aqqaneq-marluk

Points to note:

- The numeral **noor'lu** 'zero' is written with an apostrophe before the l to indicate that the r and l are pronounced separately, rather than as /rɬ/.
- The numeral **ataaseq** 'one' takes the singular case suffixes. The other numerals take the plural case suffixes.
- The variants **aqqaneq** and **aqqanillit** for 'eleven' can be used relatively interchangeably.
- The northern dialect of West Greenlandic has the variant **qulaaluat** instead of **qulingiluat** 'nine', while the southern dialect of West Greenlandic has the variant **arfineq-sisamat**.
- The northern dialect of West Greenlandic has the variant **isikkanillit** instead of **aqqaneq** or **aqqanillit** 'eleven'.
- The northern dialect of West Greenlandic has the variant **isikkaneq-marluk** instead of **aqqaneq-marluk** 'twelve'.

DOI: 10.4324/9781315160863-5

5 Numerals

Danish numerals are used instead of the Greenlandic ones when giving prices. The Danish numerals for 1–12 are shown next. Note that Danish spelling often reflects a different pronunciation than Greenlandic spelling, so we have provided an approximate pronunciation guide when the pronunciation of the Danish numerals differs markedly from what might be expected given the spelling.

1	**en**
2	**to**
3	**tre**
4	**fire** /fiə/
5	**fem**
6	**seks**
7	**syv**
8	**otte** /ɔːdə/
9	**ni**
10	**ti**
11	**elleve** /ɛlvə/
12	**tolv** /tol/

After 12, Danish numerals are usually used in all contexts. Note that the -**ten** element is pronounced as /dən/.

13	**tretten**
14	**fjorten**
15	**femten**
16	**seksten**
17	**sytten**
18	**atten**
19	**nitten**
20	**tyve**

The simple Danish numbers 1–10 listed here are also used to form numbers above 20. They are placed before the digits followed by **og** /ɒw/ 'and', with the whole construction written as one word, as follows:

21	**enogtyve**
22	**toogtyve**
23	**treogtyve**
24	**fireogtyve**
25	**femogtyve**
26	**seksogtyve**
27	**syvogtyve**
28	**otteogtyve**
29	**niogtyve**

The numerals 30 and upwards (which are also Danish) are as follows. Note that the component **halv-**, which is used to make up many of these numerals, is pronounced as /hal/, without the final v.

Cardinal

30	**tredive** /tʁaðvə/
40	**fyrre** /fœʁʌ/
50	**halvtreds** /haltʁɛs/
60	**tres**
70	**halvfjerds** /halfjæʁs/
80	**firs** /fiʁs/
90	**halvfems**
100	**hundrede** /hunʌðə/
1,000[1]	**tusind** /tusən/

If the counted noun is the subject of the sentence, it appears in the plural, e.g.:

Meeqqat tallimat silami pinnguarput.
meeqqa-t tallimat silami pinnguar-put
child-PL five outside play-3PL
Five children are playing outside.

Ilinniartut arfineq-pingasut sammisaq una pillugu allaaserinnissapput.
ilinniartu-t arfineq-pingasut sammisaq una pillugu allaaserinni-ssa-pput
student-PL eight topic this about write-FUT-3PL
Eight students will write on this topic.

If a numeral above 10 appears in conjunction with a noun, it takes a plural ending (even if written in Arabic numerals), e.g.:

Ukioq kingulleq kalaallit 250-it Danmarkimut nuupput.
ukioq kingulleq kalaalli-t 250-it danmarki-mut nuup-put
year last greenlander-PL 250-PL denmark-ALL move-3PL
Last year 250 Greenlanders moved to Denmark.

Numerals can take case suffixes and function as nouns, e.g.:

marluniit sisamanut
marlu-niit sisama-nut
two-ABL.PL five-ALL.PL
from two to five

1 Note that when large numbers are written with Arabic numerals in Greenlandic texts, there is typically a full stop after the thousands column, e.g. **5.000 kroner** '5,000 kroner'.

5
Numerals

Ilagiit <u>arfineq-marlunniit 150-inut</u> amerlisimapput.
ilagi-it arfineq-marlun-niit 150-inut amerli-sima-pput
congregation-PL seven-ABL.PL 150-ALL.PL go.up-PAST-3PL
The congregation has gone up from seven to 150.

If the counted noun is the object of the sentence, there are two different expressions depending on whether it is definite or not. If the counted object is indefinite, it appears in the instrumental plural, as does the associated numeral, e.g.:

<u>Qimminik pingasunik</u> takuvunga.
qimmi-nik pingasu-nik taku-vunga
dog-INS.PL three-INS.PL see-1SG
I see three dogs.

<u>Iipilinik qulinik</u> nerivugut.
iipili-nik quli-nik neri-vugut
apple-INS.PL ten-INS.PL eat-1PL
We ate ten apples.

If the counted noun is definite, it appears in the absolute plural, as does the associated numeral, e.g.:

<u>Qimmit pingasut</u> takuakka.
qimmi-t pingasu-t taku-akka
dog-PL three-PL see-1SG>3PL
I see the three dogs.

<u>Iipilit qulit</u> nerivavut.
iipili-t quli-t neri-vavut
apple-PL ten-PL buy-1PL>3PL
We ate the ten apples.

With certain verbs (e.g. -qarpoq 'to have', 'to be there'), the indefinite noun is incorporated into the verb (in which case there is no distinction between singular and plural), and the associated numeral appears in the instrumental plural:

<u>Pingasunik</u> qimmeqarpunga.
pingasu-nik qimme-qar-punga
three-INS.PL dog-have-1SG
I have three dogs.

<u>155 centimeterinik</u> takissuseqarpoq.
155 centimeteri-nik takissuse-qar-poq
155 centimetre-INS.PL height-have-3SG
S/he/it is 155 cm tall.

Atuarfimmi <u>aqqaneq-marlunnik</u> ilinniartoqarpoq.
atuarfim-mi aqqaneq-marlun-nik ilinniarto-qar-poq
school-LOC twelve-INS.PL student-be.there-3SG
There are twelve students in the school.

Marie <u>arfinilinnik</u> qitornaqarpoq, <u>seksteninillu</u> erngutaqarluni, <u>arfinilinnil</u>lu ernutaqqiuteqarluni.
marie arfinili-nnik qitorna-qar-poq, seksteni-nil-lu ernguta-qar-luni, arfinili-nnil-lu ernutaqqiut-eqar-luni
marie six-INS.PL child-have-3SG, sixteen-INS.PL-and grandchild-have-CONT.4SG, six great.grandchild-have-CONT.4SG
Marie has six children, 16 grandchildren, and six great-grandchildren.

Numerals can be incorporated into the verbal suffix **-uvoq** 'to be' (see section 14.2.1 for discussion of this verbal suffix), e.g.:

Atuarfimmi init <u>pingasuupput</u>.
atuarfim-mi ini-t pingasu-u-pput
school-LOC room-PL three-be-3PL
There are three rooms in the school.

As mentioned previously, when speaking about prices only the Danish numerals are used, even for numbers below twelve. The use of Danish numerals in reference to prices is illustrated in the following examples.

Londonimiikkama immiaaraq <u>fem</u> pundeqarpoq.
londoni-mi-i-kkama immiaaraq fem punde-qar-poq
london-LOC-be-CAUS.1SG beer five pound-have-3SG
When I was in London, beer cost five pounds.

Atuagaq <u>fem hundrede og halvtreds</u> koruuninik akeqarpoq.
atuagaq fem hundrede og halvtreds koruuni-nik akeqar-poq
book five hundred and fifty krone-INS.PL cost-3SG
The book costs five hundred and fifty kroner.

The numerals agree in case with their associated noun, as illustrated in the following examples.

<u>Illuni marlunni</u> najugaqarpoq.
illu-ni marlun-ni najugaqar-poq
house-LOC.PL two-LOC.PL live-3SG
S/he lives in two houses.

Cardinal

5 Numerals

Qeqertanut sisamanut angalavoq.
qeqerta-nut sisama-nut angala-voq
island-ALL.PL four-ALL.PL travel-3SG
S/he is travelling to four islands.

Napparsimasoq nakorsanit pingasunit misissortippoq.
napparsimasoq nakorsanit pingasunit misissor-tip-poq
patient doctor-ABL.PL three-ABL.PL examine-PASS-3SG
The patient was examined by three doctors.

Hans Jensenip ukiuni kingullerni femtenini Tasiilarmiut sullisimavai.
hans jensen-ip ukiu-ni kinguller-ni femten-ini tasiilar-miu-t sulli-sima-vai.
hans jensen year-LOC.PL past-LOC.PL fifteen-LOC.PL tasiilaq-resident-PL work-past-3SG>3PL
Hans Jensen has worked for the residents of Tasiilaq for the past fifteen years.

Age is indicated by putting the numeral in the instrumental case in conjunction with the verb **ukioqarpoq** 'to be an age' (literally: to have year[s]), as in the following examples:

Paniga qulinik ukioqarpoq.
pani-ga quli-nik ukio-qar-poq
daughter-1SG ten-INS.PL year-have-3SG
My daughter is 10 years old.

Anaanaga tredsinik ukioqalertussaavoq.
anaana-ga tredsi-nik ukio-qa-ler-tu-ssa-a-voq.
mother-1SG sixty-INS.PL year-have-about.to-IP-FUT-be-3SG
My mother is turning 60.

The instrumental case can also appear in other expressions to do with age and numbers of years, as illustrated in the following examples. In some instances the instrumental suffix is attached to an associated noun rather than to the numeral, as in the second example.

33-nik ukiulik Anna atuarfimmi sulisarpoq.
33-nik ukiu-lik anna atuarfim-mi suli-sar-poq
33-INS.PL year-having anna school-LOC work-HAB-3SG
The 33-year-old Anna works in a school.

Niuernermik Ilinniarfik <u>ukiunik 40</u>-nngortorsiorpoq. Cardinal
niueerner-mik ilinniarfik ukiu-nik 40-nngor-toq-sior-poq
business-INS school year-INS.PL 40-become-IP-celebrate-3SG
The Business School celebrates 40 years.

The meaning of 'in' and 'from' in conjunction with annual dates (e.g. 'in 1997', 'from 2019') is conveyed by means of the locative and ablative cases respectively, as in the following examples. The meaning of 'until' or 'to' is conveyed by putting the year in the relative case followed by postposition **tungaanut** 'until', as in the second example. See section 10.2 for discussion of postpositions. Note that annual dates themselves are said in Danish, so, for example, 1995 is said as **nitten hundrede (og) femoghalvfems**.

<u>1990-mi</u> tikippoq.
1990-mi tikip-poq
1990-LOC arrive-3SG
S/he arrived in 1990.

<u>1995-miit 2004-p tungaanut</u> ilaqutariit Møllerikkut Københavnhavnimi najugaqarput.
1995-miit 2004-p tungaanut ilaqutari-it møller-i-kkut københavni-mi najugaqar-put
1995-ABL.PL 2000-REL until family-PL møller-HV-COLL copenhagen-LOC live-3PL
The Møller family lived in Copenhagen from 1995 until 2004.

The cardinal numerals are used to answer the question 'what time is it?' as in the following examples.

West Greenlandic	English
pingasut	three o'clock
sisamat	four o'clock
arfineq-marluk	seven o'clock

To say 'it is X o'clock', the hour is followed by the verbal suffix **-nngorpoq** 'to become', e.g.:

Pingasunngorpoq.
pingasu-nngor-poq
three-become-3SG
It's three o'clock.

5 Numerals

To express 'a quarter past', 'half past', 'a quarter to', etc., the word **tanneq** (literally 'the longest', referring to the minute hand on a clock) is used, followed by the number on a clock face to which the minute hand points. For example, 'a quarter past' is **tanneq pingasut**, literally 'the minute hand [is pointing to] three'. To say, for example, 'a quarter past four', the hour 'four' is placed before the expression **tanneq pingasut** 'a quarter past' and followed by the word **qaangerlugu** 'past'. Alternatively, it is possible to put the coming hour in the allative, followed by **tanneq** and the number to which the minute hand points, for example, **sisamanut tanneq marluk** 'ten past three', literally 'the minute hand [at] two until four'. These patterns are illustrated in the following table. The expression for 'half past' consists of the word for the upcoming hour followed by the word **qeqqa** 'its half/its middle'.

West Greenlandic	English
[PREVIOUS HOUR] **qaangerlugu tanneq pingasut** [NEXT HOUR] **nut tanneq pingasut**	a quarter past
[PREVIOUS HOUR] **qaangerlugu tanneq marluk** [NEXT HOUR] **nut tanneq marluk**	ten past
[PREVIOUS HOUR] **qaangerlugu tanneq arfineq** [NEXT HOUR] **qeqqa**	half past
[PREVIOUS HOUR] **qaangerlugu tanneq qulingiluat** [NEXT HOUR] **nut tanneq qulingiluat**	a quarter to
[PREVIOUS HOUR] **qaangerlugu tanneq aqqaneq** [NEXT HOUR] **nut tanneq aqqaneq**	five to
ullup qeqqa	midday
unnuap qeqqa	midnight

Points to note:

- In addition to **qulingiluat**, 'a quarter past/to' can also be expressed by **arfineq-sisamat**, which is a synonym for 'nine' used in southern Greenland, or by **qulaaluat**, another synonym which is used in northern Greenland.
- The word **qaangerlugu** 'past' is placed after the noun (or numeral) to which it refers. For example, **pingasut qaangerlugu** 'past three' literally means 'three past'.
- In constructions meaning 'half past', the numeral is placed in the relative before **qeqqa** 'its half'. Most numerals have a plural form (ending in -t), and therefore the relative ending looks the same as the absolutive, but the numerals 6, 1, and 11 have a singular form, so they

inflect when placed in the relative before **qeqqa**, e.g. **aqqaneq** 'eleven' > **aqqarnup qeqqa** 'half past ten'.

To express the sense of 'at X o'clock', the numeral appears in the allative. Numerals ending in the plural suffix -t (e.g. **tallimat** 'five') take the allative plural.

Qulingiluanut sulillutik aallartipput.
qulingilua-nut suli-llutik aallartip-put
nine-ALL.PL work-CONT.4PL begin-3PL
They start work at nine o'clock.

Tallimanut aallartissaaq.
tallima-nut aallarti-ssaaq
five-ALL.PL start-FUT.3SG
It will start at five o'clock.

Aqagu qulinut aallartissaagut.
aqagu quli-nut aallarti-ssaagut
tomorrow ten-ALL.PL begin-FUT.1PL
We'll start at ten tomorrow.

The allative can also be used in the sense of 'to, until' in conjunction with times, e.g.:

20:00-miit nal. 22:30-imut
20:00-miit nal. 22:30-i-mut
20:00-ABL clock 22:30-HV-ALL
from 20:00 until 22:30 o'clock

As with years, the meaning of 'from' a certain time is conveyed by the ablative, e.g.:

10:00-miit 16:00-p tungaanut
10:00-miit 16:00-p tungaanut
10:00-ABL 16:00-REL until
from 10:00 until 16:00

In a compound numeral, the allative suffix is placed on the last numeral in the compound, e.g.:

Sisamanut tanneq pingasunut angerlassaaq.
sisama-nut tanneq pingasu-nut angerla-ssaaq
four-ALL.PL big.hand three-ALL.PL go.home-FUT.3SG
S/he's going home at a quarter past three.[2]

---

2 Literally: towards four the big hand is on three she goes home.

The postposition **qaangerlugu** 'past' can be used after the last full hour, as in the following example. (See section 10.2 for discussion of West Greenlandic postpositions.)

Pingasut qaangerlugu tanneq pingasunut angerlassaaq.
pingasut qaangerlugu tanneq pingasu-nut angerla-ssaaq
three past big.hand three-ALL.PL three-ALL go.home-FUT.3SG
S/he's going home at a quarter past three.[3]

As mentioned previously, the expression for 'half past X' literally means 'half of the next hour'. This is illustrated as follows.

Isiginnaagassiaq qulingiluat qeqqanut aallartissaaq.
isiginnaagassiaq qulingiluat qeqq-anut aallarti-ssaaq
film nine half-ALL.3SG begin-FUT.3SG
The film starts at half past eight.[4]

5.2 Ordinal

The West Greenlandic ordinal numerals are as follows:

Ordinal numeral	English
siulleq, siulliat	first
aappaat	second
pingajuat	third
sisamaat	fourth
tallimaat	fifth
arfern(g)at	sixth
arfineq-aappaat	seventh
arfineq-pingajuat	eighth
qulingiliuaat	ninth
qulingaat	tenth
aqqarn(g)at	eleventh
aqqaneq-aappaat	twelfth
tretteniat	thirteenth

3 Literally: s/he is going home when the big hand is on three past three.
4 Literally: half of nine.

Points to note:

- The ordinal numerals are composed of the cardinal numbers with the third-person possessive suffix -at attached (except for **siulleq**, the more common variant of the word for 'first', and **aappaa**, one of the variants for 'second').
- The ordinal numerals from 'thirteenth' upwards are based on the Danish cardinal numerals (discussed in 5.1), e.g. **femteniat** 'fifteenth', **toogtyveat** 'twenty-second'. When the Danish number ends in a consonant, -iat is used; when the Danish number ends in a vowel, -at is used.
- When an ordinal numeral appears in conjunction with a noun (e.g. 'the third house', 'the fifth child', the noun typically appears in the relative plural, while the ordinal numeral appears after it. For example, **illu** 'house' > **illut pingajuat** 'the third house' (literally: 'of the houses, their third one').
- The only exception to this rule is **siulleq** 'first', which does not take the possessive suffix -at. When **siulleq** appears in conjunction with the noun, the noun is in the absolutive case (or another case, as appropriate for the context) and **siulleq** agrees with it, e.g. **illu** 'house' > **illu siulleq** 'the first house'.
- The word **aappaat** 'second' has a closely related variant **aappaa**, which means 'one or the other (out of two)'. **Aappaa** typically appears in conjunction with a noun in the relative singular, e.g. **skooq** 'shoe' **skuup aappaa** 'one of the (two) shoes'.

The use of the ordinal numerals is illustrated in the following examples.

Illu siulleq qorsuuvoq.
illu siulleq qorsu-u-voq
house first green-be-3SG
The first house is green.

Pisiniartut pingajuat angutaavoq.
pisiniartu-t pingajuat anguta-a-voq
customer-PL third man-be-3SG
The third customer[5] was a man.

When an ordinal number needs to be inflected for case (as relevant for the context), it appears in the possessed form of that case. This is illustrated in the following example, where the ordinal **tallimaat** 'fifth' appears with a possessive locative suffix.

---

5 Literally: the third one of the customers.

Assilisat <u>tallimaanni</u> UFO takuneqarsinnaavoq.
assilisa-t tallima-anni UFO taku-neqar-sinnaa-voq
photo-PL fifth-LOC.3PL see-PASS-be.able-3SG
A UFO can be seen in the fifth photo.

The equative is used when one finishes in a certain position in a competition, as in the following example.

Iron Manimi unamminermi <u>tallimaattut</u> naammassivoq.
iron mani-mi unamminer-mi tallima-attut naammassi-voq
iron mani-LOC competition-LOC fifth-EQU.3PL finish/complete-3SG
S/he finished fifth in the Iron Man competition.

The Danish versions of the smaller ordinals ('first' through 'twelfth') are often used instead of the West Greenlandic ones in conjunction with the word **etage** 'floor (of a multi-story building)' (which is itself a Danish loanword). The smaller Danish ordinals are as follows:

Danish ordinal numeral	English
første /fœɐ̯sdə/	first
anden /anən/	second
tredje	third
fjerde /fjɛʌ/	fourth
femte	fifth
sjette /ɕɛdə/	sixth
syvende	seventh
ottende /ʌdənə/	eighth
niende	ninth
tiende	tenth
ellevte /ɛlfdə/	eleventh
tolvte /tʌldə/	twelfth

The use of these Danish ordinals in conjunction with **etage** 'floor' is illustrated here.

<u>Tredje</u> etagemi najugaqarput.
tredje etage-mi najugaqar-put
third floor-LOC live-3PL
They live on the third floor.

Illoorara blok k-mi <u>femte</u> etagemi ineqarpoq.
illoora-ra blok k-mi femte etage-mi ineqar-poq.
cousin-1SG block k-LOC fifth floor-LOC live-3SG
My cousin lives in block K on the fifth floor.

Ordinal

The days of the month are expressed by putting the name of the month in the relative, followed by the ordinal with a possessive suffix in the appropriate case. This type of construction is illustrated in the following examples.

<u>Septemberip pingajuat</u> ataasinngorneruvoq.
septemberi-p pingajuat ataasinngorner-u-voq
september-REL third monday-be-3SG
The third of September is a Monday.

Aggustusip <u>qulinganni</u> tikissaanga.
aggustusi-p qulinga-nni tiki-ssa-anga
august-REL tenth-PL.LOC.3SG arrive-FUT-1SG
I'm arriving on the tenth of August.

<u>Januaarip sisamaani</u> inuueqarpunga.
januaari-p sisama-ani inuue-qar-punga
january-REL fourth-PL.LOC.3SG birthday-have-1SG
My birthday is on the fourth of January.

Tusarnaartitsineq <u>maajip treogtyveani</u> pissaaq.
tusarnaartitsineq maaji-p treogtyve-ani pi-ssaaq
concert may-REL 23rd-PL.LOC.3SG happen-FUT.3SG
The concert will be on the 23rd of May.

<u>aggustip 25-aniit 29-anut</u>
aggusti-p 25-aniit 29-anut
august-REL 25-PL.ABL.3SG 29-PL.ALL.3SG
from the 25th to the 29th of August

For the first day or week of a period of time, the expression **aallaqqaat** 'beginning' is used in the same type of possessive construction as those discussed previously. This is illustrated in the following example.

<u>Januaarip aallaqqaataa</u> ukiortaajuvoq.
januaari-p aallaqqaata-a ukior-taa-ju-voq
january-REL first-3SG year-new-be-3SG
The first of January is New Year's Day.

For the adverbs 'for the first time', 'for the third time' etc. the suffix -**saat** is used in transitive clauses and -**saanik** is used in intransitive clauses (with the exception of 'for the first time', which is **aatsaat**). This is illustrated in the following examples. (See section 7.2.1.1 for discussion of transitive and intransitive clauses.)

<u>Aatsaat</u> Kalaallit Nunaanniippunga.
aatsaat kalaalli-t nuna-anni-ip-punga
for.the.first time greenlander-PL country-LOC.3PL-be-1SG
I'm in Greenland for the first time.

Sisimiut <u>pingajussaat</u> tikippara.
sisimiut pingajussaat tikip-para
sisimiut for.the.third.time arrive-1SG>3SG
I arrived in Sisimiut for the third time.

Piitaq <u>sisamassaanik</u> piniarpoq.
piitaq sisamassaanik piniar-poq
piitaq for.the.fourth.time hunt-3SG
Piitaq is hunting for the fourth time.

The contemporative forms -**saaneerluni** (SG) and -**saaneerlutik** (PL) can also be used with the same meaning. This is illustrated in the following examples. (See section 7.2.2.3 for discussion of contemporative verbs.)

Oqaasileriffik Københavnnimi <u>tallimassaaneerluni</u> ataatimiitsitsissaaq.
oqaasileriffik københavni-mi tallimassaaneerluni ataatimiitsitsi-ssaaq
language.secretariat copenhagen-LOC for.the.fifth.time hold.meeting-FUT.3SG
The Language Secretariat of Greenland is holding a meeting in Copenhagen for the fifth time.

Qimmit qitsuillu ippassaq <u>siullermeerlutik</u> kapitissimapput.
qimmi-t qitsu-il-lu ippassaq siullermeerlutik kapitis-sima-pput.
dog-PL cat-PL-and yesterday for.the.first.time be.vaccinated-PAST-3PL
The dogs and cats were vaccinated for the first time yesterday.

Chapter 6

Noun modification (= adjectives)

Unlike Indo-European languages such as English, French, and German, which have a part of speech called 'adjective' that serves to modify nouns, West Greenlandic is not typically considered to have such a grammatical category. Instead of adjectives, West Greenlandic nouns are modified by nominal or verbal forms that convey an adjectival sense. West Greenlandic has two types of such noun modification constructions, termed attributive and predicative. Attributive constructions correspond to English adjective-noun phrases (e.g. 'a white house'), while predicative constructions correspond to English sentences containing an adjective (e.g. 'the house is white'). Each of these is discussed next in turn.

6.1 Attributive modifiers

Attributive constructions consist of a noun followed by a modifier and correspond to English adjective-noun phrases such as 'a white house'. The modifier is often an intransitive participle, which has the basic meaning of 'someone/something who/which is'. The intransitive participle is formed by adding the suffix +**toq** or +**soq** to a verbal stem, as illustrated in the following table. Note that intransitive participles are marked by the abbreviation PART in the glossing.

Verb	Verbal stem and intransitive participle suffix	Resulting attributive form (in absolutive singular)
mikivoq to be small	**miki-** plus +**soq**	**mikisoq** small
qaqorpoq to be white	**qaqor-** plus +**toq**	**qaqortoq** white
inuusuppoq to be young	**inuusup-** plus +**toq**	**inuusuttoq** young

DOI: 10.4324/9781315160863-6

6 Noun modification (= adjectives)

Points to note:

- The suffix **+toq** is typically attached to verbal stems ending in a consonant, while the variant **+soq** is typically attached to stems ending in a vowel, as well as to stems ending in a historical -i. See section 8.1 for a more detailed discussion of the formation of intransitive participles.
- The intransitive participles inflect like nouns, taking case and possessive suffixes. The suffix **+toq/+soq** behaves like a weak-stem noun with the inflectional stem **+tu-/+su-** (see section 3.2.1).

Not all modifiers are intransitive participles. Some of them look more like nominal forms, and in addition some of them are borrowed forms based on Danish adjectives. When used attributively, they do not receive a special ending, but they take can take case and possessive suffixes in the same way as other nouns. Some of the more common nominal and borrowed modifiers are listed in the following table.

Modifier	English translation
nutaaq	new
utoqqaq	old (of a person)

Points to note:

- These modifiers inflect like other nouns and fall into various noun-stem categories; for example, **utoqqaq** inflects as a strong-stem noun ending in **-aq**, as discussed in section 3.2.8.
- These modifiers with nominal forms can often be used as nouns, e.g. **utoqqaq** can mean 'an old person, an elder' as well as the modifier 'old'.

Moreover, some modifiers are formed from verbal stems by means of the suffix **+tooq** (typically used following a consonant) or **+sooq** (typically used following a vowel), meaning 'very, much'. Common examples of this type of modifier include those shown in the following list. It is best to learn this type of modifier on an individual basis, as it is not always predictable when a modifier will take the form of an intransitive participle and when it will take the suffix **+tooq/+sooq**.

Verb	Modifier
angivoq to be big	**angisooq** big
mattuvoq to be tough	**mattusooq** tough
sukkavoq to be fast	**sukkasooq** fast

Point to note:

- As with modifiers like **utoqqaq** 'old', words with this ending can sometimes be used in a nominal sense, e.g. **ersivoq** 'to be scared' > **ersitooq** 'coward, scaredy-cat'.

There is another similar-looking suffix, +/-**tooq** (following a consonant) or +/-**sooq** (following a vowel or historical -**i**), which can be attached to the inflectional stem of nouns and means 'in the manner of'. It is frequently used with language names to mean 'in a certain language', but can also be used to derive other modifiers. Examples of this type of modifier are shown in the following table.

Noun	Modifier
kalaaleq Greenlander	**kalaallisooq** Greenlandic-language
tuluk English person	**tuluttooq** English-language
qallunaaq Dane	**qallunaatooq** Danish-language
savalimmiormiu Faroese person	**savalimmiormiutooq** Faroese-language

Point to note:

- It can be difficult to predict which nouns take the additive version of this suffix, and which ones take the truncative version, so it is best to learn each case individually.

There is another suffix, -**lik**, which is also attached to nouns and has a similar meaning, i.e. 'having X, possessing X', or 'having the quality associated with X'. The use of this suffix is illustrated in the following table.

Attributive modifiers

6 Noun modification (= adjectives)

Noun	Modifier
allak stripe, pattern	**allalik** striped, patterned
aappaq spouse	**aappalik** married
meqoq body hair (of human or animal)	**meqqulik** hairy

Point to note:

- The suffix -**lik** can also be used to form nouns with the meaning of 'someone/something with the quality of X', 'someone/something possessing X', e.g. **ajorti** 'sin' > **ajortilik** 'sinner', **mattak** 'whale blubber' > **mattalik** 'whale', **marluk** 'two' > **marlulik** 'double-barrelled rifle'.

Some West Greenlandic modifiers are borrowed from Danish adjectives, e.g.:

Modifier	Danish source	English translation
privatiusoq	**privat**	private
moderniusoq	**moderne**	modern
positiviusoq	**positiv**	positive (in the scientific sense – e.g. a positive ion)

Point to note:

- These borrowed modifiers are formed by attaching the verb -**uvoq** 'to be' to the loanword, and then attaching the intransitive participle +**toq**/+**soq** to the verbal stem.

An attributive modifier follows its associated noun, e.g.:

annoraaq qaqortoq
annoraaq qaqor-toq
anorak be.white-IP
a/the white anorak

nerrivik mikisoq
nerrivik miki-soq
table be.small-IP
a/the small table

computeri <u>nutaaq</u>
computeri nutaaq
computer new
a/the new computer

interneti <u>sukkasooq</u>
interneti sukka-sooq
internet be.fast-very
fast internet

suliffik <u>privatiusoq</u>
suliffik privati-u-soq
office private-be-IP
a/the private office

biibili <u>qallunaatooq</u>
biibili qallunaa-tooq
bible danish-in.the.manner.of
a/the Danish-language Bible

Qeqertaq orp<u>ilik</u> takuaa.
qeqertaq orpi-lik taku-aa
island tree-having see-3SG>3SG
S/he saw a tree-filled island.

Arnanut <u>nutaaq</u> saqqummerpoq.
arnanut nutaaq saqqummer-poq.
arnanut new come.out-3SG
The new *Arnanut* (women's magazine) has come out.

Attributive modifiers

The case and number of the modifier matches that of the associated noun. The following examples illustrate this.

qarli<u>it</u> qernertut
qarli-it qerner-tu-t
trouser-PL be.black-IP-PL
black trousers

issiavi<u>it</u> angisu<u>ut</u>
issiavi-it angi-suu-t
chair-PL be.big-very-PL
big chairs

6 Noun modification (= adjectives)

karsi<u>mi</u> qernertu<u>mi</u>
karsi-mi qerner-tu-mi
box-LOC be.black-IP-LOC
in a/the black box

pisiniarfim<u>mut</u> nutaa<u>mut</u>
pisiniarfim-mut nutaa-mut
shop-ALL new-ALL
to a/the new shop

Nuummi iliveqarfim<u>mi</u> nutaa<u>mi</u> sanningasut arlallit uppisinneqarsimapput.
nuum-mi iliveqarfim-mi nutaa-mi sanningasu-t arlalli-t uppi-sin-neqar-sima-pput
nuuk-LOC graveyard-LOC new-LOC cross-PL many-PL fall.down-VAL-PASS-PAST-3PL
Many crosses have been knocked down in the new graveyard in Nuuk.

An attributive modifier appearing in conjunction with a possessed noun does not take possessive suffixes, just case suffixes. This is shown in the following examples.

Sanilima qimmia <u>qennertoq</u> qiluppoq.
sanili-ma qimmi-a qenner-toq qilup-poq
neighbour-REL.1SG dog-3SG be.black-IP bark-3SG
My neighbour's black dog is barking.

Nukkama kjolea <u>aappalaartoq</u> errorpoq.
nukka-ma kjole-a aappalaar-toq error-poq
younger.sibling-REL.1SG skirt-3SG be.red-IP be.in.the.wash-3SG
My little sister's red skirt is in the wash.

Ikinngutima illuaraataanut <u>nuannersumut</u> angalarusuppunga.
ikinnguti-ma illuaraata-anut nuanner-su-mut angala-rusup-punga
friend-REL.1SG cottage-ALL.3SG be.lovely-IP-ALL travel-want-1SG
I want to travel to my friend's cosy cottage.

If an incorporated predicative is accompanied by a modifier (see section 14.2.1), the modifier follows the incorporated predicative and appears in the absolutive case, e.g.:

Ivalu arnaavoq <u>silatooq</u>.
ivalu arna-a-voq silatooq
ivalu woman-be-3SG clever
Ivalu is a clever woman.

Attributive modifiers

If an incorporated direct object is accompanied by a modifier (see section 14.2.2), the modifier appears in the instrumental case. The modifier tends to precede the incorporated direct object but can sometimes follow it. These types of construction are illustrated in the following examples.

<u>Qernertumik</u> kaffisorpugut.
qerner-tu-mik kaffi-sor-pugut
be.black-IP-INS coffee-consume-1PL
We are drinking black coffee.

Minik <u>moderniusumik</u> inissiaqarpoq.
minik moderniusu-mik inissia-qar-poq
minik modern-INS flat-have-3SG
Minik has a modern flat.

Hanne <u>naasulimmik</u> tujuuloqarpoq.
hanne naasu-lim-mik tujuulo-qar-poq
hanne flower-having-INS blouse-have-3SG
Hanne has a flowery blouse.

Nuussuarmi inissiaqarpugut pingasunik <u>inilimmik</u>.
nussuar-mi inissia-qar-pugut pingasu-nik ini-lim-mik
nuussuaq-LOC flat-have-1PL three-INS.PL room-having-INS
We have a three-room flat in Nuussuaq.

<u>Qorsummik</u> qaatigooqarpoq, <u>tungujortunil</u>lu koorpunik qarleqarpoq.
qorsum-mik qaatigoo-qar-poq tungujortu-nil-lu koorpu-nik qarle-qar-poq
green-INS jacket-have-3SG blue-INS.PL-and jeans-INS.PL trouser-have-3SG
She was dressed in a green jacket and blue jeans.

6
Noun modification (= adjectives)

Taartunik naatsunik nujaqarpoq.
taartu-nik naatsu-nik nuja-qar-poq
dark-INS.PL short-INS.PL hair-have-3SG
She has short, dark hair.

There are also suffixes with a specific adjectival meaning (e.g. 'big', 'small', 'old', etc.) which can be added to nominal stems. When these suffixes are attached, they form a new noun with a meaning equivalent to an English adjective-noun phrase. The following are some of the most common of these suffixes with adjectival meaning.

Suffix	Suffix attached to nominal base
-araq, -eraq, -oraq, -varaq little, small	**qitsuk** cat > **qitsuaraq** small cat **qarasaq** brain > **qarasaaraq** little brain **angut** man > **anguteeraq** little man **ini** room > **ineeraq** little room **mikisoq** small > **mikisooraq** very small, tiny **arnaq** woman > **arnavaraq** small woman
-koq old; former; ex-; ruined	**illu** house > **illukoq** ruined house **kunngi** king > **kunngikoq** former king **ui** husband > **uikoq** ex-husband
-nnguaq small and cute	**qimmeq** dog > **qimminnguaq** cute little dog
-pajuk bad; naughty; ruined; poor (as in 'poor thing'); cool, awesome	**kaffi** coffee > **kaffipajuk** bad coffee **angut** man > **angutipajuk** poor man **illit** you > **illipajuk** you're (so) cool **biilit** car > **biilipajuk** (what a; such a) cool car
-palaaq bad; nasty	**inuk** person > **inupalaaq** bad person
+(r)suaq (SG); **+(r)suit** (PL) big	**kangerluk** fjord > **kangerlussuaq** big fjord
-rujussuaq extremely big, gigantic	**illu** house > **illorujussuaq** gigantic house
+taaq, +saaq new	**oqaluffik** church > **oqaluffissaaq** new church
+tooq, +sooq having a big/long/loud/high ...	**aki** price > **akisooq** expensive, costly, high-priced **umik** beard > **umittooq** long-bearded

126

Points to note:

- The suffix **-araq** has several variants. The **-araq** variant is commonly attached to stems ending in **-a**, **-u**, and weak **k** and **q**. The **-eraq** variant is commonly attached to stems ending in **-i** (including historical **-i**, like **angut** 'man'). The **-oraq** variant is commonly attached to stems ending in **-oq** and to names ending in **-u** and **-o**. The **-varaq** variant is commonly attached to strong-stem nouns ending in **-aq**.
- The suffix **-araq** inflects like **meeraq** 'child', i.e. the inflectional stem is **-aqqa-/-eqqa-/-oqqa-/-vaqqa-**, e.g. **ineeqqami** 'in a/the small room'.
- The suffix **+tooq/+sooq** can have slightly different specific meanings depending on the word to which they are attached. These precise meanings are often unpredictable and must be learned on an individual basis.

The use of these adjectival suffixes is illustrated in the following examples.

Qatanngutiga illorsuaqarpoq.
qatannguti-ga illo-rsua-qar-poq
sibling-1SG house-big-have-3SG
My sibling has a big house.

Ataatama biilikuani cigaretsisunnippoq.
ataata-ma biili-ku-ani cigaretsi-sunnip-poq
father-REL.1SG car-old-LOC.4SG cigarette-smell-3SG
It smells of cigarettes in my father's old car.

Meeqqat qimmiaqqanik aneerussipput.
meeqqa-t qimmi-aqqa-nik aneerussi-pput
child-PL dog-small-INS.PL go.out.with-3PL
The children are walking the small dogs/puppies.

Meerannguaq inequnarpoq.
meera-nnguaq inequnar-poq
child-small be.cute-3SG
The little kid is cute.

Ilinniartitsisupajuk qasuvoq.
ilinniartitsisu-pajuk qasu-voq
teacher-poor be.tired-3SG
The poor teacher is tired.

Paalup biilipajui!
Paalu-p biili-paju-i

6 Noun modification (= adjectives)

paalu-REL car-cool-3SG
Paalu's car is so cool!

Illoqarfit<u>taaq</u> angivoq.
illoqarfit-taaq angi-voq
town-new be.big-3SG
The new part of town is big.

Some of these adjectival suffixes (e.g. +taaq/+saaq 'new' and +tooq/+sooq 'big') can themselves take a verbal suffix so as to create a verb containing an adjectival meaning, e.g.:

Suffix	Suffix attached to nominal base
+taarpoq, +saarpoq to get a new	**qarlik** trouser > **qarlittaarpoq** to get new trousers **erneq** son > **ernertaarpoq** to get a new son
+tuvoq, +suvoq to have a big	**siut** ear > **siutituvoq** to have big ears **qingaq** nose > **qingartuvoq** to have a big nose
+luppoq to have a bad	**isi** eye > **isiluppoq** to have bad eyes **kigut** tooth > **kigutiluppoq** to have bad teeth **kamik** boot > **kamilluppoq** to have bad boots

The use of these suffixes is illustrated in the following examples.

Aaqqati<u>taar</u>pit?
aaqqati-taar-pit
mitten-get.a.new-INT.2SG
Have you got new gloves?

Nagguaatsut siuti<u>tu</u>pput.
nagguaatsu-t suiti-tu-pput
elephant-PL ear-have.a.big-3PL
Elephants have big ears.

Biilinik ajutoornermik kingorna Moortat niu<u>lup</u>poq.
biili-nik ajutoorneq-mik kingorna moortat niu-lup-poq

car-INS.PL accident-INS after morten leg-be.bad-3SG
Since the car crash Morten has [had] bad legs.

6.2 Predicative modifiers

West Greenlandic constructions are sentences whereby the verb describes the subject. They correspond to English sentences containing an adjective such as 'the house is white', 'I am tall', 'they are young'. These forms take standard intransitive verbal endings, such as the first-person singular **+punga/+vunga**, the third-person singular **+poq/+voq** (which also serves as the dictionary form of verbs), the first-person plural **+pugut/+vugut**, and the third-person plural **+pput** (see section 7.1 for a complete paradigm of these verbal person endings). The following table shows how the different types of attributive modifiers discussed in 6.1 look in the predicative position.

Attributive modifier	Predicative modifier
mikisoq small	**mikivoq** to be small
qaqortoq white	**qaqorpoq** to be white
nutaaq new	**nutaavoq**, **nutaajuvoq** to be new
angisooq big	**angivoq** to be big
allalik striped, patterned	**allaliuvoq** to be striped
privatiusoq private	**privatiuvoq** to be private

Points to note:

- The modifiers whose attributive form ends in **+toq/+soq** (the intransitive participle suffix) take **+voq/+poq** in the predicative.
- The other types of modifiers take -**uvoq** 'to be' in the predicative (or its variants -**avoq** or -**juvoq**, depending on the final letter of the stem of the modifier; see section 14.2.1 for explanation of the verb 'to be').
- Some modifiers have more than one variant in the predicative, e.g. **nutaaq** 'new' can be **nutaavoq** or **nutaajuvoq** 'to be new'.

The following table illustrates the difference between attributive and predicative modificational constructions. An attributive construction is a phrase, while a predicative construction is a sentence.

6 Noun modification (= adjectives)

Attributive construction	Predicative construction
illu angisooq the big house	**Illu angivoq.** The house is big.
meeraq mikisoq the small child	**Meeraq mikivoq.** The child is small.

The following examples illustrate predicative constructions.

Qitsuit nujuarput.
qitsu-it nujuar-put
cat-PL be.wild-3PL
The cats are wild.

Pinnerpunga.
pinner-punga
be.beautiful-1SG
I am beautiful.

Qasuvugut.
qasu-vugut
be.tired-1PL
We are tired.

Atuartitsineq soqutiginarpoq.
atuartitsineq soqutiginar-poq
studying be.interesting-3SG
Studying is interesting.

If a predicative modifier indicates the outcome of a process indicated by an associated transitive verb, it is marked by the instrumental case, e.g.:

Illuni tungujortumik qalipappaa.
illu-ni tungujortu-mik qalipap-paa
house-4SG blue-INS paint-3SG>3SG
He's painting his house blue.

Note that some predicative modifiers are typically first made into intransitive participles (by means of the suffix **+toq/+soq**), and then the verb **+uvoq** 'to be' is added onto that. This is particularly common with modifiers denoting colours, e.g.:

Annoraaq qaqortuuvoq.
annoraaq qaqor-tu-u-voq
anorak be.white-IP-be-3SG
The anorak is white.

> Predicative modifiers

The suffix **+luppoq**, which means 'to have a bad' when used attributively (see section 6.1), can also be used as a predicative modifier in the sense of 'to be bad', as in the following examples. Only context will determine whether the meaning of the construction is attributive or predicative on any given occasion, and in some cases both meanings are possible.

Internetsiluppoq.
internetsi-lup-poq
internet-be.bad-3SG
The internet is bad. (Or: There is bad internet.)

Moortat niuluppoq.
moortat niu-lup-poq
morten leg-be.bad-3SG
Morten's legs are bad. (Or: Morten has bad legs.)

The suffix **-llarippoq/-llaqqippoq** 'to be good at' is slightly different as it is attached to verbs rather than nouns. It is illustrated in the following table:

Suffix	Suffix attached to verbal base
-llarippoq/-llaqqippoq to be good at	**allappoq** to write > **allallaqqippoq** to be good at writing

The use of these suffixes is illustrated in the following examples.

Maria arpallaqqippoq.
maria arpa-llaqqip-poq
maria run-be.good.at-3SG
Maria is good at running.

Anaanaga mersullaqqippoq.
anaana-ga mersu-llaqqip-poq
mother-1SG sew-be.good.at-3SG
My mother is good at sewing.

6 Noun modification (= adjectives)

Note that because predicative modifiers behave like verbs, they can be negated and take tense and aspect suffixes. The following table illustrates some of the possibilities; see section 7 on verbs for more discussion of the different verbal suffixes in West Greenlandic.

Verb form	Example	English translation
NON-FUTURE	miki**vo**q	is small
FUTURE	miki**ssa**voq/miki**ssaa**q	will be small
NEGATIVE	miki**nngila**q	is not small
PAST	miki**sima**voq	was small
CAN	miki**sinnaa**voq	can be small

6.3 Comparison

6.3.1 Comparative

West Greenlandic comparative modifiers (equivalent to English 'better', 'bigger', 'more interesting', etc.) are formed by attaching the attributive comparative suffix +neq, meaning 'more', to a modificational stem, as follows.

Comparative suffix	Example
+neq	**mikisoq** small > **mikineq** smaller **nutaaq** new > **nutaaneq** newer **sukkasooq** fast > **sukkaneq** faster

Points to note:

- The comparative suffix -neq inflects like an extra-strong-stem noun (e.g. **erneq** 'son'; see section 3.2.6).
- Like other modifiers, comparatives agree with their associated noun in case and number.
- You may also see variants of +neq with slightly different meaning, namely +nerujussuaq 'much more' and +nerumaaq 'somewhat more'. These forms are a combination of +neq with the suffix -rujussuaq 'extremely big, gigantic' and -rumaaq 'somewhat'.

- There is another comparative suffix, +(r)leq, which has a much more restricted usage than -neq and is typically found only in certain set forms, such as the noun **nukarleq** 'the younger one, the junior one', which is derived from the noun **nuka** 'younger sibling'.
- The various comparative suffixes are marked by the abbreviation COMP in the glossing.

illu mikineq
illu miki-neq
house small-COMP
(the) smaller house

mittarfiit takinerit
mittarfi-it taki-ner-it
airstrip-PL long-COMP-PL
(the) longer airstrips

aviisinit nutaanernit
aviisi-nit nutaa-ner-nit
newspaper-ABL.PL new-COMP-ABL.PL
from (the) newer newspapers

inissiami akisunermi
inissia-mi akisu-ner-mi
flat-LOC expensive-COMP-LOC
in the more expensive flat

Ullumi ippassarmit inimi mikinerujussuarmi sulivugut.
ullumi ippassar-mit ini-mi miki-ne-rujussuar-mi suli-vugut
today yesterday-ABL room-LOC small-COMP-much-LOC work-1PL
Today we are working in a much smaller room than yesterday.

The comparative suffix +neq is often followed by a verbal suffix. The verbal suffix allows the comparative to be used in predicative contexts, as in 'X is cheaper/stronger/better than Y'. The verbal comparatives are as follows.

Comparative verbal form	English translation
+neruvoq	to be more
+nerujussuuvoq	to be much more
+nerumaarpoq	to be somewhat more

6 Noun modification (= adjectives)

Points to note:

- The basic comparative verbal form is -**neruvoq** 'to be more'.
- In the forms -**nerujussuuvoq** and -**nerumaarpoq**, the comparative suffix has been augmented by an additional suffix (-**rujussuuvoq** 'to be much', from -**rujussuaq** 'much' and -**rumaarpoq** 'somewhat' respectively) to give a slightly different meaning.

When specifically comparing two options (i.e. 'the bigger of the two, the better of the two'), the form +**nerusoq** is used, as illustrated in the following example. This form consists of the verbal comparative suffix +**neruvoq** plus an intransitive participle suffix +**soq**.

Sofa <u>akisunerusoq</u> pisiaraarput.
sofa akisu-ner-u-soq pisia-raarput
sofa expensive-COMP-be-IP buy-VAL.1PL>3SG
We bought the more expensive sofa (of the two).

The West Greenlandic equivalent of English 'than' in a comparative sentence is the ablative case (singular -**mit**, plural -**nit**), as in the following examples. Note that if the comparison includes a measurement, that will appear in the instrumental (see section 3.3.6 for further examples of the instrumental used with measurements, prices, ages, and other numbers).

Henrik Anda<u>mit</u> mikineruvoq.
henrik anda-mit miki-ner-uvoq
henrik anda-ABL small-COMP-be-3SG
Henrik is smaller than Anda.

Piitaq Hansi<u>mit</u> 10 centimeteri<u>nik</u> takineruvoq.
piitaq hans-i-mit 10 centimeteri-nik taki-ner-u-voq
piitaq hans-HV-ABL 10 centimetre-INS.PL tall-COMP-be-3SG
Piitaq is 10 centimetres taller than Hans.[1]

The following examples illustrate the use of these comparative predicative modifiers.

Qimmit inunnit <u>oqilanerujussuupput</u>.
qimmi-t inun-nit oqila-ne-rujussu-u-pput
dog-PL person-ABL.PL fast-COMP-much-be-3PL
Dogs are much faster than people.

---

1 Literally: taller than Hans by 10 centimetres.

Akikinnerusunik peqanngilasi?
akikin-ner-u-su-nik pe-qa-nngila-si
cheap-COMP-be-IP-INS.PL something-have-NEG-2PL
Don't you have anything that is cheaper?

Etagehusi taanna Danmarkimi etagehusinit pukkinneruvoq.
etagehusi taanna danmarki-mi etagehusi-nit pukkin-ner-u-voq
block.of.flats this denmark-LOC block.of.flats-ABL.PL low-COMP-3SG
This block of flats is lower than the blocks of flats in Denmark.

Venedig Parisimit kusanarnerumaarpoq.
venedig paris-i-mit kusanar-ne-rumaar-poq
venice paris-HV-ABL pretty-COMP-somewhat-3SG
Venice is a bit prettier than Paris.

Note that **angivoq** 'to be big' has two comparative forms, the regular **angineq** 'bigger' and the irregular **anneq**. The latter is illustrated in the following example.

Nuuk Kangerlussuammit anneruvoq.
nuuk kangerlussuam-mit anner-u-voq
nuuk kangerlussuaq-ABL bigger-be-3SG
Nuuk is bigger than Kangerlussuaq.

Likewise, **mikivoq** 'to be small' has two comparative forms, the regular **mikineq** 'smaller' and the irregular **minneq**. The latter is illustrated in the following example.

Kangerlussuaq Nuummit minneruvoq.
kangerlussuaq nuum-mit minner-u-voq
kangerlussuaq nuuk-ABL smaller-be-3SG
Kangerlussuaq is smaller than Nuuk.

6.3.2 Superlative

The basic form of the superlative (i.e. 'the most', 'the best', etc.) is composed of the nominal suffix **+neq** 'more; the most' added to a modificational stem. As this is the same suffix that is used to mark the comparative, the superlative meaning is conveyed by particular grammatical constructions (to be discussed later in this section) or by augmenting +neq with another suffix to give it an exclusively superlative meaning. These superlative suffixes are shown in the following table. Note that

6 Noun modification (= adjectives)

the various superlative suffixes are marked by the abbreviation SUP in the glossing.

Superlative suffix	Example
+neq	**mikisoq** small > **mikineq** the smallest **nutaaq** new > **nutaaneq** the newest **sukkasooq** fast > **sukkaneq** the fastest
+nerpaaq	**mikisoq** small > **mikinerpaaq** the smallest **nutaaq** new > **nutaanerpaaq** the newest **sukkasooq** fast > **sukkanerpaaq** the fastest
+nersaq	**oqittoq** light, easy > **oqinnersaq** the lightest, the easiest **qaqortoq** white > **qaqornersaq** the whitest

Points to note:

- The suffixes **+neq** and **+nerpaaq** have the same meaning, but **+nerpaaq** is often used instead of **+neq** in order to avoid confusion with the comparative (as **+neq** can mean both).
- The suffix **+neq** is not commonly used independently; rather, it generally appears with a possessive suffix (discussed later).
- As in the comparative, the suffix **+(r)leq** can be used with superlative meaning but is typically restricted to certain set forms, e.g. **qiterleq** 'the midmost; the middle finger', **kingulleq** 'the last', **tulleq** 'the next, the closest', and **angajulleq** 'the oldest'.

In order to express a basic superlative such as 'the oldest one', 'the youngest one', 'the best one', the variant **+nerpaaq** is often used so as to avoid confusion with the comparative (as **+neq** can mean both). Thus, **takinerpaaq** means 'the tallest one' and **sukkanerpaaq** means 'the fastest one'. The following examples illustrate this type of superlative construction. Like other modifiers, the superlatives agree with their associated noun in case and number.

illu miki<u>nerpaaq</u>
illu miki-nerpaaq
house small-SUP
the smallest house

mittarfiit takinerpaat
mittarfi-it taki-nerpaa-t
airstrip-PL long-SUP-PL
the longest airstrips

aviisinit nutaanerpaanit
aviisi-nit nutaa-nerpaa-nit
newspaper-ABL.PL new-SUP-ABL.PL
from the newest newspapers

inissiami akisunerpaami
inissia-mi akisu-nerpaa-mi
flat-LOC expensive-SUP-LOC
in the most expensive flat

nunatsinni interneti sukkanerpaaq
nuna-tsinni interneti sukka-nerpaaq
country-LOC.1PL internet fast-SUP
the fastest internet in our country

Sofa akisunerpaaq pisiaraarput.
sofa akisu-nerpaaq pisia-raarput
sofa expensive-SUP buy-VAL.1PL>3SG
We bought the most expensive sofa.

The superlative suffix **+nersaq** is used in conjunction with a possessive suffix to indicate the meaning of 'the most out of us/you/them' (see section 3.4 for discussion of the possessive suffixes). This type of construction is illustrated in the following examples. It literally means 'our oldest one', 'their nicest one', etc.

utoqqaanersarput
utoqqaa-nersar-put
old-SUP-1PL
the oldest of us

nuannernersaat
nuanner-nersa-at
be.nice-SUP-3PL
the nicest of them

In order to convey the equivalent of English phrases such as 'my oldest friend', 'our nicest vase', 'their newest car', a modifier with the basic

6 Noun modification (= adjectives)

comparative/superlative suffix **+neq** is used in conjunction with a noun bearing a possessive suffix, e.g.:

qimmia an<u>neq</u>
qimmi-a an-neq
dog-3SG big-SUP
his/her biggest dog

atuarto<u>ra</u> pikkorin<u>neq</u>
atuar-to-ra pikkorin-neq
study-IP-1SG clever-SUP
my cleverest student

biili<u>i</u> sukka<u>ner</u>it
biili-i sukka-ner-it
car-PL.3PL be.fast-SUP-PL
their fastest car

When a superlative modifier is used in a phrase such as 'the biggest school' or 'the fastest ship', the superlative variant **+nersaq** is typically employed, in conjunction with a 3PL possessive suffix in the appropriate case (see section 3.4), and the associated noun appears in the absolutive/relative plural. This type of construction literally means 'the schools' biggest one', 'the ships' fastest one'. The following examples illustrate this type of construction.

atuarfi<u>it</u> an<u>nersa</u>at
atuarfi-it an-nersa-at
school-PL big-SUP-3PL
the biggest school

umiarsu<u>it</u> sukka<u>nersa</u>at
umiarsu-it sukka-nersa-at
ship-PL fast-SUP-3PL
the fastest ship

In order to express the equivalent of 'in the biggest school', 'with/by the fastest ship', etc., the superlative form takes the appropriate case, e.g.:

atuarfi<u>it</u> an<u>nersa</u>anni
atuarfi-it an-nersa-anni
school-PL big-SUP-LOC.3PL
in the biggest school

umiarsuit sukkanersaannik
umiarsu-it sukka-nersa-annik
ship-PL fast-SUP-INS.3PL
with/by the fastest ship

In order to say, for example, 'the fastest ship in the land', 'the biggest festival in the world', the expression 'in the land', 'in the world' can simply be added to the superlative phrase, e.g.:

nunarsuarmi filmfestivalit annersaasa ilaat
nunarsuar-mi film-festivali-t an-nersa-asa ilaat
world-LOC film-festival-PL big-SUP-REL.3PL one.of
one of the biggest film festivals in the world

As in the case of the comparative modifiers, the superlative modifiers can take the verbal suffix -**uvoq** 'to be'. There are two main variants, listed in the following table.

Superlative verbal suffix	Examples
+neruvoq to be the most	**pikkorinneq** the cleverest > **pikkorinneruvoq** to be the cleverest
+nerpaavoq to be the most	**sukkanerpaaq** the fastest > **sukkanerpaavoq** to be the fastest

Points to note:

- The variant **+nerpaavoq** 'to be the most' is a contraction of **+nerpaajuvoq**, i.e. **+nerpaaq** 'the most' plus -**uvoq** 'to be'.
- The variant **+nerpaavoq** is used more frequently than **+neruvoq** because the latter is ambiguous, as it can also have a comparative meaning.
- The variant **+nersaavoq** can be used instead of **+nerpaavoq**.

This type of construction is illustrated in the following examples.

Utoqqaanersaavunga.
utoqqaa-nersaa-vunga
old-be.SUP-1SG
I am the oldest.

6
Noun modification (= adjectives)

Usain Bolt <u>sukkanerpaavoq</u>.
usain bolt sukka-nerpaa-voq
usain bolt be.fast-be.SUP-3SG
Usain Bolt is the fastest.

In order to express the equivalent of 'Mount Everest is the tallest mountain', 'Usain Bolt is the fastest runner', etc., the nominal superlative suffix **+nersaq** 'the most (out of)' is combined with the transitive verbal suffix **-raa** (or its uncontracted equivalent **-rivaa**) 'to have someone/something as' (see section 14.4.7 for further discussion of this verbal suffix). The resulting form takes a transitive object suffix such as **-at** (3PL>3SG/3PL); see section 7.2.1.1.2 for a complete table of the indicative (basic) West Greenlandic transitive object suffixes.

Superlative verbal suffix	Examples
+nersaraa to be the most (out of)	**minneq** the smallest > **minnersaraat** to be the smallest out of them[1]

1 Literally: to have it as their smallest one.

This type of construction is illustrated in the following examples.

Kaju qimmit inequnar<u>nersaraat</u>.
kaju qimmi-t inequnar-nersa-ra-at
kaju dog-PL cute-SUP-have.as-3PL>3SG/3PL
Kaju is the cutest dog.[2]

Kujalleq maanna nunatsinni kommunit min<u>nersaraat</u>.
kujalleq maanna nuna-tsinni kummuni-t min-nersa-ra-at
kujalleq now land-LOC.1PL municipality-PL be.small-SUP-have.as-3PL>3SG
Kujalleq is now the smallest municipality in our country.[3]

Nuuk illoqarfiit Kalaallit Nunaanni angi<u>nersaraat</u>.
nuuk illoqarfi-it kalaalli-t nuna-anni angi-nersa-ra-at
nuuk town-PL greenlander-PL land-LOC.3PL be.big-SUP-have.as-3PL>3SG
Nuuk is the biggest town in Greenland.[4]

2 Literally: the dogs have Kaju as their cutest one.
3 Literally: the municipalities in our country have Kujalleq as their smallest one.
4 Literally: the towns in Greenland have Nuuk as their biggest one.

Kalaallit Nunaat nunarsuarmi qeqertat anginersaraat.
kalaalli-t nuna-at nunarsuar-mi qeqerta-t angi-nersa-ra-at
greenlander-PL land-3PL world-LOC island-PL be.big-SUP-have.as-3PL>3SG
Greenland is the biggest island in the world.[5]

Mount Everest nunarsuarmi qaqqat portunersaraat.
mount everest nunarsuar-mi qaqqa-t portu-nersa-ra-at
mount everest word-LOC mountain-PL be.tall-SUP-have.as-3PL>3SG
Mount Everest is the tallest mountain in the world.[6]

Comparison

---

[5] Literally: the islands in the world have Greenland as their biggest one.
[6] Literally: the mountains in the world have Mount Everest as their tallest one.

Chapter 7

Verbs

West Greenlandic has a rich verbal system with a complex morphology. Verbs all have a stem to which suffixes can be added indicating person (first, second, third, and fourth), number (singular and plural), transitivity (i.e. whether the verb takes an object or not), mood (ways of conveying different modes of action including statements, questions, causation, etc.), tense (past, present, future), aspect (completed, incomplete, etc.), and other distinctions. There are three different verbal stem types: vowel-stem, consonant-stem, and r-stem. In a dictionary verbs are listed in the indicative intransitive third-person singular form ending -**voq** or -**poq** 'he/she/it does/did', or the indicative transitive third-person singular with third-person singular object -**vaa** or -**paa** 'he/she/it does/did it'. Each of these different features of West Greenlandic verbs will be discussed in the following sections.

7.1 Person and number

7.1.1 Subject suffixes

West Greenlandic has person suffixes indicating the subject of the verb. These suffixes are more commonly used than independent personal pronouns (discussed in section 4.1), which are typically employed only for emphasis).

The subject suffixes can be either singular or plural. Modern West Greenlandic has no dual form (though older forms of the language did).

There are subject suffixes for the first person, second person, third person, and fourth person. The first person refers to the speaker, corresponding to the English 'I' in the singular and 'we' in the plural.

The second person refers to the addressee, corresponding to the English 'you' in the singular and plural.

DOI: 10.4324/9781315160863-7

The third person refers to neither the speaker or the addressee, corresponding to the English 'he', 'she', and 'it' in the singular and 'they' in the plural'. Note that West Greenlandic does not make a gender distinction in the third person, so that a single suffix corresponds to English 'he', 'she', and 'it'.

The fourth person is a feature of West Greenlandic that does not have a precise English equivalent in the pronominal system. It is a person that marks the subject of a verb in a subordinate clause which is the same as the subject of the verb in an associated main clause. It is restricted to the West Greenlandic subordinate verbal moods (see section 7.2.2). In order to understand the use of the West Greenlandic fourth person, consider the English sentence 'Aggusti made the phone call when he was at his house'. This sentence contains a main clause, 'Aggusti made the phone call', and a subordinate clause, 'when he was at his house'. In the English sentence, it is impossible to know whether the 'he' in the subordinate clause refers to Aggusti or to another person (e.g. Aggusti could have made the phone call when a friend was at Aggusti's house). In West Greenlandic, by contrast, in a sentence like this the subject of the subordinate clause would be in the fourth person and would thus clearly refer back to Aggusti rather than to anyone else.

Person and number

7.1.2 Object suffixes

In addition to subject suffixes, West Greenlandic has person suffixes which are used to indicate the object of a verb. These suffixes correspond to the English object pronouns 'me', 'you', 'him', 'her', 'it', 'us', and 'them'.

The object suffixes are used only in conjunction with transitive verbs (i.e. verbs which take a direct object; see section 7.2.1.1.2). The suffix indicates both the subject and the object of the verb. For example, the single West Greenlandic suffix **-vara** simultaneously denotes a first-person subject and a third-person object; thus, the verb **takuvara** means 'I see/saw him/her', where **taku-** is a verbal stem meaning 'see' and the ending indicates both 'I' and 'him/her'. The transitive suffixes are presented in the following section on West Greenlandic moods, where the full paradigms of the different verbal forms are given.

The four subordinate moods (causative, conditional, contemporative, and participial; see 7.2) can have a fourth-person object in addition to a third-person object. The fourth-person object is used when the object of the subordinate verb is the same as the subject of the main verb. For an example of this phenomenon, see section 7.2.2.1.2 regarding the transitive causative mood.

7.2 Mood

West Greenlandic verbs conjugate in eight different moods. Four of the moods are used only in independent or main clauses, while the other four are used only in subordinate clauses. The following table illustrates the West Greenlandic verbal system, including the eight moods and the characteristic markers of each one. (Note that the following applies only to the affirmative moods; the negative moods have different markers, discussed in 7.11.)

Independent/Main		Subordinate	
Indicative	-vu-, -va-	Causative	-ga-, -ma-
Interrogative	-vi-, -va-	Conditional	-gu-, -pa-
Imperative	-li-, -la-	Contemporative	-lu-
Optative	-li-, -la-	Participial	-tu-, -su-, -gi-

Points to note:

- Some of the forms of the indicative and the interrogative (e.g. the 3SG) are the same.
- The imperative and the optative have similar functions (i.e. they are both used to give commands and to make requests and suggestions) but appear in complimentary distribution, i.e. the imperative is only used with the 2SG, 1PL, and 2PL, while the optative is only used with the 1SG, 3SG, and 3PL.
- The causative is used for subordinate clauses indicating reason, cause, and consecutive action. It can also be used as a past tense in everyday language.
- The conditional is used for potential and hypothetical situations (i.e. 'If ... then').
- The contemporative is used for simultaneous action (e.g. 'I listened to music while I was cooking').
- The participial forms complement clauses (i.e. clauses beginning with 'that' in English, e.g. 'I saw that he had cleaned the house', 'I know that you are reliable'; see section 14.5.3 for discussion of this clause type).
- All of these moods have separate negative version, which will be described in section 7.11.

The following examples illustrate a single verb in the first- and second-person singular in all of the different main and subordinate verb forms.

Independent/main		Subordinate	
INDICATIVE	**sulivunga** I work/worked	CAUSATIVE	**suligama** when I worked
INTERROGATIVE	**sulivit?** do/did you work?	CONDITIONAL	**suliguma** if I work/worked
IMPERATIVE	**suligit!** work!	CONTEMPORATIVE	**sulillunga** while working
OPTATIVE	**sulilanga** let me work	PARTICIPIAL	**sulisunga** that I worked

7.2.1 Independent/main moods

7.2.1.1 Indicative

The basic mood of West Greenlandic verbs is the indicative. The indicative is used to denote actions in affirmative statements (as opposed to questions or negative statements). Indicative verbs in West Greenlandic can refer to either present or past actions. For example, the verb **sulivoq** can mean either 's/he is working' or 's/he worked'. (Note that it does not usually express the equivalent of English 's/he works', which refers to a habitual action and is conveyed by means of a specific suffix, **+tarpoq/+sarpoq** 'to do something usually/habitually'). See section 7.4.2 for discussion of **+tarpoq/+sarpoq**.) The wider context can make clear whether a given verb has a present or past sense, and in addition, specific tense and aspect suffixes can be added to the verbal stem in order to make this information explicit. The indicative can be divided into two subcategories, intransitive and transitive, as detailed in the following sections.

7.2.1.1.1 INTRANSITIVE

West Greenlandic intransitive verbs (i.e. verbs which do not take a direct object) and transitive verbs (i.e. verbs which take a direct object) take different sets of suffixes. The following table illustrates the suffixes for intransitive indicative verbs.

7 Verbs

Intransitive indicative suffixes		
	Vowel-stem	Consonant-stem, r-stem
1SG	**+vunga**	**+punga**
2SG	**+vutit**	**+putit**
3SG	**+voq**	**+poq**
1PL	**+vugut**	**+pugut**
2PL	**+vusi**	**+pusi**
3PL	**+pput**	**+put**

Points to note:

- Consonant-stem and r-stem verbs take the same suffixes.
- The final consonant of consonant-stem verbs always becomes -p- before the suffixes are added. For example, the final **k** at the end of the stem **sinik-** 'sleep (noun)' is assimilated with the -p- in the ending, e.g. **sinippoq** 's/he sleeps/slept'.
- the 3PL form vowel-stem suffix starts with +pp, not +v as might be expected.

The following table shows the complete intransitive indicative conjugation of a model vowel-stem verb (**nerivoq** 'to eat'), consonant-stem verb (**sinippoq** 'to sleep'), and r-stem verb (**atuarpoq** 'to read').

Intransitive indicative verbs			
Subject	Vowel-stem **nerivoq** to eat	Consonant-stem **sinippoq** to sleep	R-stem **atuarpoq** to read
1SG	**nerivunga**	**sinippunga**	**atuarpunga**
2SG	**nerivutit**	**sinipputit**	**atuarputit**
3SG	**nerivoq**	**sinippoq**	**atuarpoq**
1PL	**nerivugut**	**sinippugut**	**atuarpugut**
2PL	**nerivusi**	**sinippusi**	**atuarpusi**
3PL	**neripput**	**sinipput**	**atuarput**

The following examples illustrate the use of intransitive indicative verbs.

Timmisartoq Nuummut tikippoq.
timmisartoq nuum-mut tikip-poq
plane nuuk-ALL arrive-3SG
The plane is arriving/arrived in[1] Nuuk.

Qitsuk siniffimmi sinippoq.
qitsuk siniffim-mi sinip-poq
cat bed-LOC sleep-3SG
The cat is sleeping/slept in the bed.

Iggumi nerivugut.
iggu-mi neri-vugut
iggu-LOC eat-1PL
We are eating/ate at Iggu.[2]

Allafimmi sulivunga.
allafimmi sulivunga
office-LOC work-1SG
I am working/worked in the office.

Sukkavallaartumik pisupputit.
sukka-vallaar-tu-mik pisup-putit
fast-too-IP-INS walk-2SG
You are walking/walked too fast.

| 7.2.1.1.2 | TRANSITIVE |

In West Greenlandic, transitive verbs (i.e. verbs which take a direct object) take a different set of suffixes than intransitive verbs. The transitive suffixes include both the subject of the verb and the direct object, i.e. in the verb **asavaanga** 's/he loves me' the subject 's/he' and the direct object 'me' are both conveyed by the suffix -**vaanga**. Like their intransitive counterparts, transitive verbs in the indicative mood can convey either present or past actions, with context (or additional tense or aspect suffixes) distinguishing the two meanings. The following table illustrates the suffixes for transitive indicative verbs.

1 Literally: to.
2 A restaurant in Nuuk.

7 Verbs

| Subject | Transitive indicative suffixes ||||||
| | Object ||||||
	1SG	1PL	2SG	2PL	3SG	3PL
1SG	–	–	+(p/v)akkit	+(p/v)assi	+(p/v)ara	+(p/v)akka
2SG	+(p/v)arma	+(p/v)atsigut	–	–	+(p/v)at	+(p/v)atit
3SG	+(p/v)aanga	+(p/v)aatigut	+(p/v)aatit	+(p/v)aasi	+(p/v)aa	+(p/v)ai
1PL	–	–	+(p/v)atsigit	+(p/v)assi	+(p/v)arput	+(p/v)avut
2PL	+(p/v)assinga	+(p/v)atsigut	–	–	+(p/v)arsi	+(p/v)asi
3PL	+(p/v)aannga	+(p/v)aatigut	+(p/v)aatsit	+(p/v)aasi	+(p/v)aat	

Points to note:

- Consonant- and r-stem verbs take suffix variants beginning in +p, e.g. **ornippaa** 'to approach him/her/it' and **ikiorpaa** 'to help him/her/it'.
- Vowel-stem verbs whose stem ends in -a- or -i- take suffix variants starting in +v, e.g. **asavaa** 'to love him/her/it', **akivaa** 'to answer him/her/it'.
- Vowel-stem verbs whose stem ends in -u- take suffix variants without +v, e.g. **takuaa** 'to see him/her/it', **tiguaa** 'to take him/her/it'.
- Note that in the glosses of transitive suffixes, the subject appears first, followed by an arrow and then the object; for example, the suffix -vaanga 's/he ... me' is glossed as 3SG>1SG.
- If a third-person object is a noun (rather than simply a pronoun), the third-person object suffix is still used in addition to the noun. For example, 'I saw the polar bear' is **nanoq taku_ara_**, with the object **nanoq** 'polar bear' encoded in the object suffix -ara (1SG>3SG) in addition to appearing independently as a noun. The same object suffix appears when there is no explicit nominal object, e.g. **taku_ara_** 'I saw him/her/it'.

The following tables show the complete transitive indicative conjugation of a model vowel-stem verb (**asavaa** 'to love him/her/it'), consonant-stem verb (**ornippaa** 'to approach him/her/it'), and r-stem verb (**ikiorpaa** 'to help him/her/it').

	Transitive indicative vowel-stem verb **asavaa** to love him/her/it					
Subject	Object					
	1SG	1PL	2SG	2PL	3SG	3PL
1SG	–	–	asavakkit	asavassi	asavara	asavakka
2SG	asavarma	asavatsigut	–	–	asavat	asavatit
3SG	asavaanga	asavaatigut	asavaatit	asavaasi	asavaa	asavai
1PL	–	–	asavatsigit	asavassi	asavarput	asavavut
2PL	asavassinga	asavatsigut	–	–	asavarsi	asavasi
3PL	asavaannga	asavaatigut	asavaatsit	asavaasi	asavaat	

Point to note:

- In order to use this and subsequent transitive verb tables, you need to first locate the subject person by using the vertical column on the left. Then locate the object person by using the horizontal row running across the top of the column. For example, if the subject is 1SG and the object is 2SG, the resulting form will be **asavakkit** 'I love you'. If the subject is 3PL and the object is 1PL, the resulting form will be **asavaatigut** 'they love us'.

	Transitive indicative consonant-stem verb **ornippaa** to approach him/her/it					
Subject	Object					
	1SG	1PL	2SG	2PL	3SG	3PL
1SG	–	–	ornippakkit	ornippassi	ornippara	ornippakka
2SG	ornipparma	ornippatsigut	–	–	ornippat	ornippatit
3SG	ornippaanga	ornippaatigut	ornippaatit	ornippaasi	ornippaa	ornippai
1PL	–	–	ornippatsigit	ornippassi	ornipparput	ornippavut
2PL	ornippassinga	ornippatsigut	–	–	ornipparsi	ornippasi
3PL	ornippaannga	ornippaatigut	ornippaatsit	ornippaasi	ornippaat	

Point to note:

- This verb means 'approach' in the sense of 'go up to someone/something'.

7 Verbs

Transitive indicative r-stem verb **ikiorpaa** to help him/her/it						
Subject	Object					
	1SG	1PL	2SG	2PL	3SG	3PL
1SG	–	–	ikiorpakkit	ikiorpassi	ikiorpara	ikiorpakka
2SG	ikiorparma	ikiorpatsigut	–	–	ikiorpat	ikiorpatit
3SG	ikiorpaanga	ikiorpaatigut	ikiorpaatit	ikiorpaasi	ikiorpaa	ikiorpai
1PL	–	–	ikiorpatsigit	ikiorpassi	ikiorparput	ikiorpavut
2PL	ikiorpassinga	ikiorpatsigut	–	–	ikiorparsi	ikiorpasi
3PL	ikiorpaannga	ikiorpaatigut	ikiorpaatsit	ikiorpaasi	ikiorpaat	

The following examples illustrate the use of transitive verbs. Note that the subject of a transitive verb is in the relative case, while the direct object is in the absolutive case. (See sections 3.3.1 and 3.3.2 for discussion of the absolutive and relative cases.)

Air Greenlandip Nuummi mittarfik <u>nersualaarpaa</u>.
air greenlandi-p nuum-mi mittarfik nersualaar-paa
air greenland-REL nuuk-LOC airport praise-3SG>3SG
Air Greenland praises the airport in Nuuk.

Inuuneq <u>toqqarpara</u>.
inuuneq toqqar-para
life choose-1SG>3SG
I chose life.

Pisortap nutaap Kujataa <u>nittarsaatissavaa</u>.
pisorta-p nutaa-p kujataa nittarsaati-ssa-vaa
manager-REL new-REL south.greenland advertise-FUT-3SG>3SG
A new manager will promote South Greenland.

Nerrivik <u>asappara</u>.
nerrivik asap-para
table clean-1SG>3SG
I cleaned the table.

Mittarfimmi <u>naapippaatigut</u>.
mittarfim-mi naapip-paatigut
airport-LOC meet-3PL>1PL
They met us at the airport.

Iipili nerivara.
iipili neri-vara
apple eat-1SG>3SG
I ate the apple.

Taskit kusagaara.
taski-t kusagaa-ra
bag-2SG like-1SG>3SG
I like your bag.

7.2.1.2 Interrogative

West Greenlandic has a distinct interrogative mood which is used for asking questions. The interrogative mood has its own set of suffixes. As in the case of the indicative mood, the interrogative mood can be used to convey actions in either the present or past, with the broader context distinguishing the meaning. For example, **nerivit?** means 'are you eating, have you eaten?' as opposed to **nerivoq** 's/he is eating, s/he ate', and **sinippa?** means 'is s/he sleeping, did s/he sleep?' as opposed to **sinippoq** 's/he is sleeping, s/he slept'.

As in the case of the indicative verbs discussed in the previous section, interrogative verbs have two different forms, transitive and intransitive, which will be discussed in turn.

Note that interrogative verbal forms are accompanied by falling intonation (see section 2.4).

The verbal suffix -**laarpoq** 'to be a little bit' often appears in conjunction with verbs in the interrogative mood when the speaker is making a request. The suffix serves to soften the tone of the request and make it more polite.

7.2.1.2.1 INTRANSITIVE

The following table illustrates the suffixes for intransitive interrogative verbs.

	Intransitive interrogative suffixes	
	Vowel-stem	Consonant-stem, r-stem
1SG	**+vunga?**	**+punga?**
2SG	**+vit?**	**+pit?**
3SG	**+va?**	**+pa?**
1PL	**+vugut?**	**+pugut?**
2PL	**+visi?**	**+pisi?**
3PL	**+ppat?**	**+pat?**

7 Verbs

Points to note:

- The 1SG and 1PL intransitive interrogative suffixes are the same as their intransitive indicative counterparts.
- As in the indicative, the 3PL form vowel-stem suffix starts with +pp, not +v as might be expected.
- The interrogative is indicated by the abbreviation INT in the glossing.

The following table shows the complete intransitive indicative conjugation of a model vowel-stem verb (**nerivoq** 'to eat'), consonant-stem verb (**sinippoq** 'to sleep'), and r-stem verb (**atuarpoq** 'to read').

	Intransitive interrogative verbs		
	Vowel-stem **nerivoq** to eat	Consonant-stem **sinippoq** to sleep	R-stem **atuarpoq** to read
1SG	**nerivunga?**	**sinippunga?**	**atuarpunga?**
2SG	**nerivit?**	**sinippit?**	**atuarpit?**
3SG	**neriva?**	**sinippa?**	**atuarpa?**
1PL	**nerivugut?**	**sinippugut?**	**atuarpugut?**
2PL	**nerivisi?**	**sinippisi?**	**atuarpisi?**
3PL	**nerippat?**	**sinippat?**	**atuarpat?**

The following examples illustrate the use of the intransitive interrogative.

Assat annernarpa?
assa-t annernar-pa
hand-2SG hurt-INT.3SG
Does your hand hurt?

Aqagu aamma pulaartoqassavisi?
aqagu aamma pulaarto-qa-ssa-visi
tomorrow also guest-have-FUT-INT.2PL
Are you going to have guests tomorrow as well?

Sinippat?
sinip-pat
sleep-INT.3PL
Are they sleeping?

Unnugu anissavisi?
unnugu ani-ssa-visi
tonight go.out-FUT-INT.2PL
Are you guys going out tonight?

Uffarpit?
uffar-pit
bathe-INT.2SG
Are you taking a shower?

The following example illustrates an interrogative with the suffix -**laarpoq** 'to be a little bit', which gives an added element of politeness to requests.

Pisinialaarsinnaavit?
pisi-niar-laar-sinnaa-vit
buy-go-a.little-be.able-INT.2SG
Could you please go and buy (it)?

7.2.1.2.2 TRANSITIVE

The following table illustrates the suffixes for transitive interrogative verbs.

Subject	Transitive interrogative suffixes					
	Object					
	1SG	1PL	2SG	2PL	3SG	3PL
1SG	–	–	+(p/v)akkit?	+(p/v)assi?	+(p/v)ara?	+(p/v)akka?
2SG	+(p/v)inga?	+(p/v)isigut?	–	–	+(p/v)iuk?	+(p/v)igit?
3SG	+(p/v)aanga?	+(p/v)aatigut?	+(p/v)aatit?	+(p/v)aasi?	+(p/v)aa?	+(p/v)ai?
1PL	–	–	+(p/v)atsigit?	+(p/v)assi?	+(p/v)arput?	+(p/v)avut?
2PL	+(p/v)isinga?	+(p/v)isigut?	–	–	+(p/v)isiuk?	+(p/v)isigit?
3PL	+(p/v)aannga?	+(p/v)aatigut?	+(p/v)aatsit?	+(p/v)aasi?	+(p/v)aat?	

Points to note:

- The interrogative suffixes highlighted in grey are different from their indicative counterparts. The rest of the interrogative forms are the same as in the indicative (see section 7.2.1.1.2).
- Consonant- and r-stem verbs take suffix variants beginning in +p.

7 Verbs

- Vowel-stem verbs whose stem ends in -a- or -i- take suffix variants starting in +v.
- Vowel-stem verbs whose stem ends in -u- take suffix variants without +v.

The following tables shown the complete transitive interrogative conjugation of a model vowel-stem verb (**asavaa** 'to love him/her/it'), consonant-stem verb (**ornippaa** 'to approach him/her/it'), and r-stem verb (**ikiorpaa** 'to help him/her/it').

Transitive interrogative vowel-stem verb **asavaa** to love him/her/it						
Subject	Object					
	1SG	1PL	2SG	2PL	3SG	3PL
1SG	–	–	asavakkit?	asavassi?	asavara?	asavakka?
2SG	**asavinga?**	**asavisigut?**	–	–	asaviuk?	asavigit?
3SG	asavaanga?	asavaatigut?	asavaatit?	asavaasi?	asavaa?	asavai?
1PL	–	–	asavatsigit?	asavassi?	asavarput?	asavavut?
2PL	**asavisinga?**	**asavisigut?**	–	–	**asavisiuk?**	**asavisigit?**
3PL	asavaannga?	asavaatigut?	asavaatsit?	asavaasi?	asavaat?	

Point to note:

- The interrogative suffixes highlighted in grey are different from their indicative counterparts. The rest of the interrogative forms are the same as in the indicative (see section 7.2.1.1.2).

Transitive interrogative consonant-stem verb **ornippaa** to approach him/her/it						
Subject	Object					
	1SG	1PL	2SG	2PL	3SG	3PL
1SG	–	–	ornippakkit?	ornippassi?	ornippara?	ornippakka?
2SG	**ornippinga?**	**ornippisigut?**	–	–	ornippiuk?	ornippigit?
3SG	ornippaanga?	ornippaatigut?	ornippaatit?	ornippaasi?	ornippaa?	ornippai?
1PL	–	–	ornippatsigit?	ornippassi?	ornipparput?	ornippavut?
2PL	**ornippisinga?**	**ornippisigut?**	–	–	**ornippisiuk?**	**ornippisigit?**
3PL	ornippaannga?	ornippaatigut?	ornippaatsit?	ornippaasi?	ornippaat?	

Mood

Transitive interrogative r-stem verb **ikiorpaa** to help him/her/it						
Subject	Object					
	1SG	1PL	2SG	2PL	3SG	3PL
1SG	–	–	ikiorpakkit?	ikiorpassi?	ikiorpara?	ikiorpakka?
2SG	ikiorpinga?	ikiorpisigut?	–	–	ikiorpiuk?	ikiorpigit?
3SG	ikiorpaanga?	ikiorpaatigut?	ikiorpaatit?	ikiorpaasi?	ikiorpaa?	ikiorpai?
1PL	–	–	ikiorpatsigit?	ikiorpassi?	ikiorparput?	ikiorpavut?
2PL	ikiorpisinga?	ikiorpisigut?	–	–	ikiorpisiuk?	ikiorpisigit?
3PL	ikiorpaannga?	ikiorpaatigut?	ikiorpaatsit?	ikiorpaasi?	ikiorpaat?	

The following sentences illustrate the use of the transitive interrogative with various object suffixes.

Tuttup neqaa pisiarissavisiuk?
tuttu-p neqa-a pisiari-ssa-visiuk
reindeer-REL meat-3SG buy-FUT-INT.2PL
Are you going to buy the reindeer meat?

Ikiorsinnaavinga?
ikior-sinnaa-vinga
help-be.able-INT.2SG>1SG
Can you help me?

Cigaritsit pisiarivigit?
cigaritsi-t pisiari-vigit
cigarette-PL buy-INT.2SG>3PL
Did you buy the cigarettes?

Ornippisigut?
ornip-pisigut
approach-INT.2SG/PL>1PL
Are you on your way to us?

Meeraq uffassaviuk?
meeraq uffa-ssa-viuk
child bathe-FUT-INT.2SG>3SG
Are you going to give the child a bath?

Ikiulaarsinnaavinga?
ikiu-laar-sinnaa-vinga
help-a.little-be.able-INT.2SG>1SG
Could you please help me?

Pingasunut itersalaarsinnaaviuk?
pingasu-nut itersa-laar-sinnaa-viuk
three-ALL wake.up-a.little-be.able-INT.2SG>3SG
Can you please wake him/her up at three?

7.2.1.3 Imperative

West Greenlandic has an imperative mood, which is used for giving commands and making requests. As with the indicative and interrogative moods, the imperative has separate intransitive and transitive suffixes. Note that the imperative only exists in the 2SG, 2PL, and 1PL. The 1PL imperative is equivalent to English constructions with 'let's'. The imperative is marked by the abbreviation IMP in the glossing.

As in the case of interrogative verbs (discussed in 7.2.1.2), imperatives are often accompanied by the suffix -**laarpoq**, which means 'to be a little bit' and is used to soften their force or make them sound more polite.

The suffix +**niarpoq** 'to intend to; to try to; to want to' is also often used with imperatives. It adds an element of extra emphasis to the imperative. In some cases it can also add an element of politeness, like -**laarpoq**, and can be translated roughly as 'just' or 'please'. However, in other cases it can be used to intensify the strength of the order rather than softening it. Context will usually distinguish the intended sense of the suffix.

7.2.1.3.1 INTRANSITIVE

The intransitive imperative has the following forms.

	Intransitive imperative suffixes		
Subject	Vowel-stem	Consonant-stem	R-stem
2SG	+git	-git	+it
1PL	+sa	+ta	+ta
2PL	+gitsi	-gitsi	+itsi

Points to note:

- When the 2SG and 2PL suffixes **-git** and **-gitsi** are attached to a consonant-stem verb, the final consonant of the verbal stem is dropped, e.g. **sinipputit** 'you (SG) sleep' > **sinigit** 'sleep (SG)!'; **sinippusi** 'you (PL) sleep' > **sinigitsi** 'sleep (PL)!'
- The 1PL imperative suffix is the same for consonant-stem and r-stem verbs.

The following table shows the complete intransitive imperative conjugation of a model vowel-stem verb (**nerivoq** 'to eat'), consonant-stem verb (**sinippoq** 'to sleep'), and r-stem verb (**atuarpoq** 'to read').

	Intransitive imperative verbs		
Subject	Vowel-stem **nerivoq** to eat	Consonant-stem **sinippoq** to sleep	R-stem **atuarpoq** to read
2SG	**nerigit**	**sinigit**	**atuarit**
1PL	**nerisa**	**sinigitta**	**atuarta**
2PL	**nerigitsi**	**sinigitsi**	**atuaritsi**

The use of the intransitive imperative is illustrated in the following examples.

Peqataagit!
peqataa-git
participate-IMP.2SG
Take part!

Arpagitsi!
arpa-gitsi
run-IMP.2PL
Run!

Makitta!
makit-ta
get.up-IMP.1PL
Let's get up (out of bed)!

Skåleerta pitsaammik taakkuulluta!
skåleer-ta pitsaam-mik taakku-u-lluta
toast-IMP.1PL excellent-INS those-be-CONT.1PL
Let us who are here raise a good toast!³

Tamaaniigitsi uternissama tungaanut!
tamaani-i-gitsi uter-neq-ssa-ma tugaanut
here-be-IMP.2PL return-AP-FUT-REL.1SG until
Stay here until I come back!⁴

Unnuaq naallugu qititta!
unnuaq naallugu qitit-ta
night through dance-IMP.1PL
Let's dance the whole night through!

The use of the suffix -laarpoq 'to be a little bit' to soften the force of an imperative is illustrated in the following examples.

Angerlaruit sms-ilaarit.
angerlar-uit sms-i-laar-it
come.home-COND.2SG text-HV-a.little-IMP.2SG
Please text when you get home.

Nanoq takussagukku sissamut ammukalaarit.
nanoq taku-ssa-gukku sissa-mut ammuka-laar-it
polar.bear see-FUT-COND.2SG>3SG beach-ALL go.down-a.little-IMP.2SG
If you want to see the polar bear, just go down to the beach.

The suffix +niarpoq 'to intend to; to try to; to want to' can be used with an imperative in the sense of English 'please', e.g.:

Tamassa, inginniaritsi!
tamassa ingin-niar-itsi
come.in sit.down-want-IMP.2PL
Please, come in and sit down!

Peerniaritsi!
peer-niar-itsi
go.away-want-IMP.2PL
Please go away!

3 From a popular Greenlandic birthday song.
4 Literally: until my return.

Assiliiniarit!
assilii-niar-it
take.photo-want-IMP.2SG
Please take a photo!

7.2.1.3.2 TRANSITIVE

The following table illustrates the suffixes for transitive imperative verbs.

Subject	Transitive imperative suffixes			
	Object			
	1SG	1PL	3SG	3PL
2SG	-nnga	+t(s)igut	+(j)uk, -guk	+kit, -kkit
1PL	–	–	+t(s)igu	+t(s)igit
2PL	+singa	+t(s)igut	+siuk	+sigit

Points to note:

- For the 2SG>3SG, there are several different variants. The variant +uk is used with vowel-stem verbs whose stem ends in -i- or -u-, e.g. **akiuk!** 'answer him/her/it!', **tiguuk!** 'take him/her/it!', and with r-stem verbs, e.g. **ikioruk!** 'help him/her!' The variant +juk is used with vowel-stem verbs whose stem ends in -a-, e.g. **asajuk!** 'love him/her!' Finally, -guk is used with consonant-stem verbs, e.g. **orniguk!** 'approach him/her/it!'
- For the 2SG>3PL, the variant -kkit is used with vowel-stem and r-stem verbs, e.g. **akikkit!** 'answer them!', **ikiokkit** 'help them!' The variant +kit is used with consonant-stem verbs, e.g. **ornikkit!** 'approach them!'
- For the suffixes beginning with +t(s), the variant +ts is used with consonant-stem verbs, whereas the variant +t is used with vowel-stem and r-stem verbs, e.g. **ornitsigut!** 'approach us!' vs. **akitigut!** 'answer us!'.

The following tables shown the complete transitive imperative conjugation of a model vowel-stem verb (**akivaa** 'to answer him/her/it'), consonant-stem verb (**ornippaa** 'to approach him/her/it'), and r-stem verb (**ikiorpaa** 'to help him/her/it').

7 Verbs

Transitive imperative vowel-stem verb
akivaa to answer him/her/it

Subject	Object			
	1SG	1PL	3SG	3PL
2SG	**akinnga**	**akitigut**	**akiuk**	**akikkit**
1PL	–	–	**akitigu**	**akitigit**
2PL	**akisinga**	**akitigut**	**akisiuk**	**akisigit**

Transitive imperative consonant-stem verb
ornippaa to approach him/her/it

Subject	Object			
	1SG	1PL	3SG	3PL
2SG	**orninnga**	**ornitsigut**	**orniguk**	**ornikkit**
1PL	–	–	**ornitsigu**	**ornitsigit**
2PL	**ornissinga**	**ornitsigut**	**ornissiuk**	**ornissigit**

Transitive imperative r-stem verb
ikiorpaa to help him/her/it

Subject	Object			
	1SG	1PL	3SG	3PL
2SG	**ikiunnga**	**ikiortigut**	**ikioruk**	**ikiukkit**
1PL	–	–	**ikiortigu**	**ikiortigit**
2PL	**ikiorsinga**	**ikiortigut**	**ikiorsiuk**	**ikiorsigit**

The use of the transitive imperative is shown in the following examples.

Eqqaamajuk!
eqqaama-juk
remember-IMP.2SG>3SG
Remember it!

App-erput downloaderuk!
app-e-rput downloader-uk
app-HV-1PL download-IMP.2SG>3SG
Download our app!

Biibili internettikkut atuaruk!
biibili internetti-kkut atuar-uk
bible internet-PRO read-IMP.2SG>3SG
Read the Bible online!

Apeqqutit ukua marluk akikkit!
apeqquti-t ukua marluk aki-kkit
question-PL these two answer-IMP.2SG>3PL
Answer these two questions!

Qerititsivik immeruk!
qerititsivik immer-uk
freezer fill.up-IMP.2SG>3SG
Fill up the freezer!

Kalaaliaraq takusartigu!
kalaaliaraq takusar-tigu
kalaaliaraq have.a.look.at-IMP.1PL>3SG
Let's go and have a look at Kalaaliaraq[5]!

Nuuk bussinik angalaaruk!
nuuk bussi-nik angalaar-uk
nuuk bus-INS.PL travel.around-IMP.2SG>3SG
Travel around Nuuk by bus!

The suffix -laarpoq used in conjunction with transitive imperatives to soften their force is illustrated in the following example.

5 Greenlandic food market in Nuuk.

Tiiliutilaannga.
tii-liu-ti-laa-nnga
tea-make-VAL-a.little-IMP.2SG>1SG
Please make me some tea.

The suffix **+niarpoq** 'to intend to; to try to; to want to' in conjunction with transitive imperatives, in the sense of 'please', is illustrated in the following example.

Mattak neriniaruk.
mattak neri-niar-uk
whale.blubber eat-want-IMP.2SG>3SG
Please eat the whale blubber.

7.2.1.4 Optative

The final independent/main mood in West Greenlandic is the optative. The optative form is used only with the 1SG, 3SG, and 3PL. It complements the imperative in that it is used to express wishes and indirect requests with the persons for which there are no imperative forms. It is equivalent to English first-person constructions with 'let me' and third-person constructions with 'let him/her, let them'. Like the other moods discussed previously, the optative has different intransitive and transitive suffixes. Note that the optative is marked by the abbreviation OPT in the glossing.

7.2.1.4.1 INTRANSITIVE

The intransitive optative suffixes are listed in the following table.

Intransitive optative suffixes	
Subject	All stem types
1SG	**+langa**
3SG	**+li**
3PL	**+(l)lit**

Point to note:

- In the 3PL, vowel-stem verbs take +llit, whereas consonant-stem and r-stem verbs take +lit.

The following table shows the complete intransitive imperative conjugation of a model vowel-stem verb (**nerivoq** 'to eat'), consonant-stem verb (**sinippoq** 'to sleep'), and r-stem verb (**atuarpoq** 'to read').

Subject	Intransitive optative verbs		
	Vowel-stem **nerivoq** to eat	Consonant-stem **sinippoq** to sleep	R-stem **atuarpoq** to read
1SG	**nerilanga**	**sinillanga**	**atuarlanga**
3SG	**nerili**	**sinilli**	**atuarli**
3PL	**nerillit**	**sinillit**	**atuarlit**

The use of the intransitive optative is illustrated in the following examples.

Ghanamiillanga!
ghana-mi-il-langa
ghana-in be-OPT.1SG
I wish I were in Ghana!

Ikiorneqarli.
ikior-neqar-li
help-PASS-OPT.3SG
If only s/he could get help.

Pizzatorlanga!
pizza-tor-langa
pizza-eat-OPT.1SG
I wish I was eating pizza!

Sulineq massakkut aallartilli!
sulineq massakkut aallartil-li
work now start-OPT.3PL
Let them start the work now!

Mobiilitaarlanga!
mobiili-taar-langa
mobile-new-OPT.1SG
If only I could have a new mobile phone!

7.2.1.4.2 TRANSITIVE

The transitive optative suffixes are listed in the following table.

Subject	Transitive optative suffixes					
	Object					
	1SG	1PL	2SG	2PL	3SG	3PL
1SG	–	–	+lakkit	+lassi	+lara	+lakka
3SG	+linga	+lisigut	+lisit	+lisi	+liuk	+ligit
3PL	+linnga				+lissuk	+lisigit

Points to note:

- All stem types take the same transitive optative suffixes.
- There is an infrequently used transitive optative form for 1PL subjects which exists in parallel with the 1PL transitive imperative forms discussed in 7.2.1.3.2. For reference, the forms are as follows: **+latsigit** (1PL>2SG), **+lassi** (1PL>2PL), **+larput** (1PL>3SG), and **+lavut** (1PL>3PL). Note that there are no corresponding 1PL forms in the intransitive optative.

The following tables shown the complete transitive optative conjugation of a model vowel-stem verb (**akivaa** 'to answer him/her/it'), consonant-stem verb (**ornippaa** 'to approach him/her/it'), and r-stem verb (**ikiorpaa** 'to help him/her/it').

Subject	Transitive optative vowel-stem verb **akivaa** to answer him/her/it					
	Object					
	1SG	1PL	2SG	2PL	3SG	3PL
1SG	–	–	akilakkit	akilassi	akilara	akilakka
3SG	akilinga	akilisigut	akilisit	akilisi	akiliuk	akiligit
3PL	akilinnga				akilissuk	akilisigit

Transitive optative consonant-stem verb
ornippaa to approach him/her/it

Subject	Object					
	1SG	1PL	2SG	2PL	3SG	3PL
1SG	–	–	ornillakkit	ornillassi	ornillara	ornillakka
3SG	ornillinga	ornillisigut	ornillisit	ornillisi	ornilliuk	ornilligit
3PL	ornillinnga				ornillissuk	ornillisigit

Transitive optative r-stem verb
ikiorpaa to help him/her/it

Subject	Object					
	1SG	1PL	2SG	2PL	3SG	3PL
1SG	–	–	ikiorlakkit	ikiorlassi	ikiorlara	ikiorlakka
3SG	ikiorlinga	ikiorlisigut	ikiorlisit	ikiorlisi	ikiorliuk	ikiorligit
3PL	ikiorlinnga				ikiorlissuk	ikiorlisigit

The use of the transitive optative is shown here.

Ikiorlakkit.
ikior-lakkit
help-OPT.1SG>2SG
Let me help you.

Ilagilakka.
ilagi-lakka
accompany-OPT.1SG>3PL
Let me go with them.

7.2.2 Subordinate moods

In addition to the four independent moods introduced in section 7.2.1, Greenlandic has four moods that are only used in subordinate clauses, namely the causative, conditional (glossed as COND), contemporative (glossed as CONT), and participial (glossed as PART). Each of these moods is discussed in turn.

7.2.2.1 Causative

The causative is used in subordinate clauses to express temporal and causal meanings corresponding to English 'when' and 'because', for example 'I stayed at home because I was ill'. It is also known as the conjunctive. Like the independent moods discussed in section 7.2.1, the causative has different endings for transitive and intransitive verbs. Note that the causative is marked by the abbreviation CAUS in the glossing.

7.2.2.1.1 INTRANSITIVE

The intransitive causative suffixes are shown in the following table.

Subject	Vowel-stem	Consonant-stem	R-stem
1SG	+gama	+kama	+ama
2SG	+gavit	+kavit	+avit
3SG	+mmat	+mat	+mat
4SG	+gami	+kami	+ami
1PL	+gatta	+katta	+atta
2PL	+gassi	+kassi	+assi
3PL	+mmata	+mata	+mata
4PL	+gamik	+kamik	+amik

Points to note:

- The suffixes for all stem types are the same except for the first letter (detailed in the following points).
- Where vowel-stem suffixes start with +g, consonant-stem suffixes start with +k and r-stem suffixes start with a vowel.
- Where vowel-stem suffixes start with +mm, consonant-stem and r-stem suffixes start with +m.
- In contrast to the independent/main moods, the causative and most other subordinate moods have fourth-person forms. These are used when the subject of the subordinate mood is the same as that of the main mood.

The following table shows the complete intransitive causative conjugation of a model vowel-stem verb (**nerivoq** 'to eat'), consonant-stem verb (**sinippoq** 'to sleep'), and r-stem verb (**atuarpoq** 'to read').

Mood

	Intransitive causative verbs		
Subject	Vowel-stem **nerivoq** to eat	Consonant-stem **sinippoq** to sleep	R-stem **atuarpoq** to read
1SG	nerigama	sinikkama	atuarama
2SG	nerigavit	sinikkavit	atuaravit
3SG	nerimmat	sinimmat	atuarmat
4SG	nerigami	sinikkami	atuarami
1PL	nerigatta	sinikkatta	atuaratta
2PL	nerigassi	sinikkasi	atuarassi
3PL	nerimmata	sinimmata	atuarmata
4PL	nerigamik	sinikkamik	atuaramik

The use of the intransitive causative is illustrated in the following examples. Note that the causative verb may appear either at the beginning of the sentence or after a verb in an independent/main mood.

Isermata iterpoq.
iser-mata iter-poq
come.in-CAUS.3PL wake.up-3SG
When they came in s/he woke up.

Sianermata Lisep matu mapperpaa.
sianer-mata lise-p matu mapper-paa
ring-CAUS.3PL lise-REL door open-3SG>3SG
After they have rung [the doorbell] Lise opens the door.

Majuarassi imaqqa qasuvusi.
majuar-assi imaqqa qasu-vusi
climb-CAUS.2PL maybe be.tired-2PL
Having climbed up, you may be tired.

Qaqqasiorama paarmartarpunga nattoralimmillu takullunga.
qaqqasior-ama paarmar-tar-punga nattoralim-mil-lu taku-llunga
mountaineer-CAUS.1SG berry-collect-1SG eagle-INS-and see-CONT.1SG
When I went into the mountains, I collected berries and saw an eagle.

Qujanaq iserassi.
qujanaq iser-assi
thanks come-CAUS.2PL
Thanks for coming.

Kalaallit Nunaat Finlandilu <u>unammimmata</u> isaatitsisoqangaatsiarpoq.
kalaalli-t nuna-at finlandi-lu unammi-mmata isaatitsiso-qa-ngaatsiar-poq
greenlander-PL land-3PL finland-and compete-CAUS.3PL goal-have-quite.a.lot-3SG
When Greenland and Finland played there were quite a lot of goals.

Suleqatiga <u>piniartuugami</u> arfininngornikkut angalasarpoq.
suleqati-ga piniartu-u-gami arfininngorni-kkut angala-sar-poq
colleague-1SG hunter-be-CAUS.1SG saturday-PRO travel-HAB-3SG
Because my colleague is a hunter, he goes out (hunting) on Saturdays.

Kalaaliminertortarpunga ullut tamaasa, <u>piniartuugama</u>.
kalaaminer-tor-tar-punga ullu-t tamaasa piniar-toq-u-gama
greenlandic.food-consume-HAB-1SG day-PL all hunt-IP-be-CAUS-1SG
I eat Greenlandic food every day because I am a hunter.

1992-mi <u>naammassigama</u> Qaqortormi ilinniartitsisunngorpunga.
1992-mi naammassi-gama qatorqor-mi ilinniartitsisu-nngor-punga
1992-LOC graduate-CAUS.1SG qaqortoq-LOC teacher-become-1SG
After I had graduated in 1992 I became a teacher in Qaqortoq.

A sentence may contain a sequence of causatives, each of which can be translated slightly differently, as in the following example.

Pisiniarfimmi <u>kaffisigama</u> <u>angerlarama</u> kaffiliorpunga.
pisiniarfim-mi kaffi-si-gama angerlar-ama kaffi-lior-punga
shop-LOC coffee-buy-CAUS.1SG go.home-CAUS.1SG coffee-make-1SG
I had bought coffee at the shop, (and) when I went home I made coffee.

The causative can be modified with the suffix +gaangat/-raangat/-kkaangat 'when, every time, whenever' to give the meaning of 'when, every time', as in the following example.

Qimmit <u>nuannaanngikkaangama</u> paasilertortarpaat.
qimmi-t nuannaa-nngi-kkaang-ama paasi-lertor-tar-paat
dog-PL be.happy-NEG-whenever-CAUS.1SG understand-quickly-HAB-3PL>3SG
The dogs understand (it) quickly when I am not in a good mood.

<u>Unnukkaangat</u> ullorissat nuisarput.
unnu-kkaangat ullorissa-t nui-sar-put
become.evening-whenever star-PL appear-HAB-3PL
When the evening comes, the stars usually appear.

The suffix -**riarpoq** 'as soon as' (and its variants -**kkiarpoq** and -**giarpoq**) can be added to the causative used to convey the meaning of 'as soon as; just as' in the past, as in the following example.

Aneriarmat iserpunga.
ane-riar-mat iser-punga
go.out-as.soon.as-CAUS.3SG go.in-1SG
As soon as he went out, I went in.

The causative can be modified by the suffix -**nngikkallarpoq** 'not yet' to convey the sense of the conjunction 'before', as in the following example.

Ataataga <u>pensiuuninngikkallarami</u> nalunaarasuartaaserisutut sulivoq.
ataata-ga pensiuuni-nngikkallar-ami nalunaarasuartaaserisu-tut suli-voq
father-1SG retire-before-CAUS.4SG telegraphist-EQU work-3SG
My father worked as a telegraphist before he retired.

In addition to the meaning of 'because' or 'when', in everyday speech the causative is often used as a simple past tense without any explicit causative sense. In such cases the causative is often part of a larger narrative sequence. The following examples illustrate this use of the causative.

Unnukkut <u>innajaarassi</u> ...
unnu-kkut inna-jaar-assi
evening-PRO go.to.bed-early-CAUS.2PL
In the evening you (PL) went to bed early ...

Ulluni pingasuni <u>napparsimagama</u> ...
ullu-ni pingasu-ni nappar-sima-gama
day-LOC.PL three-LOC.PL be.sick-PAST-CAUS.1SG
I've been sick for three days ...

Ippassaq <u>nalukkama</u> ...
ippassaq naluk-kama
yesterday swim-CAUS.1SG
Yesterday I went swimming ...

7 Verbs

Kaasipat <u>anillakkami</u> aamma kaffisoriartoqquneqarpoq.
kaasipat anillak-kami aamma kaffi-so-riar-to-qqu-neqar-poq
kaasipat come.out-CAUS.4SG and coffee-consume-going.to-IP-invite-PASS-3SG
Kaasipat came out and was invited to come and have coffee.

7.2.2.1.2 TRANSITIVE

The transitive causative suffixes are listed in the following table.

Subject	Object							
	1SG	1PL	2SG	2PL	3SG	3PL	4SG	4PL
1SG	–	–	+(g/k)akkit	+(g/k)assi	+(g/k)akku	+(g/k)akkit	+(g/k)anni	+(g/k)atsik
2SG	+(g/k)amma	+(g/k)atsigut	–	–				
3SG	+(m)manga	+(m)matigut	+(m)matit	+(m)masi	+(m)magu	+(m)magit	+(m)mani	+(m)matik
4SG	+(g/k)aminga	+(g/k)amisigut	+(g/k)amisit	+(g/k)amisi	+(g/k)amiuk	+(g/k)amigit	–	–
1PL	–	–	+(g/k)atsigit	+(g/k)assi	+(g/k)atsigu	+(g/k)atsigit	+(g/k)atsinni	+(g/k)atsik
2PL	+(g/k)assinga	+(g/k)atsigut	–	–	+(g/k)assiuk	+(g/k)assigit	+(g/k)assinni	
3PL	+(m)mannga	+(m)matigut	+(m)matsit	+(m)masi	+(m)massuk	+(m)matigit	+(m)manni	+(m)matik
4PL	+(g/k)aminnga	+(g/k)amisigut	+(g/k)amitsit	+(g/k)amisi	+(g/k)amikku	+(g/k)amikkit	–	–

Points to note:

- Vowel-stem verbs take the variants starting in +g and +mm.
- Consonant-stem verbs take the variants starting in +k and +m.
- R-stem verbs take the variants starting in +a and +m.
- The fourth-person object forms are used when the object of the causative verb is the same as the subject of verb in the associated main clause.

The following tables show the complete transitive causative conjugation of a model vowel-stem verb (**asavaa** 'to love him/her/it'), consonant-stem verb (**ornippaa** 'to approach him/her/it'), and r-stem verb (**ikiorpaa** 'to help him/her/it').

Transitive causative vowel-stem verb
asavaa to love him/her/it

Subject	Object							
	1SG	1PL	2SG	2PL	3SG	3PL	4SG	4PL
1SG	–	–	asagakkit	asagassi	asagakku	asagakkit	asaganni	asagatsik
2SG	asagamma	asagatsigut						
3SG	asammanga	asammatigut	asammatit	asammasi	asammagu	asammagit	asammani	asammatik
4SG	asaganinga	asagamisigut	asagamisit	asagamisi	asagamiuk	asagamigit	–	–
1PL	–	–	asagatsigit	asagassi	asagatsigu	asagatsigit	asagatsinni	asagatsik
2PL	asagassinga	asagatsigut	–	–	asagassiuk	asagassigit	asagassinni	
3PL	asammannga	asammatigut	asammatsit	asammasi	asammassuk	asammatigit	asammanni	asammatik
4PL	asagaminnga	asagamisigut	asagamitsit	asagamisi	asagamikku	asagamikkit	–	–

Transitive causative consonant-stem verb
ornippaa to approach him/her/it

Subject	Object							
	1SG	1PL	2SG	2PL	3SG	3PL	4SG	4PL
1SG	–	–	ornikkakkit	ornikkassi	ornikkakku	ornikkakkit	ornikkanni	ornikkatsik
2SG	ornikkamma	ornikkatsigut	–	–				
3SG	ornimmanga	ornimmatigut	ornimmatit	ornimmasi	ornimmagu	ornimmagit	ornimmani	ornimmatik
4SG	ornikkaminga	ornikkamisigut	ornikkamisit	ornikkamisi	ornikkamiuk	ornikkamigit	–	–
1PL	–	–	ornikkatsigit	ornikkassi	ornikkatsigu	ornikkatsigit	ornikkatsinni	ornikkatsik
2PL	ornikkassinga	ornikkatsigut	–	–	ornikkassiuk	ornikkassigit	ornikkassinni	
3PL	ornimmannga	ornimmatigut	ornimmatsit	ornimmasi	ornimmassuk	ornimmatigit	ornimmanni	ornimmatik
4PL	ornikkaminnga	ornikkamisigut	ornikkamitsit	ornikkamisi	ornikkamikku	ornikkamikkit	–	–

Transitive causative r-stem verb
ikiorpaa to help him/her/it

Subject	Object							
	1SG	1PL	2SG	2PL	3SG	3PL	4SG	4PL
1SG	–	–	ikiorakkit	ikiorassi	ikiorakku	ikiorakkit	ikioranni	ikioratsik
2SG	ikioramma	ikioratsigut	–	–		ikiorakkit	ikioranni	ikioratsik
3SG	ikiormanga	ikiormatigut	ikiormatit	ikiormasi	ikiormagu	ikiormagit	ikiormani	ikiormatik
4SG	ikioraminga	ikioramisigut	ikioramisit	ikioramisi	ikioramiuk	ikioramigit	–	–
1PL	–	–	ikioratsigit	ikiorassi	ikioratsigu	ikioratsigit	ikioratsinni	ikioratsik
2PL	ikiorassinga	ikioratsigut	–	–	ikiorassiuk	ikiorassigit	ikiorassinni	ikioratsik
3PL	ikiormannga	ikiormatigut	ikiormatsit	ikiormasi	ikiormassuk	ikiormatigit	ikiormanni	ikiormatik
4PL	ikioraminnga	ikioramisigut	ikioramitsit	ikioramisi	ikioramikku	ikioramikkit	–	–

Mood

The following example illustrate the use of the transitive causative.

Ilinniartut <u>takugatsigit</u> ilassivavut.
ilinniartu-t taku-gatsigit ilassi-vavut
student-PL see-CAUS.1PL>3PL greet-1PL>3PL
When we saw the students we greeted them.

The following example illustrates a causative verb with a fourth-person object suffix. The fourth-person object suffix is used because the object of the causative verb (i.e. Lisa) is the same as the subject of the main verb.

Lisa nuannaarpoq <u>ikioranni</u>.
lisa nuannaar-poq ikior-anni
lisa be.happy-3SG help-CAUS.1SG>4SG
Lisa was happy because I helped her (i.e. Lisa).

By contrast, in the following example, the third-person object suffix is used because the object of the transitive verb is different to the subject of the main verb.

Lisa nuannaarpoq <u>ikiorakku</u>.
lisa nuannaar-poq ikior-akku
lisa be.happy-3SG help-CAUS.1SG>3SG
Lisa was happy because I helped her (i.e. someone other than Lisa).

The following examples illustrate the use of the transitive causative in contexts where it can be translated as a simple past tense.

Suna pisari<u>gakku</u>?
suna pisari-gakku
what catch-CAUS.2SG>3SG
What is it that you have caught?

Qarlitit nammineq ilaar<u>akkit</u>?
qarli-tit nammineq ilaar-akkit
trouser-PL.2SG oneself mend-CAUS.2SG>3PL
Did you mend your trousers yourself?

7.2.2.2 Conditional

The conditional mood is used to convey actions that may take place in the future if a given condition is met. It corresponds to English real conditional sentences starting with 'if' or 'when' that refer to the future, e.g. 'if I have time I'll go to the cinema' or 'when I have time I'll go to the cinema'. It can also be used for hypothetical and counterfactual statements, such as 'if I had time, I would go to the cinema' or 'if I had had time, I would have gone to the cinema'. As in the case of the other moods examined thus far, it has different intransitive and transitive forms. Note that the conditional is marked by the abbreviation COND in the glossing.

7.2.2.2.1 INTRANSITIVE

The intransitive conditional suffixes are shown in the following table.

Subject	Vowel-stem	Consonant-stem	R-stem
1SG	+guma	+kuma	+uma
2SG	+guit	+kuit	+uit
3SG	+ppat	+pat	+pat
4SG	+guni	+kuni	+uni
1PL	+gutta	+kutta	+utta
2PL	+gussi	+kussi	+ussi
3PL	+ppata	+pata	+pata
4PL	+gunik	+kunik	+unik

Intransitive conditional suffixes

Points to note:

- The suffixes for all stem types are the same except for the first letter (detailed in the following points).
- Where vowel-stem suffixes start with +g, consonant-stem suffixes start with +k and r-stem suffixes start with a vowel.
- Where vowel-stem suffixes start with +pp, consonant-stem and r-stem suffixes start with +p.

The following table shows the complete intransitive conditional conjugation of a model vowel-stem verb (**nerivoq** 'to eat'), consonant-stem verb (**sinippoq** 'to sleep'), and r-stem verb (**atuarpoq** 'to read').

7 Verbs

Subject	Intransitive conditional verbs		
	Vowel-stem **nerivoq** to eat	Consonant-stem **sinippoq** to sleep	R-stem **atuarpoq** to read
1SG	**neriguma**	**sinikkuma**	**atuaruma**
2SG	**neriguit**	**sinikkuit**	**atuaruit**
3SG	**nerippat**	**sinippat**	**atuarpat**
4SG	**neriguni**	**sinikkuni**	**atuaruni**
1PL	**nerigutta**	**sinikkutta**	**atuarutta**
2PL	**nerigussi**	**sinikkusi**	**atuarussi**
3PL	**nerippata**	**sinippata**	**atuarpata**
4PL	**nerigunik**	**sinikkunik**	**atuarunik**

The following examples illustrate the use of the conditional endings in real (i.e. possible) conditions.

Imeq 100 gradinngor<u>uni</u> qalassaaq.
imeq 100 gradi-nngor-uni qala-ssaaq
water 100 degree-become-COND.4SG boil-FUT.3SG
If water reaches 100 degrees, it will boil.

<u>Kiatsippat</u> siku aassaaq.
kiatsip-pat siku aa-ssaaq
get.warm-COND.3SG ice melt-FUT.3SG
If (the weather) gets warm, the ice will melt.

<u>Taxanngikkutta</u> timmisartoq inortussavarput.
taxa-nngik-kutta timmisartoq inortu-ssa-varput
taxi-NEG-COND.1PL flight miss-FUT-1PL
If we don't take a taxi, we will miss the flight.

The conditional can also be combined with tense suffixes to indicate a more precise time reference, such as past, future, etc., as in the following examples. See section 7.3 for discussion of tense suffixes in West Greenlandic.

<u>Arpareeruma</u> uffassaanga.
arpa-reer-uma uffa-ssa-anga
run-PERF-COND.1SG shower-FUT-1SG
When I have been running I will take a shower.

Arfininngorpat <u>piffissaqassaguma</u> aggissaanga.
arfininngorpat piffissa-qa-ssa-guma aggi-ssa-anga
on.saturday time-have-FUT-COND.1SG visit-FUT-1SG
If I have time on Saturday I will come.

<u>Kaffisoreerussi</u> ikani pujortagassaqarpoq.
kaffi-so-reer-ussi ikani pujortagassa-qar-poq
coffee-consume-PERF-COND.2PL there smoking.supplies-have-3SG
If you've finished drinking coffee, there's tobacco over there.

The following example illustrates the use of the conditional suffixes in hypothetical/counterfactual conditions. The main clause (i.e. the one with a verb in an independent/main mood) of these conditions typically includes the hypothetical suffix +galuarpoq/-raluarpoq/-kkaluarpoq 'if only ... then; would'.

<u>Innajaarsimaguit</u> qasusimanavianngilatit.
inna-jaar-sima-guit qasu-sima-navianngila-tit
go.to.bed-early-PAST-COND.2SG be.tired-PAST-certainly.not-2SG
If you had gone to bed early you would not be tired.

Note that it is possible to combine the verb in the main clause with the past tense suffix -**simavoq** with the future tense suffix -**ssaaq** (along with the counterfactual suffix +**galuarpoq/-raluarpoq/-kkaluarpoq** 'if only ... then; would') to construct the equivalent of an English counterfactual condition set in the past, i.e. 'would have done X', e.g.:

<u>Ilinniagassalerinerusimasuuguit</u> angusisimassagaluarputit.
ilinniagassa-leri-ner-u-sima-su-u-guit angusi-sima-ssa-galuar-putit
homework-work.with-COMP-be-PAST-IP-be-COND.2SG pass.exam-PAST-FUT-would-2SG
If you had done more homework you would have passed the exam.

<u>Silagissimagaluarpat</u> qaqqaliarsimassagaluarpunga.
silagis-sima-galuar-pat qaqqaliar-sima-ssa-galuar-punga
be.good.weather-PAST-would-COND.3SG mountaineer-PAST-FUT-would-1SG
If the weather had been good I would have gone to the mountains.

The suffix -**riarpoq** 'as soon as' (and its variants -**kkiarpoq** and -**giarpoq**) can be added to the conditional used to convey the meaning of 'as soon as; just as' in the future, as in the following example.

7 Verbs

Seqineq nueriarpat avalassaanga.
seqineq nue-riar-pat avala-ssaanga
sun rise-as.soon.as-COND.3SG sail.out-FUT.1SG
As soon as the sun rises I'll sail out.

7.2.2.2.2 TRANSITIVE

The transitive conditional suffixes are shown in the following table.

Subject	Transitive conditional suffixes — Object							
	1SG	1PL	2SG	2PL	3SG	3PL	4SG	4PL
1SG	–	–	+(g/k)ukkit	+(g/k)ussi	+(g/k)ukku	+(g/k)ukkit	+(g/k)unni	+(g/k)utsik
2SG	+(g/k)umma	+(g/k)utsigut	–	–	+(g/k)ukku	+(g/k)ukkit	+(g/k)unni	+(g/k)utsik
3SG	+(p)panga	+(p)patigut	+(p)patit	+(p)pasi	+(p)pagu	+(p)pagit	+(p)pani	+(p)patik
4SG	+(g/k)uninga	+(g/k)unisigut	+(g/k)unisit	+(g/k)unisi	+(g/k)uniuk	+(g/k)unigit	–	–
1PL	–	–	+(g/k)utsigit	+(g/k)ussi	+(g/k)utsigu	+(g/k)utsigit	+(g/k)utsinni	+(g/k)utsik
2PL	+(g/k)ussinga	+(g/k)utsigut	–	–	+(g/k)ussiuk	+(g/k)ussigit	+(g/k)ussinni	+(g/k)utsik
3PL	+(p)pannga	+(p)patigut	+(p)patsit	+(p)pasi	+(p)passuk	+(p)patigit	+(p)panni	+(p)patik
4PL	+(g/k)unninga	+(g/k)unisigut	+(g/k)unitsit	+(g/k)unisi	+(g/k)unikku	+(g/k)unikkit	–	–

Points to note:

- Vowel-stem verbs take the variants starting in +g and +pp.
- Consonant-stem verbs take the variants starting in +k and +p.
- R-stem verbs take the variants starting in +u and +p.

The following tables shown the complete transitive conditional conjugation of a model vowel-stem verb (**asavaa** 'to love him/her/it'), consonant-stem verb (**ornippaa** 'to approach him/her/it'), and r-stem verb (**ikiorpaa** 'to help him/her/it').

Mood

Transitive conditional vowel-stem verb
asavaa to love him/her/it

Subject	Object							
	1SG	1PL	2SG	2PL	3SG	3PL	4SG	4PL
1SG	–	–	asagukkit	asagussi	asagukku	asagukkit	asagunni	asagutsik
2SG	asagumma	asagutsigut	–	–				
3SG	asappanga	asappatigut	asappatit	asappasi	asappagu	asappagit	asappani	asappatik
4SG	asaguninga	asagunisigut	asagunisit	asagunisi	asaguniuk	asagunigit	–	–
1PL	–	–	asagutsigit	asagussi	asagutsigu	asagutsigit	asagutsinni	asagutsik
2PL	asagussinga	asagutsigut	–	–	asagussiuk	asagussigit	asagussinni	
3PL	asappannga	asappatigut	asappatsit	asappasi	asappassuk	asappatigit	asappanni	asappatik
4PL	asagunninnga	asagunisigut	asagunisit	asagunisi	asagunikku	asagunikkit	–	–

Transitive conditional consonant-stem verb
ornippaa to approach him/her/it

Subject	Object							
	1SG	1PL	2SG	2PL	3SG	3PL	4SG	4PL
1SG	–	–	ornikkukkit	ornikkussi	ornikkukku	ornikkukkit	ornikkunni	ornikkutsik
2SG	ornikkumma	ornikkutsigut	–	–				
3SG	ornippanga	ornippatigut	ornippatit	ornippasi	ornippagu	ornippagit	ornippani	ornippatik
4SG	ornikkuninga	ornikunisigut	ornikunisit	ornikkunisi	ornikkuniuk	ornikkunigit	–	–
1PL	–	–	ornikkutsigit	ornikkussi	ornikkutsigu	ornikkutsigit	ornikkutsinni	ornikkutsik
2PL	ornikkussinga	ornikkutsigut	–	–	ornikkussiuk	ornikkussigit	ornikkussinni	
3PL	ornippannga	ornippatigut	ornippatsit	ornippasi	ornippassuk	ornippatigit	ornippanni	ornippatik
4PL	ornikkunninnga	ornikkunisigut	ornikkunitsit	ornikkunisi	ornikkunikku	ornikkunikkit	–	–

Transitive conditional r-stem verb
ikiorpaa to help him/her/it

Subject	Object							
	1SG	1PL	2SG	2PL	3SG	3PL	4SG	4PL
1SG	–	–	ikiorukkit	ikiorussi	ikiorukku	ikiorukkit	ikiorunni	ikiorutsik
2SG	ikiorumma	ikiorutsigut	–	–				
3SG	ikiorpanga	ikiorpatigut	ikiorpatit	ikiorpasi	ikiorpagu	ikiorpagit	ikiorpani	ikiorpatik
4SG	ikioruninga	ikiorunisigut	ikiorunisit	ikiorunisi	ikioruniuk	ikiorunigit	–	–
1PL	–	–	ikiorutsigit	ikiorussi	ikiorutsigu	ikiorutsigit	ikiorutsinni	ikiorutsik
2PL	ikiorussinga	ikiorutsigut	–	–	ikiorussiuk	ikiorussigit	ikiorussinni	
3PL	ikiorpannga	ikiorpatigut	ikiorpatsit	ikiorpasi	ikiorpassuk	ikiorpatigit	ikiorpanni	ikiorpatik
4PL	ikiorunninnga	ikiorunisigut	ikiorunitsit	ikiorunisi	ikiorunikku	ikiorunikkit	–	–

The use of the transitive conditional is illustrated in the following examples. See section 7.2.2.2.1 for discussion of the various tense and other suffixes that can be used in conjunction with the conditional.

Arlaata <u>takusimasorippassuk</u> tusarusuttorujussuuarput.
arlaata taku-sima-sori-ppassuk tusa-rusut-to-rujussuu-arput.
someone taku-PAST-believe-COND.3SG>3SG hear-want-IP-very.much-1PL>3SG
If someone believes that they have seen him, we would very much like to hear about it.

Assammiora <u>nanigunikku</u> sianissapput.
assammio-ra nani-ppassuk siani-ssa-pput
ring-1SG find-COND.4PL>3SG phone-FUT-3PL
If they find my ring, they'll phone.

Brugseni app <u>atorsinnaasimasuugukku</u> pisisimassagaluarpara.
brugseni app ator-sinnaa-simasuu-gukku pisi-sima-ssa-galuar-para
brugseni app use-be.able-COND.1SG>3SG buy-PAST-FUT-would-1SG>3SG
If I could have used the Brugseni app, I would have bought it.

7.2.2.3 Contemporative

The contemporative mood is used to indicate an action that occurs at the same time as a main-clause action (e.g. 'she drank tea and worked; she drank tea while working') or the manner in which something happens (e.g. 'she came running'). It can also be used in a similar way to the causative, in the meaning of 'when', 'after', 'having done'.

The contemporative does not have third-person forms. Instead, it uses the fourth person, which serves to mark the subject of a subordinate clause as being the same as the subject of an associated main clause. (See 7.1.1 for discussion of the concept of the fourth person.) This is because traditionally the subject of a contemporative verb is always the same as that of the verb in an associated main clause. Note that the contemporative can also have a different subject from the verb in the main clause, but in such cases the fourth person is still used instead of the third person.

Contemporatives can be easily identified because the contemporative marker in all persons is +lu- (for consonant-stem and r-stem verbs) or +llu- (for vowel-stem verbs). The contemporative is marked by the abbreviation CONT in the glossing. As in the case of the other moods discussed earlier, there are different transitive and intransitive paradigms.

7.2.2.3.1 INTRANSITIVE

The intransitive contemporative suffixes are shown in the following table.

Intransitive contemporative suffixes		
Subject	Vowel-stem	Consonant-stem and r-stem
1SG	+llunga	+lunga
2SG	+llutit	+lutit
4SG	+lluni	+luni
1PL	+lluta	+luta
2PL	+llusi	+lusi
4PL	+llutik	+lutik

Point to note:

- As mentioned earlier, the contemporative mood does not exist in the third person. Because the subject of a contemporative verb is always the same as that of the verb in the main clause, the fourth person is used instead.

The following table shows the complete intransitive contemporative conjugation of a model vowel-stem verb (**nerivoq** 'to eat'), consonant-stem verb (**sinippoq** 'to sleep'), and r-stem verb (**atuarpoq** 'to read').

Intransitive contemporative verbs			
Subject	Vowel stem	Consonant-stem	R-stem
1SG	**nerillunga**	**sinillunga**	**atuarlunga**
2SG	**nerillutit**	**sinillutit**	**atuarlutit**
4SG	**nerilluni**	**sinilluni**	**atuarluni**
1PL	**nerilluta**	**sinilluta**	**atuarluta**
2PL	**nerillusi**	**sinillusi**	**atuarlusi**
4PL	**nerillutik**	**sinillutik**	**atuarlutik**

The use of the intransitive contemporative is illustrated in the following examples. Note that the verb in the contemporative mood can either precede or follow the main verb.

Nerillunga fjernsynerpunga.
neri-llunga fjernsyner-punga
eat-CONT.1SG watch.tv-1SG
I watch TV while I eat (or: while I eat, I watch TV).

Sikutorpunga kaagisorlungalu.
siku-tor-punga kaagi-sor-lunga-lu
ice.cream-consume-1SG cake-consume-CONT.1SG-and
I eat ice cream and I eat cake.

Mariamik ateqarpoq aqqanilinnillu ukioqarluni.
maria-mik ate-qar-poq aqqinilinnit-lu ukioq-qar-luni
maria-INS name-have-3SG eleven-and year-have-CONT.4SG
She is called Maria and is eleven years old.

Unnukkut timmisartorit unnuinissarlu sipaarlugu.
unnu-kkut timmisartor-it unnui-ni-ssar-lu sipaar-lugu
evening-PRO fly-IMP.2SG stay.overnight-AP-FUT-and save-CONT.4SG
Fly in the evening and avoid an overnight stay.

Ilaannigooq angut utoqqaq puisinniarluni qajartorpoq.
ilaannigooq angut utoqqaq puisinniar-luni qajartor-poq
once.upon.a.time man old hunt.seal-CONT.4SG go.by.kayak-3SG
Once upon a time an old man was out kayaking and hunting seals.

The contemporative can also be used in the construction of complement clauses, that is, clauses conveying the meaning of 'that' after verbs of perception and utterance, as in 'He said that he would come'. Contemporative verbs are used in this type of construction only when the subject of the main verb is the same as the subject of the contemporative verb. The verb in the main clause will make it clear whether the contemporative has this sense or not. The following example illustrates this type of usage.

Oqarpoq aggerniarluni.
oqar-poq agger-niar-luni
say-3SG come-intend.to-CONT.4SG
S/he said s/he was planning to come.

The contemporative can be augmented by a number of suffixes that lend a more specific meaning to the construction, e.g. 'just as', 'just after', 'while'. Some of the most commonly used of these compound suffixes are shown in the following table.

Suffix	English translation
+gallarluni, -kkallarluni, -rallarluni	just as, while
-qqaarluni	only when, not until
+sinnarluni	only when, not until
-reerluni	as soon as, just after
-riarluni	as soon as, just after
+niariarluni	as soon as, just after
-ruttorluni	just as
-ajutigaluni, -itigaluni, -utigaluni	while, at the same time as
+/-t(s)illuni	while

Point to note:

- The suffixes are listed here with the 4SG contemporative ending, but they can take the other contemporative endings as well.

The use of these augmented contemporatives is illustrated in the following examples.

Igatillunga utaqqissaatit.
iga-til-lunga utaqqi-ssaatit
cook-while-CONT.1SG wait-FUT.2SG
Wait while I'm cooking.

Canadami piniartoq aavartilluni qilalugarniartillunilu nannu-mit saassunneqarpoq.
canada-mi piniartoq aavar-til-luni qilaluganniar-til-luni-lu nannu-mit saassun-neqa-poq
canada-LOC hunter hunt.reindeer-while-CONT.4SG catch.narwhal-while-4SG-and bear-ABL attack-PASS-3SG
While hunting reindeer and narwhals in Canada, the hunter was attacked by a bear.

Decemberimi nannut piaqqisarput <u>apissiminiitillutik</u>.
decemberi-mi nannu-t piaqqi-sar-put apissi-mini-i-til-lutik
december-LOC polar.bear-PL give.birth-HAB-3PL bear.den-PL.LOC.4PL-be-while-CONT.4PL
Polar bears give birth in December while they are in their dens.

The suffix +niarpoq 'to intend to; to try to; to want to' can be used in conjunction with a contemporative verb to convey the meaning of 'in order to', e.g.:

Neriniarluni ingippoq.
neri-niar-luni ingip-poq
eat-intend.to-CONT.4SG sit.down-3SG
He sat down in order to eat.

7.2.2.3.2 TRANSITIVE

The transitive contemporative suffixes are shown in the following table.

Subject	Transitive contemporative suffixes							
	Object							
	1SG	1PL	2SG	2PL	3SG	3PL	4SG	4PL
4SG/PL	+(l)lunga	+(l)luta	+(l)lutit	+(l)lusi	+(l)lugu	+(l)lugit	+(l)luni	+(l)lutik

Points to note:

- The transitive contemporative is typically used only with the 4SG/PL subject suffixes listed in the table, since verbs in the contemporative typically have the same subject as those in the associated main clause.
- Even when the subject of the contemporative verb is different from that of the main clause, the fourth person is still used instead of the third person.
- While the transitive contemporative is typically employed only with fourth-person subjects, you may occasionally see transitive contemporative subject suffixes in other persons, such as 1PL>3PL +(l)lutigit, 2PL>1SG +(l)lusinga, etc. Combinations not listed here are typically straightforward to recognise as they closely resemble the transitive suffixes found in the other subordinate moods.

The following tables shown the complete transitive contemporative conjugation of a model vowel-stem verb (**asavaa** 'to love him/her/it'), consonant-stem verb (**ornippaa** 'to approach him/her/it'), and r-stem verb (**ikiorpaa** 'to help him/her/it').

Transitive contemporative vowel-stem verbs **asavaa** to love him/her/it								
Subject	Object							
	1SG	1PL	2SG	2PL	3SG	3PL	4SG	4PL
4SG/PL	asallunga	asalluta	asallutit	asallusi	asallugu	asallugit	asalluni	asallutik

Transitive contemporative consonant-stem verbs **ornippaa** to approach him/her/it								
Subject	Object							
	1SG	1PL	2SG	2PL	3SG	3PL	4SG	4PL
4SG/PL	ornillunga	ornilluta	ornillutit	ornillusi	ornillugu	ornillugit	ornilluni	ornillutik

Transitive contemporative consonant-stem verbs **ikiorpaa** to help him/her/it								
Subject	Object							
	1SG	1PL	2SG	2PL	3SG	3PL	4SG	4PL
4SG/PL	ikiorlunga	ikiorluta	ikiorlutit	ikiorlusi	ikiorlugu	ikiorlugit	ikiorluni	ikiorlutik

The use of the transitive contemporative is illustrated in the following examples.

Anaanama <u>ikiorlunga</u> tassani inissarsivaanga.
anaana-ma ikior-lunga tassani inissar-si-vaanga
mother-REL.1SG help-4SG>1SG there apartment-buy-3SG>1SG
My mother is helping me by buying a flat for me there.

As in the intransitive (7.2.2.3.1), the transitive contemporative can be used in the construction of complement clauses when the subject of the main verb and the contemporative verb are the same, e.g.:

Oqarpoq takureerlunga.
oqar-poq taku-reer-lunga
say-3SG see-PERF-CONT.4SG>1SG
S/he said that s/he had seen me.

The augmented transitive contemporative suffix -**qqullugu** (the transitive verbal suffix -**qquaa** 'to make/ask/invite someone to do something' in the contemporative) can be used in the meaning of 'in order to', as in the following example. The contemporative verb with -**qqullugu** does not necessarily have a direct object, despite the transitive form.

Taamaaliorpoq illaqqullugu.
taammaa-lior-poq illa-qqu-llugu
this-do-3SG laugh-cause-CONT.4SG>3SG
S/he did this so that s/he would laugh (or: in order to make him/her laugh).

When used in conjunction with a verb indicating a command or order, the suffix -**qqullugu** can be used to mark the commanded action, equivalent to an English construction such as 'to tell someone to do something'. Again, in such instances a contemporative verb with this suffix does not necessarily have a direct object. The following example illustrates this type of construction.

Oqarfigaa aallaqqullugu.
oqar-figaa aalla-qqu-llugu
tell-VAL.3SG>3SG leave-cause-CONT.4SG>3SG
S/he told him/her to go.

7.2.2.4 Participial

The participial mood is used in complement clauses, which correspond to English clauses starting with 'that' (e.g. 'I thought that he would still be at work'). The subject of the participial verb is usually different than that of the main clause verb. The participial is marked by the abbreviation PART in the glossing. As in the case of the other moods discussed earlier, there are distinct intransitive and transitive paradigms for the participial.

7.2.2.4.1 INTRANSITIVE

The intransitive participial suffixes are shown in the following table.

Intransitive participial suffixes		
Subject	Vowel-stem	Consonant-stem and r-stem
1SG	+sunga	+tunga
2SG	+sutit	+tutit
3SG	+soq	+toq
1PL	+sugut	+tugut
2PL	+susi	+tusi
3PL	+sut	+tut

Points to note:

- The intransitive participial suffixes are composed of the intransitive participle +toq/+soq (see section 8.1) plus a person ending.
- The third-person participial suffixes are identical to the intransitive participle (+toq/+soq in the singular and +tut/+sut in the plural).
- There are no fourth-person participial forms. This is because the participial mood is typically used with a different subject than the subject of the associated main clause.
- Some verbs ending in a consonant may take +soq, e.g. **aggerpoq** 'to arrive' > participial **aggersoq**. These forms are best learnt individually. (See also section 2.5.1.)
- Some consonant-stem verbs have -t as the final consonant of their stem, but this is not usually visible, as it assimilates into the person suffixes. Such verbs may take -ts instead of -t in the intransitive participial mood. An example of this is **akikippoq** 'to be cheap' > participial **akikitsoq**. It is difficult to predict which verbs follow this pattern, so they must be learned individually.

The following table shows the complete intransitive participial conjugation of a model vowel-stem verb (**nerivoq** 'to eat'), consonant-stem verb (**sinippoq** 'to sleep'), and r-stem verb (**atuarpoq** 'to read').

7
Verbs

	Intransitive participial verbs		
Subject	Vowel stem	Consonant-stem	R-stem
1SG	**nerisunga**	**sinittunga**	**atuartunga**
2SG	**nerisutit**	**sinittutit**	**atuartutit**
4SG	**nerisoq**	**sinittoq**	**atuartoq**
1PL	**nerisugut**	**sinittugut**	**atuartugut**
2PL	**nerisusi**	**sinittusi**	**atuartusi**
4PL	**nerisut**	**sinittut**	**atuartut**

The use of the intransitive participial is illustrated in the following examples. Note that in these examples the subject of the participial verb is different than the subject of the main verb.

Naalakkaersuisoq neriorsuivoq aaqqinneqassasoq.
naalakkaersuisoq neriorsui-voq aaqqin-neqa-ssa-soq
minister promise-3SG solve-PASS-FUT-PART.3SG
The minister promised that it will be solved.

Neriuppugut atsa aqagu takutissasoq.
neriup-pugut atsa aqagu takuti-ssa-soq
hope-1PL aunt tomorrow make.an.appearance-FUT-PART.3SG
We hope that auntie will make an appearance tomorrow.

Eqqumiitsuliortup nalunaarutigaa sisamanngorpat qalipagaq saqqumissasoq.
eqqumiitsuliortu-p nalunaarutig-aa sisamanngorpat qalipagaq saqqumi-ssa-soq
artist-REL announce-3SG>3SG on.thursday painting be.revealed-FUT-PART.3SG
The artist has announced that the painting will be revealed on Thursday.

Ilinniartitsisoq oqarpoq suliassarput tallimanngorpamut piariissasoq.
ilinniartitsisoq oqar-poq suliassar-put tallimanngorpa-mut piarii-ssa-soq
teacher say-3SG assignment-1PL friday-ALL be.ready-FUT-PART.3SG
The teacher said that our assignment is to be ready on Friday.

Mood

Silaannaap allanngoriartornera ilutigalugu nannut saassussi-sartut amerleriassasut ilimagineqarpoq.
silaannaa-p allanngoriartorner-a ilutigalugu nannu-t saassussisartu-t amerleria-ssa-sut ilimagi-neqar-poq
climate-REL change-3SG because.of bear-PL attack-PL increase-FUT-PART.3PL expect-PASS-3SG
It is expected that polar bear attacks will increase in the future because of climate change.

Kalaallit takutippaatigut kalaallit aamma operamik erinarsorsinnaasut.
kalaalli-t takutip-paatigut kalaalli-t aamma opera-mik erinarsor-sinnaa-sut
greelander-PL show-1PL>3PL greenlander-PL also opera-INS sing-be.able-PART.3PL
She showed Greenlandic people that Greenlandic people can also sing opera.

In addition to subordinate clauses with 'that', the participial mood can be used to convey the equivalent of English indirect questions such as 'do you know where the cat is?'. This usage is illustrated in the following example.

Alersikka sumiittut nalunngiliuk?
alersi-kka sumiit-tut nalu-nngiliuk
sock-PL.1SG be.where-PART.3PL be.unknowing-NEG.INT.2SG>3SG
Do you know where my socks are?

The augmented participial form **+nersoq** can be used to form indirect questions without a question word, corresponding to English indirect questions with 'whether', as in the following example. (The augmented version can also be used in indirect questions containing a question word, but this is not obligatory.)

Naluara aninersoq.
nalu-ara ani-ner-soq
be.unknowing-1SG>3SG go.out-whether-PART.3SG
I don't know whether he has gone out.

7.2.2.4.2 TRANSITIVE

The transitive participial suffixes are shown in the following table.

7
Verbs

Subject	Transitive participial suffixes — Object							
	1SG	1PL	2SG	2PL	3SG	3PL	4SG	4PL
1SG	–	–	+(g/k)ikkit	+(g/k)issi	+(g/k)iga	+(g/k)ikka	+(g/k)inni	+(g/k)itsik
2SG	+(g/k)imma	+(g/k)itsigut	–	–	+(g/k)it	+(g/k)itit		
3SG	+(g/k)aanga	+(g/k)aatigut	+(g/k)aatit	+(g/k)aasi	+(g/k)aa	+(g/k)ai	+(g/k)aani	+(g/k)aatik
1PL	–	–	+(g/k)itsigit	+(g/k)issi	+(g/k)ipput	+(g/k)ivut	+(g/k)itsinni	+(g/k)itsik
2PL	+(g/k)issinga	+(g/k)itsigut	–	–	+(g/k)issi	+(g/k)isi	+(g/k)issinni	
3PL	+(g/k)aannga	+(g/k)aatigut	+(g/k)aatsit	+(g/k)aasi	+(g/k)aat		+(g/k)aanni	+(g/k)aatik

Points to note:

- Vowel-stem verbs take the variants starting in +g.
- Consonant-stem verbs take the variants starting in +k.
- R-stem verbs take the variants starting in a vowel.

The following tables shown the complete transitive causative conjugation of a model vowel-stem verb (**asavaa** 'to love him/her/it'), consonant-stem verb (**ornippaa** 'to approach him/her/it'), and r-stem verb (**ikiorpaa** 'to help him/her/it').

Subject	Transitive participial vowel-stem verb **asavaa** to love him/her/it — Object							
	1SG	1PL	2SG	2PL	3SG	3PL	4SG	4PL
1SG	–	–	asagikkit	asagissi	asagiga	asagikka	asaginni	asagitsik
2SG	asagimma	asagitsigut	–	–	asagit	asagitit		
3SG	asagaanga	asagaatigut	asagaatit	asagaasi	asagaa	asagai	asagaani	asagaatik
1PL	–	–	asagitsigit	asagissi	asagipput	asagivut	asagitsinni	asagitsik
2PL	asagissinga	asagitsigut	–	–	asagissi	asagisi	asagissinni	
3PL	asagaannga	asagaatigut	asagaatsit	asagaasi	asagaat		asagaanni	asagaatik

Mood

Transitive participial consonant-stem verb
ornippaa to approach him/her/it

Subject	Object							
	1SG	1PL	2SG	2PL	3SG	3PL	4SG	4PL
1SG	–	–	ornikkikkit	ornikkissi	ornikkiga	ornikkikka	ornikkinni	ornikkitsik
2SG	ornikkimma	ornikkitsigut	–	–	ornikkit	ornikkitit		
3SG	ornikkaanga	ornikkaatigut	ornikkaatit	ornikkaasi	ornikkaa	ornikkai	ornikkaani	ornikkaatik
1PL	–	–	ornikkitsigit	ornikkissi	ornikkipput	ornikkivut	ornikkitsinni	ornikkitsik
2PL	ornikkissinga	ornikkitsigut	–	–	ornikkissi	ornikkisi	ornikkissinni	
3PL	ornikkaannga	ornikkaatigut	ornikkaatsit	ornikkaasi	ornikkaat		ornikkaanni	ornikkaatik

Transitive participial r-stem verb
ikiorpaa to help him/her/it

Subject	Object							
	1SG	1PL	2SG	2PL	3SG	3PL	4SG	4PL
1SG	–	–	ikiorikkit	ikiorissi	ikioriga	ikiorikka	ikiorinni	ikioritsik
2SG	ikiorimma	ikioritsigut	–	–	ikiorit	ikioritit		
3SG	ikioraanga	ikioraatigut	ikioraatit	ikioraasi	ikioraa	ikiorai	ikioraani	ikioraatik
1PL	–	–	ikioritsigit	ikiorissi	ikioripput	ikiorivut	ikioritsinni	ikioritsik
2PL	ikiorissinga	ikioritsigut	–	–	ikiorissi	ikiorisi	ikiorissinni	
3PL	ikioraannga	ikioraatigut	ikioraatsit	ikioraasi	ikioraat		ikioraanni	ikioraatik

The use of the transitive participial is illustrated in the following examples.

Takuarput suliarisimagaat.
taku-arput suliari-sima-gaat
see-1PL>3SG work.on-PAST-PART.3PL>3SG
We can see that they have done it.

Anaanap illu asassimagaa takuara.
Anaana-p illu asas-sima-gaa taku-ara
mother-REL clean-PAST-PART.3SG>3SG see-1SG>3SG
I see that mother has cleaned the house.

Isumaqarpunga Cristinap ikiussagaanga unnuk manna.
isumaqar-punga cristina-p ikiu-ssa-gaanga unnuk manna

think-1SG cristina-REL help-FUT-3SG>1SG evening this
I think that Cristina will help me this evening.

7.3 Tense

The eight West Greenlandic verbal moods discussed in 7.2 do not generally convey a specific tense on their own (with the exception of the indicative, which can be used as a past or present tense, and the causative, which can be used as a past tense). Instead, tense (past, present, and future) is most commonly expressed by means of verbal suffixes employed in conjunction with one of the moods, and/or by means of independent adverbials (e.g. 'yesterday', 'tomorrow'). The ways of expressing present, past, and future tense in West Greenlandic are discussed in the following subsections.

7.3.1 Present tense

The indicative forms of West Greenlandic verbs can denote either past or present tense, with only the context indicating which interpretation is correct in any given instance. This is illustrated in the following table, in which a single West Greenlandic indicative form is shown with its possible English equivalents.

West Greenlandic indicative verb	Possible English equivalents
naluppugut	we are swimming we swam

Point to note:

- English present simple forms such as 'we swim' usually indicate a habitual action, which is expressed differently in Greenlandic, by means of the habitual suffix **+tarpoq/+sarpoq**; see section 7.4.2.

However, adverbials can be used in order to make it clearer that a given indicative verb has present rather than past tense value. This is illustrated in the following example, in which the adverb **maanna** 'now' clearly gives the verb present reference.

<u>Maanna</u> naluttarfimmi Malimmi <u>naluppugut</u>.
maanna naluttarfim-mi malim-mi nalup-pugut
now swimming.pool-LOC malik-LOC swim-1PL
We are swimming in the Malik swimming pool now.

7.3.2 *Past tense*

7.3.2.1 Past tense with adverbials

While the past tense in West Greenlandic can technically be conveyed simply by means of the indicative mood, in practice an adverbial of time is typically used in such contexts in order to make the past context clear. This is illustrated in the following example, in which the adverb **ipassaq** 'yesterday' serves to give the verb **naluppugut** 'we are swimming/we swam' unequivocal past tense reference.

Ipassaq naluttarfimmi Malimmi naluppugut.
ipassaq naluttarfim-mi malik-mi nalup-pugut
yesterday swimming.pool-LOC malik-LOC swim-1PL
Yesterday we swam in the Malik swimming pool.

7.3.2.2 Past tense with suffixes

In addition to adverbials, it is possible to specify a past tense meaning for a given verb by means of the addition of a past tense suffix. There are three such suffixes, shown in the following table. There is some overlap in meaning between all three, but each one can sometimes be used with a slightly different meaning. The suffixes **+nikuuvoq** and **+simavoq** are marked by PAST in the glossing, while the suffix **+/-reerpoq** is indicated by the abbreviation PERF.

Suffix	English meaning	Example
+/-reerpoq	• present perfect (i.e. a past action with present relevance)	**nerireerpoq** has eaten
+nikuuvoq	• general past (which the speaker has witnessed) • historic past (once, formerly, used to)	**nakorsaanikuuvoq** was a doctor used to be a doctor
+simavoq	• general past • present perfect (i.e. a past action with present relevance) • reported general past or present perfect (i.e. an action which the speaker has not witnessed)	**apisimavoq** it snowed it has snowed it is reported to have snowed

The following examples illustrate the use of the first suffix, +/-reerpoq.

Angallammik angalaareerpunga.
angallam-mik angalaa-reer-punga
boat-INS travel-PERF-1SG
I have travelled by boat.

Qitsuk nerereerpoq.
qitsuk nere-reer-poq
cat eat-PERF-3SG
The cat has eaten.

The following example illustrates the use of the second past tense suffix, +nikuuvoq.

Assiliivik pisiarigatsigu 5.000 kr.-qarnikuuvoq maannakkut 2.000 kr.-nik naleqarpoq.
assiliivik pisiari-gatsigu 5.000 kr.-qar-nikuu-voq maannakkut 2.000 kr.-nik nale-qar-poq
camera buy-CAUS.1PL>3SG 5.000 kroner-cost-PAST-3SG now 2.000 kroner value-have-3SG
When we bought the camera, it cost 5.000 kroner, (but) now it's worth 2.000 kroner.

The use of **+nikuuvoq** to indicate historic past is illustrated next. In such instances, it is usually accompanied by the habitual suffix **+tarpoq/+sarpoq** 'usually' (see section 7.4.2 for further discussion of this suffix).

Kaffisortarnikuuvunga.
kaffisor-tar-nikuu-vunga
coffee-consume-HAB-PAST-1SG
I used to drink coffee.

Illup ilua assut qiianartarnikuuvoq.
illu-p ilu-a assut qiianar-tar-nikuu-voq
house-REL inside-3SG very be.cold-HAB-PAST-3SG
It used to be very cold inside the house.

Mobiilimik attaveqarnissamut Kalaallit Nunaanni Danmarkimilu isumaqatigiissuteqarnikuupput.
mobiili-mik attaveqarnissa-mut kalaalli-t nuna-anni danmarki-mi-lu isumaqatigiissute-qar-nikuu-pput

mobile.phone-INS connection-ALL greenlander-REL.PL land-LOC.3PL denmark-LOC-
and agreement-have-PAST-3PL
Denmark and Greenland used to have an agreement regarding mobile phone connections.

The third past tense suffix, +simavoq, is illustrated in the following example.

Isiginnaagassiaq soqutiginarsimavoq.
isiginnaagassiaq soqutiginar-sima-voq
film be.interesting-PAST-3SG
The film was interesting.

The suffix **+simavoq** often contains an element of the sense of the English adverb 'apparently, allegedly, reportedly', indicating that the speaker has not personally witnessed the action. The following examples illustrate this type of usage. This sense of **+simavoq** is frequently seen in news reports, in which the writers often discuss past actions which they have not personally observed.

Ilaqutariit Motzfeldtikkut Tasiilamut nuussimapput.
ilaqutari-it motzfeldt-i-kkut tasiila-mut nuus-sima-pput
family-PL motzfeldt-HV-COLL tasiila-ALL move-PAST-3PL
The Motzfeldt family has (apparently) moved to Tasiilaq.

Angut maanna inissiisarfimmut utersimavoq.
angut manna inissiisarfim-mut uter-sima-voq
man now open.prison-ALL return-PAST-3SG
(Reportedly) the man has now returned to the open prison.

Aningaarooq Igalikumut aallarsimavoq.
aningaa-rooq igaliku-mut aallar-sima-voq
aningaaq-apparently igaliku-ALL travel-PAST-3SG
(Apparently) Aningaaq has travelled to Igaliku.

Finlandip præsidentikua seks og halv-femsinik ukioqarluni toqusimavoq.
findlandi-p præsidenti-ku-a seks.og.half.femsi-nik ukio-qar-luni toqu-sima-voq
finland-REL president-former-3SG ninety.six-INS.PL year-have-CONT.4SG die-PAST-3SG
Finland's former president (is reported to have) died at the age of 96.

Ilulissani ukiut 90-it matuma siorna nannumik takusoqarsimavoq.
ilulissa-ni ukiu-t 90-it matuma siorna nannu-mik taku-so-qar-sima-voq
ilulissa-LOC.PL year-PL 90-PL this past.year polar.bear-INS see-IP-have-PAST-3SG
(Apparently) no one has seen a polar bear in Ilulissat for the past 90 years.

Using +simavoq in the first-person singular often means that the speaker does not remember what happened. The following examples illustrate this usage.

Taxanik sisamanut <u>angerlarsimavunga</u>.
taxa-nik sisama-nut angerlar-sima-vunga
taxi-INS.PL four-ALL.PL come.home-PAST-1SG
Apparently I came home at 4 a.m. by taxi.

Meeraallunga <u>qiajasimavunga</u>.
meera-a-llunga qia-ja-sima-vunga
child-be-CONT.1SG cry-easily-PAST-1SG
They say I cried easily when I was a child.

Note that the past tense suffixes can be combined with the various West Greenlandic moods in addition to the indicative. For example, the underlined verb in the following sentence contains two past tense suffixes in conjunction with the contemporative mood suffix.

Ukiut 30-t <u>katisimareerluni</u> Nuka uillarninngorpoq.
ukiu-t 30-t kati-sima-reer-luni nuka uillarni-nngor-poq
year-PL 30-PL get.married-PAST-PERF-CONT.4SG nuka widow-become-3SG
After being married for 30 years Nuka became a widow.

7.3.2.3 Past tense with causative mood

In addition to past tense suffixes, the causative mood (discussed in 7.2.2.1) is commonly used in everyday speech as a narrative past tense, for example when a speaker is telling another person what they did yesterday. In contrast to the actual causative sense of the mood, when used as a generic past tense, the clause containing the causative verb does not necessarily have a subordinate sense. Context usually distinguishes the causative meaning of this mood ('because', 'since', 'when') from the more general past tense meaning. There can only be one causative verb in this use, as any subsequent actions will be in the indicative mood. The following examples illustrate the past tense use of the causative mood.

Ippassaq neriniartarfimmi <u>nerigama</u> ...
ippassaq neriniartarfim-mi neri-gama
yesterday restaurant-LOC eat-CAUS.1SG
I ate in a restaurant yesterday ...

Qaqortormiut sissiukkami Dronning Margrethe niuffioramikku ...   Tense
qaqortormiu-t sissiukka-mi dronning margrethe niuffior-amikku
qaqortoq-resident-PL jetty-LOC queen margrethe greet-4PL>3SG
The people of Qaqortoq greeted Queen Margrethe at the jetty ...

Paniga aanaamini tukkugami ullaaq angerlarpoq.
pani-ga aanaa-mini tukku-gami ullaaq angerlar-poq
daughter-1SG grandmother-LOC.4SG sleep-CAUS.4SG this.morning come.home-3SG
My daughter slept over at her grandmother's and came home this morning.

7.3.3 Future tense

7.3.3.1 Future tense with -ssavoq/-saaq

In contrast to the present and past, which can both be expressed by means of the indicative mood on its own or in conjunction with adverbials of time (see 7.3.1 and 7.3.2.1 for the present and past respectively), the future tense in West Greenlandic has a dedicated verbal suffix, -ssavoq, which must be employed in future contexts.

The future suffix looks slightly irregular in form in the intransitive indicative paradigm because the full form -ssavoq is archaic and is not generally used in everyday speech or writing (though it may appear in poetry and song lyrics). The shortened form -ssaaq is used instead. The short forms are listed in the following table. Note that the future suffix is marked by the abbreviation FUT in the glossing.

Intransitive indicative of -**ssaaq**	
Subject	All stem types
1SG	**-ssaanga**
2SG	**-ssaatit**
3SG	**-ssaaq**
1PL	**-ssaagut**
2PL	**-ssaasi**
3PL	**-ssapput**

7 Verbs

Point to note:

- The archaic long variant **-ssavoq** conjugates like a regular vowel-stem verb, e.g. **-ssavunga**, **-savugit**, etc.

The rest of the future tense forms are formed predictably by treating **-ssavoq** as a regular vowel-stem verb and attaching the appropriate suffixes in the relevant mood and person. The following table illustrates some of the possibilities.

Form	Example	English translation
Transitive indicative 1pl>3sg	**nerissavarput**	we are going to eat it
Intransitive interrogative 2sg	**nerissavit?**	are you going to eat?
Intransitive conditional 3sg	**nerissappat**	if s/he eats
Transitive conditional 1pl>3sg	**nerissagutsigu**	if we eat it
Intransitive contemporative 2pl	**nerissallusi**	while you eat
Transitive contemporative 4sg>3sg	**nerissallugu**	while eating it
Intransitive participial 1sg	**nerissasunga**	that I will eat
Transitive participial 2sg>3sg	**nerissagit**	that you will eat it

Points to note:

- The future suffix does not tend to be used with the imperative.
- The future suffix can also be combined with other suffixes, such as the habitual **+tarpoq/+sarpoq** (discussed in section 7.4.2), the negative suffixes (discussed in 7.11), the passive suffixes (discussed in 7.9), etc.

The following examples illustrate the use of the future tense suffix.

Dronningi tupermi <u>sinissaaq</u>.
dronningi tupeq-mi sini-ssaaq
queen tent-LOC sleep-FUT.3SG
The Queen will sleep in a tent.

Illu ullumi <u>pisiarissavara</u>.
illu ullumi pisiari-ssa-vara
house today buy-FUT-1SG>3SG
I am going to buy the house today.

Aleqama ornissavaanga.
aleqa-ma orni-ssa-vaanga
big.sister.to.a.boy-REL.1SG visit-FUT-3SG>1SG
My big sister is going to visit me.

Aputsiap Ivalu aassavaa.
aputsia-p ivalu aa-ssa-vaa
aputsiaq-REL ivalu pick.up-FUT-3SG>3SG
Aputsiaq will pick Ivalu up.

Arpassagama nerinngilanga.
arpa-ssa-gama neri-nngi-langa
run-FUT-CAUS.1SG eat-NEG-1SG
I'm not eating because I'm going to run.

Tamanna Nuummi aqagu Hotel Hans Egedemi pissaaq.
tamanna nuum-mi aqagu arfininngorner-mi hotel hans egede-mi pi-ssaaq
this nuuk-LOC tomorrow saturday-LOC hotel hans egede-LOC happen-FUT.3SG
This is happening tomorrow in Hotel Hans Egede in Nuuk.

Suliniut Sisimiuni suliffinnik 28-nik pilersitsisinnaassaaq.
suliniut sisimiu-ni suliffin-nik 28-nik pilersitsi-sinnaa-ssaaq.
project sisimiut-LOC.PL job-INS.PL 28-INS.PL create-be.able-FUT.3SG
The project is expected to be able to create 28 jobs in Sisimiut.

Inuuissiortoq poortukkamik tunissavat.
inuuissiortoq poortukka-mik tuni-ssa-vat
birthday.person present-INS give-FUT-2SG>3SG
You will give the birthday person a present.

Marluulluta illaqatigiittaqaagut, taava katissaagut.
marlu-u-lluta illa-qatigiitta-qaagut taava kati-ssagut
two-be-CONT.1PL laugh-together-a.lot.1PL so get.married-FUT.1PL
The two of us laugh a lot together, so we're going to get married.

The future tense -ssaaq/-ssavoq can be augmented with other suffixes to create compound future suffixes. For example the suffix -ssamaarpoq means 'to plan', e.g.:

Aappaagu katissamaarput.
aappaagu kati-ssamaar-put
next.year get.married-plan-3SG
They plan to get married next year.

7.3.3.2 Future suffix -**ssaq** on nouns

The future tense can also be attached to nouns in the form -ssaq. In such instances it has the meaning of 'a future X'.

Base noun	Suffixed noun
illu house	**illussaq** future house
suliffik workplace	**suliffissaq** future workplace
angalaneq trip, excursion	**angalanissaq** future trip, planned trip

Point to note:

- These constructions can often be translated into English with a phrase such as 'the house where they were going to live', 'the new house', 'the place where they were going to start working', 'the future job', 'the new job', etc. It can also often be left untranslated.

In many cases this suffix has become somewhat lexicalised and can be translated with a single English noun, e.g.:

aniffissaq 'exit' (lit: 'future going out place')
imissaq 'drinking water' (lit: 'water to be drunk in the future')
inissaq 'lodging place' (lit: 'future room')
nerisassat 'food' (lit: 'things to be eaten in the future')
nuliassaq 'fiancée' (lit: 'future wife')
palasissaq 'theology student' (lit: 'future priest')
suliassaq 'task', 'work' (lit: 'something to be done in the future')
uissaq 'fiancé' (lit: 'future husband')
viinissaq 'grape' (lit: 'future wine')

The suffix is quite commonly found in words denoting materials, e.g.:

annoraassaq 'anorak material', 'cotton' (lit: 'future anorak')
ikummatissaq 'fuel' (lit: 'something to be burnt in the future')
orsussaq 'petrol' (lit: 'future fat, oil') (can also mean 'battery')
sanaassaq 'raw material' (lit: 'something to be made in the future')

In some cases the future suffix appears in conjunction with a noun where the future meaning is not obvious, e.g.:

anaanassaq 'stepmother'
ataatassaq 'stepfather'
ernissaq 'stepson'
panissaq 'stepdaughter'

The following sentences illustrate the use of this construction.

Illussara Nuummiippoq.
illu-ssa-ra nuum-mi-ip-poq
house-FUT-1SG nuuk-LOC-be-3SG
My future house is in Nuuk.

Suliffissat qulit illit ujaasininnut tulluarpoq.
suliffi-ssa-t qulit illit ujaasini-nnut tulluar-poq
job-FUT-PL ten you search-ALL.2SG match-3SG
Ten potential jobs match your search.

Sikumi aalisarfissaminnukarput.
siku-mi aalisarfi-ssa-min-nukar-put
ice-LOC fishing-place-FUT-ALL.4PL-go-3PL
They're going to their future fishing place on the ice.

Kalaaliminernik misiliinissamut pisiniarnissamullu periarfissiisoqarsimavoq.
kalaaliminer-nik misilii-ni-ssa-mut pisiniar-ni-ssa-mul-lu periarfissiiso-qar-sima-voq
greenlandic.food-INS.PL try-AP-FUT-ALL buy-AP-FUT-ALL-and possibility-have-PAST-3SG
There were lots of opportunities for tasting and buying Greenlandic food.

The suffix -ssaq can be combined with -galuaq/-kkaluaq/-raluaq, a nominal version of the hypothetical verbal suffix -galuarpoq/-kkaluarpoq/-raluarpoq (see section 7.2.2.2 and 14.5.1.2) to convey a meaning similar to the English 'a hypothetical future X', e.g.:

Tuluit ministeriunerat uppernarsaavoq brexitimut taasinissaraluaq kinguartinneqartoq.
tulu-it ministeriuner-at uppernarsaa-voq brexiti-mut taasini-ssa-raluaq kinguartin-neqar-toq
brit-PL prime.minister-3PL confirm-3SG brexit-ALL vote-FUT-hypothetical postpone-PASS-PART.3SG
The British prime minister confirmed that the intended Brexit vote had been postponed.

7.3.3.3 Future tense with -lerpoq

In addition to the basic future suffix -ssaaq, the verbal suffix -lerpoq can also be used to express future plans, corresponding to English future plans with 'going to' or the use of the progressive in English for future events. The action is more likely to happen with -lerpoq than -ssaaq and it is closer to the present time. (Otherwise, it functions as an inchoative suffix with the meaning 'begin'; see 7.4.3.)

Nerilerpoq.
neri-ler-poq
eat-going.to-3SG
S/he is going to eat.

Amerikamut aallalerpunga.
amerika-mut alla-ler-punga
america-ALL travel-going.to-1SG
I am going to go to America.

Unnugu Anna uffalerpoq.
unnugu anna uffa-ler-poq
tonight anna shower-going.to-3SG
Anna is going to shower tonight.

Mobiilikkut oqaluusilerpugut.
mobiili-kkut oqaluusi-ler-pugut
mobile.phone-PRO speak-going.to-1PL
We are going to speak on the phone.

Puisip neqaa igalerpara.
puisi-p neqa-a iga-ler-para
seal-REL meat-3SG cook-going.to-1SG>3SG
I am going to cook seal meat.

The suffix -lerpoq may also be used to indicate an imminent action, similar to the English 'about to', as in the following example.

Umiarsuup Nuuk tikilerpaa.
umiarsu-up nuuk tiki-ler-paa
boat-REL nuuk arrive-about.to-3SG>3SG
The boat is about to arrive in Nuuk.

7.4 Aspect

West Greenlandic has a number of verbal suffixes that can be used to convey various aspectual nuances. These suffixes indicate whether an action happens once or habitually, or serve to present it as ongoing as opposed to a finite event. Aspectual suffixes can be used in conjunction with any of the verbal moods (see 7.2) and with the various tense suffixes (see 7.3). The different aspectual suffixes are detailed in the following sections.

7.4.1 Completed

Completed actions can be conveyed by means of the past tense suffixes -reerpoq, nikuuvoq, and -simavoq (see 7.3.2 for discussion of the different past tense nuances of these suffixes).

7.4.2 Habitual

Habitual actions (i.e. actions that occur on a frequent or regular basis) are typically marked in West Greenlandic by adding the suffix +tarpoq/+sarpoq to a verbal stem, as illustrated in the following table. The habitual suffix is marked by the abbreviation HAB in the glossing.

Base verb	Verb with habitual suffix
naluppugut we are swimming (right now)	**naluttarpugut** we swim (usually, regularly)
sulivunga I am working (right now)	**sulisarpunga** I work (usually, regularly)
neripput they are eating (right now)	**nerisarput** they eat (usually, regularly)

Points to note:

- The variant +sarpoq is used in conjunction with vowel-stem verbs, as well as with verbs that historically ended in -i, such as **aggerpoq** 'to approach' > **aggersarpoq** 'to approach regularly'.
- The variant +tarpoq is used in conjunction with consonant-stem and r-stem verbs.

This habitual suffix is a much more frequent feature of Greenlandic than the English adverbs 'usually' or 'habitually'; indeed, it is a standard feature of any Greenlandic verb that denotes an action which recurs on a regular basis. Thus, in most cases it is best left untranslated, as it does not have a natural equivalent in, for example, English: whereas in English the present or past simple of most verbs may imply a habitual nuance, e.g. 'I work in Nuuk', in Greenlandic the habitual suffix +**tarpoq**/+**sarpoq** must be added in order for this nuance to be present in the verb. This point can be seen in the following examples, in which the suffix is generally untranslated.

Kaffimut sukkulertarpit?
kaffi-mut sukkuler-tar-pit
coffee-ALL take.sugar-HAB-INT.2SG
Do you take sugar in coffee?

Ukiut tamaasa sisorartarput.
ukiu-t tamaasa sisorar-tar-put
year-PL all ski-HAB-3PL
They go skiing every year.

Puisinniartarpunga.
puisinniar-tar-punga
hunt.seal-HAB-1SG
I go seal-hunting (regularly/often).

Nuannaartarpugut.
nuannaar-tar-pugut
be.happy-HAB-1PL
We tend to be happy.

Cafémi ikinngutikka takusarpakka.
café-mi ikinngut-ikka taku-sar-pakka
café-LOC friend-PL.1SG see-HAB-1SG>3PL
I usually see my friends in the café.

Unnukkut arsartarpoq.
unnu-kkut asar-tar-poq
evening-PRO play.ball-HAB-3SG
S/he plays ball in the evenings.

Sanilima naasut <u>imertertarpai</u>.
sanili-ma naasu-t imerter-tar-pai
neighbour-REL.1SG flower-PL water-HAB-3SG>3PL
My neighbour waters the flowers (regularly).

West Greenlandic has another suffix, +juarpoq/+tuarpoq/+uarpoq, which is also used to convey habitual action. However, the meaning of +juarpoq/+tuarpoq/+uarpoq is somewhat different than that of +tarpoq/+sarpoq; rather than conveying habitual action in general, it is used in the more specific sense of 'continually', 'always', e.g.:

Base verb	Verb with habitual suffix
naluppugut we are swimming	**naluttuarpugut** we always swim
sulivunga I am working	**suliuarpunga** I work and work
neripput they are eating	**neriuarput** they eat all the time

Points to note:

- The variant **+juarpoq** is used with stems ending in **-u** and **-a**, e.g. **qasuvoq** 'to be tired' > **qasujuarpoq** 'to be tired all the time'; **ammavoq** 'to be open' > **ammajuarpoq** 'to be open all the time'.
- The variant **+tuarpoq** is used with consonant-stem and r-stem verbs, e.g. **naluppoq** 'to swim' > **naluttuarpoq** 'to swim all the time'; **nuannaarpoq** 'to be happy' > **nuannaartuarpoq** 'to be happy all the time'.
- The variant **+uarpoq** is used with stems ending in **-i**, e.g. **sulivoq** 'to work' > **suliuarpoq** 'to work all the time'.

The use of +juarpoq/+tuarpoq/+uarpoq is illustrated in the following examples:

Nuannaartuarpoq.
nuannaar-tuar-poq
be.happy-always-3SG
S/he is always happy.

Qasujuarpunga.
qasu-juar-punga
be.tired-always-1SG
I am always tired.

Aspect

Uffarfimmi erinarsortuarpugut.
uffarfim-mi erinarsor-tuar-pugut
shower-LOC sing-always-1PL
We always sing in the shower.

Palernerluttuarpoq.
palerner-lut-tuar-poq
tan-bad-always-3SG
S/he always gets a sunburn.

Danmarkimi atuarnini oqaluttuariuarpaa.
danmarki-mi atuarner-ni oqaluttuari-uar-paa
denmark-LOC studies-4SG tell-always-3SG>3SG
S/he is always telling (people) about his/her studies in Denmark.

Asajuassavakkit.
asa-jua-ssa-vakkit
love-always-FUT-1SG>2SG
I will always love you.

Takornarissat apersortuarpaanga sumiuunersunga.
takornarissa-t apersor-tuar-paanga sumiu-u-ner-sunga
tourist-PL ask-always-3PL>1SG where.from-be-AP-PART.1SG
Tourists are always asking me where I am from.

7.4.3 Inchoative

The term 'inchoative' refers to a verb form that marks the start of an action, equivalent to English constructions with 'start to', 'begin to', or sometimes more specific expressions such as 'burst into tears', 'fall asleep'. In West Greenlandic, inchoative actions are expressed by the suffix **-lerpoq** 'to start', which is added to a verbal stem. (Note that **-lerpoq** can also mean 'to be going to, to be about to'; see section 7.3.3.3.) The following examples illustrate the use of the inchoative.

Imeq qalaalerpoq.
imeq qalaa-ler-poq
water boil-start-3SG
The water has started/is starting to boil.

Seqinnilerpoq.
seqinni-ler-poq

sun.shine-start-3SG
The sun has started to shine.

Ippassaq nukaga hotelimi <u>sulilerpoq</u>.
ippassaq nuka-ga hoteli-mi suli-ler-poq
yesterday little.sister-1SG hotel-LOC work-start-3SG
Yesterday my little sister started working in the hotel.

Qitsuk miavimik <u>ateqalerpoq</u>.
qitsuk miavi-mik ate-qa-ler-poq
cat meow-INS name-have-start-3SG
The cat has just been given the name Meow.[6]

Naatiiat <u>naalerput</u>.
naatiia-t naa-ler-put
potato-PL grow-start-3PL
The potatoes have started/are starting to grow.

Nalunaaqutaq sisamanut aatsaat <u>sinilerpoq</u>.
nalunaaqutaq sisama-nut aatsaat sini-ler-poq
clock four-ALL.PL first/only sleep-start-3SG
S/he only fell asleep at four o'clock.

Illalerpunga.
illa-ler-punga.
laugh-start-1SG
I started to laugh.

7.5 Modality

Modality refers to the expression of nuances such as possibility, desire, obligation, and ability. West Greenlandic has a number of suffixes that can express modal meanings. These suffixes are comparable to English modal verbs such as 'can', 'may', 'must', 'should', etc. The modal suffixes can be used in conjunction with any of the verbal moods (see 7.2) and with the various tense and/or aspect suffixes (see 7.3 and 7.4 respectively). The following are some of the most common West Greenlandic suffixes with modal meanings:

---

6 Literally: has started to be called Meow.

Modal suffix	English translation
+sinnaavoq	to be able to
+niarpoq	to want to; to intend to
-rusuppoq, -kkusuppoq	to want to
-jumavoq, -kkumavoq, -rumavoq, -umavoq	to want to
+tariaqarpoq, +sariaqarpoq	to have to
+ssagaluarpoq	should

Points to note:

- The variant +tariaqarpoq is used with consonant-stem and r-stem verbs, while the variant +sariaqarpoq is used with vowel-stem verbs.
- The variant -rusuppoq is used with vowel-stem and r-stem verbs. The variant -kkusuppoq is used with consonant-stem verbs.
- The suffix +niarpoq can also mean 'to intend to' and 'to try to' (as well as 'to hunt').
- The variant -jumavoq is used with verbal stems ending in -aa, -kkumavoq is used with vowel-stem verbs, -rumavoq is used with r-stem verbs, and -umavoq is used with stems ending in -i.

The following examples illustrate the use of the modal suffixes.

Kalaallisut oqalussinnaavit?
kalaallisut oqalus-sinnaa-vit
greenlandic speak-be.able-INT.2SG
Can you speak Greenlandic?

Inuuneq ilunngersunarsinnaasarpoq.
inuuneq ilunngersunar-sinnaa-sar-poq
life be.difficult-be.able-HAB-3SG
Life can sometimes be difficult.

Piitaq ipeqarami uffartariaqarpoq.
piitaq ipe-qar-ami uffar-tariaqar-poq
piitaq dirt-have-CAUS.4SG shower-have.to-3SG
Piitaq has to have a shower because he is dirty.

Ippassaq <u>itiaartariaqarnikuuvugut</u> Kujataani angalaartussaagatta. Evidentiality
ippassaq iti-aar-tariaqar-nikuu-vugut kujata-ani angalaar-tu-ssa-atta
yesterday wake.up-early-have.to-PAST-1PL south-LOC.3PL travel-IP-FUT-CAUS.1PL
Yesterday we had to wake up early because we were going on a trip in South Greenland.

Aarhusimi kalaallit avatangiisaannik uummaarinnerusumik <u>pilersitsiniarpugut</u>.
aarhusi-mi kalaalli-t avatangiisa-annik uummaarin-ner-u-su-mik pilersitsi-niar-pugut
århus-LOC greenlander-PL environment-INS.3PL vibrant-more-be-IP-INS create-intend-1PL
We intend to create a more vibrant Greenlandic environment in Århus.

Nunatta internetikkut illersornissani nammineq <u>aqukkusuppaa</u>.
nuna-tta interneti-kkut illernorni-ssa-ni nammineq aqu-kkusup-paa
land-REL.1PL internet-PRO defence-FUT-4SG oneself manage-want-3SG>3SG
Greenland wants to manage its own cyber defence.

Meeraq qilalerami <u>imissagaluarpoq</u>.
meeraq qilaler-ami imi-ssagaluar-poq
child be.very.thirsty-CAUS.4SG drink-should-3SG
The child should drink because s/he is very thirsty.

Qitsuk saluttoq <u>nerilluassagaluarpoq</u>.
qitsuk salut-toq neri-llua-ssagaluar-poq
cat be.skinny-IP eat-properly-should-3SG
The skinny cat should eat properly.

7.6 Evidentiality

Evidentiality is a verbal category that refers to the indication of how much evidence there is for a given action – that is, whether the speaker has seen the action take place or has only heard about it second-hand, and how likely or unlikely it is that the action did indeed happen. English does not have special evidential markers for verbs, but evidential information can be supplied by means of helping verbs such as 'seem to', 'be believed to', 'appear to', etc., or by means of adverbs such as 'apparently', 'allegedly', 'supposedly', etc. In West Greenlandic, specific suffixes can be attached to verbal stems in order to convey evidential meanings. The evidential suffixes can be used in conjunction with the different verbal moods and in combination with other verbal suffixes (e.g. modal suffixes, aspectual suffixes, tense suffixes etc.). Some of the more common evidential suffixes are as follows.

Evidential suffix	Example
+(r)pallappoq they say, allegedly	**qiavoq** s/he is crying > **qiarpallappoq** they say s/he is crying
+(r)paluppoq to seem like, to look like, to sound like, apparently	**anivoq** s/he is going out > **anerpaluppoq** it sounds like s/he is going out
+(r)pasippoq to seem like, to look like, apparently	**qasuvoq** s/he is tired > **qasorpasippoq** it looks like s/he is tired
+nerarpoq s/he says that	**Nuummiippoq** s/he is in Nuuk > **Nuummiinnerarpaat** they say that s/he is in Nuuk
+gunarpoq, -kkunarpoq, -runarpoq to seem like, apparently	**sulipput** they are working > **suligunarpput** they seem to be working
-gooq, -nngooq, -rooq they say, apparently, I've heard	**pisaraa** s/he has caught it > **pisaraagooq** apparently s/he has caught it **uanga** I > **uangagooq** ... they say that I ...

Points to note:

- Most of these evidential suffixes lack a specific tense value; as indicative verbs, they can be used in present or past contexts.
- The variants +(r)pallappoq, +rpaluppoq, and +rpasippoq are used with vowel-stem verbs, e.g. **anivoq** 's/he is going out' > **anerpallappoq** 'they say s/he is going out'; **anerpaluppoq** 'it sounds like s/he is going out'; **anerpasippoq** 'it seems like s/he is going out'.
- The variant +gunarpoq is used with vowel-stem verbs, while -kkunarpoq is used with consonant-stem verbs and -runarpoq is used with r-stem verbs.
- The suffix -gooq/-rooq/-nngooq is enclitic. This means it is attached at the end of the word in focus in the sentence, which may be the subject, the object, or the verb itself.
- The variant -gooq is used following a vowel, while -nngooq is used following a consonant other than -q-, and -rooq is used following -q-.

- The past tense markers presented in section 7.3.2.2 can have evidential functions: +**nikuuvoq** is often used when the speaker is witnessed the event, whereas +**simavoq** is often used when the speaker has not witnessed the event themself.

The uses of the evidential suffixes are illustrated here:

Najaaraq suliffimmini <u>ulapippasippoq</u>.
najaaraq suliffim-mini ulapip-pasip-poq
najaaraq work-LOC.4SG be.busy-seem-3SG
It seems like Najaaraq is busy at work.

Inuit <u>tigulluarpasippaat</u>.
inu-it tigu-lluar-pasip-paat
person-PL receive-well-seem-3PL>3SG
People seem to have received it well.

Meeqqat silami <u>pinnguarpalupput</u>.
meeqqa-t sila-mi pinnguar-palup-put
child-PL outside-LOC play-sound.like-3PL
It sounds like the children are playing outside.

Ataata soraareerluni <u>iserpaluppoq</u>.
ataata soraa-reer-luni iser-palup-poq
father get.off.work-PERF-CONT.4SG enter-sound.like-3SG
It sounds like father is coming in after getting off work.

Qarasaasiaq <u>ajorunarpoq</u>.
qarasaasiaq ajo-runar-poq
computer be.broken-seem-3SG
The computer seems to be broken.

Ivik <u>anigunarpoq</u>.
ivik ani-gunar-poq
ivik go.out-seem-3SG
Ivik seems to have gone out.

Barcelonami <u>tammarunarpugut</u>.
barcelona-mi tamma-runar-pugut
barcelona-LOC get.lost-seem-1PL
We seem to have lost our way in Barcelona.

Evidentiality

Qimmeq Anthonimik atilik Pisiffiup eqqaani <u>takuvaanngooq</u>.
qimmeq anthon-i-mik atilik pisiffiu-p eqqaani taku-vaa-nngooq
dog anthon-HV-INS named pisiffik-REL outside see-3PL>3SG-reportedly
Reportedly they saw Anthon the dog outside (the supermarket) Pisiffik.

7.7 Causativity

West Greenlandic has various suffixes that can be added to verbal stems in order to make the verb causative (i.e. 'to cause someone to do something'). The most common West Greenlandic causative suffixes are listed next. Each of the causative suffixes has a slightly different sense. Note that causative suffixes are always transitive, as by definition they take a direct object. Note also that the causative suffixes discussed here are not related in form or meaning to the causative verbal mood (discussed in section 7.2.2.1).

Causative suffix	English translation
+tippaa, +sippaa	to make someone do something
-qquaa	to ask someone do something
+tarpaa, +sarpaa	to (try to) make someone do something

Points to note:

- The variants **+tippaa** and **+tarpaa** are used with consonant-stem and r-stem verbs, whereas the variants **+sippaa** and **+sarpaa** are used with vowel-stem verbs and with verbs that historically ended in -i.
- There is another causative suffix, **+taarpaa/+saarpaa**, which has a similar function to **+tarpaa/+sarpaa** 'to try to make someone/something do/be something', but with the additional meaning of 'as much as possible', e.g. **kusanarpoq** 'to be pretty' > **kusanarsaarpaa** 'to try to make something as pretty as possible'.

The function of the causative suffixes is illustrated in the following examples. In each example, a basic intransitive verb (shown on the left) is augmented by a causative suffix, which turns the subject of the intransitive verb into the object of the newly created causative transitive verb (shown on the right).

Causativity

Intransitive verb	Verb with causative suffix
Qimmeq nerivoq. qimmeq neri-voq dog eat-3SG The dog is eating.	**Qimmeq nerisippara.** qimmeq neri-sip-para dog eat-cause-1SG>3SG I am feeding the dog.
Mads ingippoq. Mads ingip-poq Mads sit.down-3SG Mads sat down.	**Lisep Mads ingeqquaa.** lise-p mads inge-qqu-aa lise-REL mads sit.down-invite-3SG>3SG Lise asked Mads to sit down.
Atuartoq atuarfimmut aggerpoq. atuar-toq atuarfim-mut agger-poq study-IP school-ALL come-3SG The student is coming to school.	**Ilinniartitsisup atuartoq atuarfimmut aggersarpaa.** ilinniartitsisu-p atuar-toq atuarfim-mut agger-sar-paa teacher-REL study-IP school-ALL come-try.to.make-3SG>3SG The teacher is trying to make the student come to school.

The use of the causative suffixes is illustrated in the following examples.

Ilinniartut kalaallisut oqaluttippakka.
ilinniartu-t kalaallisut oqalut-tip-pakka
student-PL greenlandic speak-cause-1SG>3PL
I am getting the students to speak Greenlandic.

Fjernsynimik isiginnaarteqqippaatit.
fjernsyni-mik isiginnaar-te-qqip-paatit
television-INS watch-cause-again-3SG>2SG
S/he is making you watch television again.

Niviugak anisippat.
niviugak ani-sip-pat
fly go.out-cause-2SG>3SG
You are making the fly go out.

Perorsaanermik Ilinniarfiup ilinniartuni ilinniartitsisullu angerlartippaat.
perorsaaner-mik ilinniarfiu-p ilinniartu-ni ilinniartitsisu-l-lu angerlar-tip-paat
pedagogy-INS institute-REL student-4SG teacher-PL-and go.home-cause-3PL>3PL
The Institute of Education has sent their students and teachers home.

Nakorsap ullumi aggeqquaa.
nakorsaq-p ullumi agge-qqu-aa
doctor-REL today come-invite-3SG>3SG
The doctor asked him/her to come today.

Suliffeqarfiup sulisoq tunumut suliartoqquaa.
suliffeqarfiu-p sulisoq tunu-mut suliarto-qqu-aa
employer-REL employee east-ALL go.to.work-cause-3SG>3SG
The employer made the employee go to work in East Greenland.

Ataatap itersajaarpaanga.
ataata-p iter-sa-jaar-paanga
dad-REL wake.up-cause-early-3SG>1SG
Dad woke me up early.

There is a special suffix, +**narpoq**, which is used specifically to indicate that something (usually a situation or impersonal entity such as work or the weather) causes someone to feel a physical or emotional sensation. The subject is typically the third-person singular, referring to the entity causing the sensation. The use of this suffix is illustrated in the following table.

Base verb	Verb with +**narpoq**
qasuvoq to be tired	**qasunarpoq** to be tiring
kissappoq to become warm	**kissannarpoq** to be warming
mamiagaa to be angry about it	**mamianarpoq** to be annoying, to be infuriating, to be shocking, to make one annoyed

Sulineq assut qasunarpoq.
suli-neq assut qasu-nar-poq
work-AP be.tired-cause-3SG
Work is very tiring.

Illup akia mamianarpoq.
illu-p aki-a mamia-nar-poq
house-REL price-3SG be.angry-cause-3SG
The price of the house is shocking.

7.8 Reflexivity and reciprocity

7.8.1 Reflexivity

Reflexive verbs can be formed by taking a causative or valency suffix (as discussed in 7.7 and 7.10) and replacing the transitive ending with an intransitive ending. Some of the reflexive verbal suffixes are shown in the following table.

Reflexive suffix	English translation
+tarpoq, **+sarpoq**	to make oneself do something
+tippoq, **+sippoq**	to make oneself do something
-ssippoq	to give something to oneself; to get something for oneself
+lerpoq	to get something for oneself
+/-uppoq, **-appoq**	to do something with/for oneself

Points to note:

- The variants +tippoq and +tarpoq are used with consonant-stem and r-stem verbs, whereas the variants +sippoq and +sarpoq are used with vowel-stem verbs and with verbs that historically ended in -i.
- The variant +/-uppoq can be used with verbal stems ending in -i, a consonant, or -r.
- The variant -appoq can be used with verbal stems ending in -a, a consonant, or -r.
- The choice of variant +/-uppoq or -appoq can be somewhat unpredictable, so it may be best to learn each verb individually.

The following examples illustrate the use of these reflexive suffixes. See also section 4.4 for discussion of reflexive pronouns.

Transitive or causative verb	Verb with reflexive suffix
Piareersarpakka.	**Piareersarpunga.**
piareer-sar-pakka	piareer-sar-poq
get.ready-cause-1SG>3PL	get.ready-cause-3SG
I got them ready.	I got myself ready.
Qimmeq nerisippara.	**Nerisippunga.**
qimmeq neri-sip-para	neri-sip-punga
dog eat-cause-1SG>3SG	eat-cause-1SG
I am feeding the dog.	I am feeding myself.
Illussippavut.	**Illussippugut.**
illu-ssip-pavut	illu-ssip-pugut
house-get-1PL>3SG	house-get-1PL
We got them a house.	We got ourselves a house.
Tupalerpara.	**Tupalerpunga.**
tupa-ler-para	tupa-ler-punga
tobacco-get-1SG>3SG	tobacco-get-1SG
I got him/her tobacco.	I got myself tobacco.

7.8.2 Reciprocity

Reciprocal action can be indicated in West Greenlandic by taking a normally transitive verb and replacing the transitive suffix with an intransitive plural suffix, as illustrated in the following examples.

Transitive verb	Reciprocal verb
naapippaa to meet him/her/it	**naapipput** to meet each other

The following suffixes can also mark reciprocity.

Reciprocal suffix	Example
+/-upput, -apput	**kamappoq** s/he is angry > **kamaapput** they are angry at each other
-qatigiipput	**allappoq** s/he writes > **allaqatigiippugut** they write to each other

Points to note:

- The suffix +/-**upput**, +**apput** is the plural of the reflexive suffix +/-**uppoq**, +**appoq** discussed in 7.8.1.
- The variant +/-**upput** can be used with verbal stems ending in -i, a consonant, or -r.
- The variant -**apput** can be used with verbal stems ending in -a, a consonant, or -r.
- The choice of variant +/-**upput** or -**apput** can be somewhat unpredictable, so it may be best to learn each verb individually.

See also section 4.5 for discussion of reciprocal pronouns and further discussion of reciprocal suffixes.

7.9 Passivity

Passive sentences are those in which the subject of the verb is the one to which the action of the verb is done, e.g. 'the news was read', 'the food has been cooked', etc. West Greenlandic conveys passive meaning by adding a passive suffix to a verbal stem. Like other West Greenlandic verbal suffixes, passive suffixes can be used with all different verbal moods and in combination with other verbal suffixes (e.g. aspectual suffixes, causative suffixes, modal suffixes, tense suffixes, etc.). The chief passive suffix in West Greenlandic is +**neqarpoq**, meaning 'to be ...ed'. This suffix is marked by the abbreviation PASS in the glossing.

Active clause	Passive clause
Illu sanavaa.	**Illu sananeqarpoq.**
illu sana-vaa	illu sana-neqar-poq
house build-3SG>3SG	house make-PASS-3SG
S/he is building the house.	The house is being built.
Sanasup illu sanavaa.	**Illu sanasumit sananeqarpoq.**
sanasu-p illu sana-vaa	illu sanasu-mit sana-neqar-poq
builder-REL house build-3SG>3SG	house builder-ABL make-PASS-3SG
The builder is building the house.	The house is being built by the builder.

7 Verbs

Points to note:

- The subject of a passive sentence is in the absolutive case.
- If the passive sentence has an agent (i.e. someone performing the passive action), the agent is in the ablative case.

The use of the passive suffix +neqarpoq is illustrated here.

Allagarsiaq nassiunneqarpoq.
allagarsiaq nassiun-neqar-poq
letter send-PASS-3SG
The letter is sent.

Nuummi piniartut aalisartullu peqatigiiffiat aallartinneqarpoq.
nuum-mi piniartu-t aalisartu-l-lu peqatigiiffi-at aallartin-neqar-poq.
nuuk-LOC hunter-PL fisherman-PL-and association-3PL start-PASS-3SG
The hunters' and fishermen's association in Nuuk has been started.

Meeqqat illersuisuat aamma oqalugiartussatut qaaqquneqarsimavoq.
meeqqa-t illersuisu-at aamma oqalugiar-tu-ssa-tut qaaqqu-neqar-sima-voq
child-PL protector-3PL also give.a.speech-IP-FUT-EQU invite-PASS-PAST-3SG
The child protection officer was also invited to give a speech.

Suliassaq Folketingimi suliarineqarpoq.
suliassaq folketing-i-mi suliari-neqar-poq
matter folketing-HV-LOC work.with-PASS-3SG
The matter is being handled in the Folketing (the Danish parliament).

Kangerlussuaq amerikarmiut sakkutooqarfiattut 1941-mi tunngavilerneqarpoq.
kangerlussuaq amerikarmiu-t sakkutooqarfi-attut 1941-mi tunngaviler-neqar-poq
kangerlussuaq american-PL military.base-EQU.3PL 1941-LOC found-PASS-3SG
Kangerlussuaq was founded in 1941 as an American military base.

Saviit qinngutillu tunilluarneqarput.
savi-it qinnguti-l-lu tuni-lluar-neqar-put
knife-PL binocular-PL-and sell-well-PASS-3PL
The knives and binoculars have sold well.[7]

---

7 Literally: have been sold well.

Nunarsuami qeqertat annersaat eqqornerusumik assiliorneqassaaq.
nunarsua-mi qeqarta-t annersa-at eqqor-ner-u-su-mik assi-lior-neqa-ssaaq
world-LOC island-PL biggest.one-3PL precise-COMP-be-IP-INS picture-make-PASS-FUT.3SG
The world's biggest island is to be mapped more precisely.

Umiarsualivik pisortatigoortumik ammaanersiorneqarpoq.
umiarsualivik pisortatigoortu-mik ammaanersior-neqar-poq
harbour official-INS inaugurate-PASS-3SG
The harbour has now been officially inaugurated.

There are also a number of other suffixes that can have a passive interpretation in some cases. The most common of these are shown in the following table.

Passive suffix	English translation
+tippoq	to be done
+qqusaavoq	to be allowed to do something
+simavoq	to have been done
+tariaqarpoq, +sariaqarpoq	ought to be done

Points to note:

- The suffix **+tippoq** is actually the intransitive version of the causative suffix **+tippaa** 'to make someone do something' discussed in section 7.7. This intransitive variant is used as a passive in colloquial contexts.
- The suffix **+qqusaavoq** is derived from the causative suffix **+qquaa** 'to ask someone to do something' discussed in section 7.7.
- The suffix **+simavoq** is one of the past tense suffixes discussed in section 7.3.2.2. When attached to a verbal stem that is normally transitive, it takes on a passive meaning, e.g. **ulippaa** 'to cover (something)' > **ulissimavoq** 'it was covered'.
- The suffix **+tariaqarpoq/+sariaqarpoq** is one of the modal suffixes discussed in section 7.5. When attached to a verbal stem that is normally transitive, it takes on a passive meaning, e.g. **ikiorpaa** 'to help (someone)' > **ikiortariaqarpoq** 's/he ought to be helped'.
- The variant **+tariaqarpoq** is used with consonant-stem and r-stem verbs, while the variant **+sariaqarpoq** is used with vowel-stem verbs as well as with verbs that historically ended in -i.

The use of these suffixes is illustrated in the following examples.

Meeraq aatippoq.
meeraq aa-tip-poq
child pick.up-cause-3SG
The child was picked up.

Nuka, aatissaatit.
nuka aa-ti-ssaatit
Nuka pick.up-cause-FUT.2SG
Nuka, you'll be picked up.

Illumi pujortaqqusaavoq.
illu-mi pujorta-qqusaa-voq
house-LOC smoke-be.allowed-3SG
S/he is allowed to smoke in the house.

Biilit apummit ulissimapput.
biili-t apum-mit ulis-sima-pput
car-PL snow-ABL cover-PAST-3PL
The car is covered in snow.

Utoqqaq angerlarsimaannaqqusaasoq ikiortariaqarpoq.
utoqqaq angerlarsimaannaqqusaa-soq ikior-tariaqar-poq
elderly.person quarantine-IP help-ought.to.be-3SG
The elderly person who is in quarantine ought to be helped.

In addition to the suffixes outlined, the passive participle -aq/-gaq/-raq/-taq/-saq can also be used to form passive verbs. The West Greenlandic passive participle is a suffix that can be attached to verbal stems to create forms with a meaning equivalent to English passive participle constructions such as 'baked potato', 'woven fabric', 'a closed door', etc. See section 8.2 for more detailed discussion of the passive participle. The passive participle is used in conjunction with the verb -avoq 'to be' (see section 14.2) to form passive verbal constructions. This type of passive is illustrated in the following examples. Note that the passive participle is marked by the abbreviation PP in the glossing.

Tillinniaq paasisaavoq.
tillinniaq paasi-sa-a-voq
thief identify-PP-be-3SG
The thief has been identified.

Kommuneqarfik Sermersuumi borgermesteritut qinigaavoq.
kommuneqarfik sermersuu-mi borgermesteri-tut qini-ga-a-voq
municipality sermersooq-LOC mayor-EQU elect-PP-be-3SG
S/he was elected as the mayor of Sermersooq municipality.

Qimmeq tammarsimasoq <u>ujagaavoq</u>.
qimmeq tammar-sima-soq uja-ga-a-voq
dog go.missing-PAST-IP look.for-PP-be-3SG
The missing dog is being looked for.

Inissiaq <u>akigisaangajalerpoq</u>.
inissiaq akigi-sa-a-ngaja-ler-poq
flat sell-PP-be-soon-FUT-3SG
The flat will be sold soon.

7.10 Valency

The term valency refers to the number of participants (subjects and objects) in a sentence. For example, the English sentence 'I read' has only one participant (the subject), whereas 'I read the book' has two participants (the subject and the direct object), and 'I read the book to the children' has three participants (the subject, the direct object, and the indirect object). In West Greenlandic, a change in valency (i.e. an increase or decrease in the number of participants) can be changed by means of verbal suffixes. The valency-changing suffixes are all marked by the abbreviation VAL in the glossing.

Some of the most common valency-changing suffixes are shown and exemplified in the following table. They are always transitive, and all serve to add a direct object to the clause.

Valency-changing suffix	Verb	Verb with valency-changing suffix
+figaa	**oqarpoq** to say	**oqarfigaa** to say something to him/her
	iserpoq to enter	**iserfigaa** to enter it
+/-atigaa, +tigaa, +utigaa	**oqarpoq** to say	**oqaatigaa** to tell it
	nalunaarpoq to announce	**nalunaarutigaa** to announce it

Points to note:

- The forms +figaa and +tigaa (and their variants) are contracted versions of +figivaa and +tigivaa (and their variants).

- The variant **+atigaa** is used after -a. The variant **+utigaa** is used after r stems as well as after -i and -u. The variant **-atigaa** is sometimes used after r stems. It can be difficult to predict when an r-stem verb will take -atigaa and when +utigaa, so each instance must be learnt individually.
- The variant **+tigaa** can cause gemination in the preceding consonant, e.g. **maalavoq** 'to moan' > **maallatigaa** 'to complain about it'. Such instances must be learnt individually.
- The long versions are not used very often in the modern language, but their forms can sometimes be encountered; their conjugation is regular, e.g. 2SG>1SG **+figivarma**.
- The short forms have a slightly irregular conjugation, like the shortened future suffix **-ssaaq** discussed in section 7.3.3.1. The conjugation of the short forms is shown next.

The conjugation of **+figaa** is shown in the following tables. The conjugation of **+tigaa** follows the same pattern.

Subject	Object					
	1SG	1PL	2SG	2PL	3SG	3PL
1SG	–	–	+figaakkit	+figaassi	+figaara	+figaakka
2SG	+figaarma	+figaatsigut	–	–	+figaat	+figaatit
3SG	+figaanga	+figaatigut	+figaatit	+figaasi	+figaa	+figai
1PL	–	–	+figaatsigit	+figassi	+figaarput	+figaavut
2PL	+figaassinga	+figaatsigut	–	–	+figaarsi	+figaasi
3PL	+figaannga	+figaatigut	+figaatsit	+figaasi	+figaat	+figaat

Transitive indicative suffix **+figaa**

Point to note:

- The contracted forms of the interrogative are the same as those of the indicative except for 2SG>3SG **+figaajuk**, 2SG>3PL **+figaagit**, 2PL>3SG **+figaasiuk**, and 2PL>3PL **+figaasigit**.

	Transitive imperative suffix +**figaa**			
Subject	Object			
	1SG	1PL	3SG	3PL
2SG	**+figinga**	**+figitigut**	**+figiuk**	**+figigit**
2PL	**+figisinga**	**+figisigut**	**+figisiuk**	**+figisigit**

Point to note:

- Some of the endings shown here are identical to the standard transitive imperative endings shown in 7.2.1.3.2, but others are slightly different.

Points to note about these suffixes in the remaining moods:

- The contracted forms of the optative for these suffixes are formed predictably by attaching the relevant vowel-stem transitive endings to +figi- or +tigi-.
- The contracted forms of the contemporative for these suffixes are formed predictably by attaching the relevant r-stem transitive endings to +figa- or +tiga-.

There is a third suffix with a similar meaning to +figaa and +tigaa, as shown in the following table.

Valency-changing suffix	Verb	Verb with valency-changing suffix
+/-uppaa, -appaa	**tikippoq** to arrive	**tikiuppaa** to arrive with it

Points to note:

- The variant +/-uppaa can be used with verbal stems ending in -i, a consonant, or -r.
- The variant -appaa can be used with verbal stems ending in -a, a consonant, or -r.
- The choice of variant can be somewhat unpredictable, so it may be best to learn each verb individually.

When one of these valency suffixes is added to an intransitive verb with an indirect object marked by an oblique case, the verb becomes transitive, so that the indirect object (in an oblique case) becomes a direct object (in the absolutive case) and the subject changes from the absolutive case to the relative case (as is standard in transitive clauses). These contrasts are illustrated in the following table. Note that both constructions have the same meaning despite the grammatical differences.

Basic verb	Verb with valency suffix
Qimmeq sofamut nallarpoq.	**Qimmip sofa nallarfigaa.**
qimmeq sofa-mut nallar-poq	qimmi-p sofa nallar-figaa
dog sofa-ALL lie.down-3SG	dog-REL sofa lie.down-VAL.3SG>3SG
The dog lies down on the sofa.	The dog lies down on the sofa.

These valency-changing suffixes are illustrated in the following examples.

Kisimiikkami qitsuk <u>oqaluffigisarpaa</u>.
kisimiik-kami qitsuk oqaluf-figi-sar-paa
be.alone-CAUS.4SG cat speak-VAL-HAB-3SG>3SG
Because s/he is alone, s/he speaks to the cat.

Unammineq Finlandip 4–6-mik <u>ajugaaffigaa</u>.
unammineq finlandi-p 4–6-mik ajugaa-ffigaa
match finland-REL 4–6-INS beat-VAL.3SG>3SG
Finland won the match 4–6.

Allakkat timmisartukkut <u>nassiuppai</u>.
allakka-t timmisartu-kkut nassi-up-pai
letter-PL airplane-PRO send-VAL-3SG>3PL
S/he sent the letter(s) via airmail.

Some suffixes can be attached to a transitive verb in order to change the object from a specific one ('him/her/it') to an unspecified one, i.e. 'someone', 'something'. The most common of these are listed and illustrated in the following table. The first two of these suffixes are more commonly used than the third.

Valency-changing suffix	Verb	Verb with valency-changing suffix
+sivoq	**tikiuppaa** to arrive with it	**tikiussivoq** to arrive with something
+ivoq	**atorpaa** to use it	**atuivoq** to use something
+(l)lerpoq	**ujarpaa** to look for it	**ujarlerpoq** to look for something

Points to note:

- This category of valency-changing suffixes always has intransitive endings; the unspecified direct object ('someone' or 'something') is encoded within the suffix and is not expressed elsewhere in the clause.
- These suffixes can be added to a verb that already has a different valency-changing suffix. The first example, **tikiuppaa** 'to arrive with it' > **tikiussivoq** 'to arrive with something', illustrates this.
- The suffix +**sivoq** appears as +**tsivoq** when attached to certain stems, e.g. **ilinniartippaa** 'to teach him/her' > **ilinniartitsivoq** 'to teach someone'.
- The suffix +(l)lerpoq appears as +**lerpoq** following consonant-stems and r-stems, and as +**llerpoq** following vowel stems.

The following examples illustrate this type of suffix.

Umiarsuaq »Eastcoast« Aalborg-imiit Nuummut cementimik tikiussivoq.
umiarsuaq eastcoast aalborg-i-miit nuum-mut cementi-mik tikius-si-voq
ship eastcoast aalborg-HV-ABL nuuk-ALL cementi-INS arrive-VAL-3SG
The ship 'Eastcoast' arrived in Nuuk from Aalborg with cement.

Ukiukkut Nuummiut innaallagissamik assut atuisarput.
ukiu-kkut nuum-miu-t innaallagissa-mik assut atu-i-sar-put
winter-PRO nuuk-resident-PL electricity-INS much use-VAL-HAB-3PL
Nuuk residents use a lot of electricity in the winter.

The suffix +**nnippoq** can be attached to a transitive verb in order to make it intransitive, as illustrated in the following table.

Valency-changing suffix	Verb	Verb with valency-changing suffix
+nnippoq	**isor(iv)aa** to criticise it	**isorinnippoq** to be critical
	ilassivaa to greet him/her/it	**ilassinnippoq** to greet
	eqqaamavaa to remember it	**eqqaamannippoq** to reminisce

The following example illustrates this type of valency-changing suffix.

Kim ukiortaami <u>ilassinnippoq</u>.
kim ukior-taa-mi ilassi-nnip-poq
kim year-new-LOC greet-VAL-3SG
Kim is sending New Year's greetings.

There are also a number of valency-changing suffixes with more restricted meanings or less frequent use. Some of these are listed in the following table. It can be difficult to predict whether these suffixes may be attached to any given verb or what their precise meaning is when found in conjunction with a particular verb. As such, it is best to learn the meaning of each suffixed verb individually.

Valency-changing suffix	Verb	Verb with valency-changing suffix
-ssutigaa	**toquvoq** to die	**toqussutigaa** to die of it
-qqusivoq	**pilluarpoq** to be happy	**pilluaqqusivoq** to congratulate someone
-ssuppaa	**naammassivoq** to get ready	**naammassissuppaa** to get it ready for him/her/it

Point to note:

- The suffix -**ssutigaa** conjugates like +**figaa**/+**tigaa**, as discussed previously.

The following example illustrates this type of suffix.

Naalakkersuisoqarfiup <u>sulissutigaa</u>.
naalakkersuisoqarfi-up suli-ssutigaa
self.rule.government-REL work-VAL.3SG>3SG
The Greenlandic Self Rule Government is working on it.

7.11 Negation

7.11.1 Basic negative suffixes

Verbs are made negative in West Greenlandic by attaching a verbal suffix to the stem of a verb or to a verbal suffix. The basic form of the negative suffix is -**nngi(t)**-. The negative suffix conjugates for person and number. As in the case of affirmative verbs, there are different forms of the negative suffix depending on whether it is attached to an intransitive or transitive verb. Similarly, there are different forms of the negative suffix for the different verbal moods. However, all stem types take the same negative suffixes. Each set of negative forms is presented in the following sections in turn. Note that the negative suffixes are marked with the abbreviation NEG in the glossing.

Negation

7.11.1.1 Indicative

7.11.1.1.1 INTRANSITIVE

The following shows the negative intransitive indicative suffix forms.

Negative intransitive indicative suffixes	
1SG	-nngilanga
2SG	-nngilatit
3SG	-nngilaq
1PL	-nngilugut
2PL	-nngilasi
3PL	-nngillat

Points to note:

- The negative endings are very similar to their affirmative counterparts (e.g. negative 1SG -nngi<u>langa</u> vs. affirmative 1SG -pu<u>nga</u>).
- These endings can be added predictably to all stem types, e.g. **nerivunga** 'I eat' > **nerinngilanga** 'I don't eat'; **sinippunga** 'I sleep' > **sininngilanga** 'I don't sleep'; **atuarpunga** 'I read' > **atuanngilanga** 'I don't read'. The negative endings are truncative, so consonant- and vowel-stem verbs lose the final letter of their stem.

The following examples illustrate the use of the negative intransitive indicative suffixes.

Festimut aggilinngilanga.
festi-mut aggi-li-nngi-langa
part-ALL come-FUT-NEG-1SG
I'm not going to the party.

Ullumi tamaani nerinianngillat.
ullumi tamaani neri-nia-nngi-llat
today here eat-be.going.to-NEG-3PL
They are not going to eat here today.

7 Verbs

Ajunngilaq.
aju-nngi-laq
be.bad-NEG-3SG
It's good.

Akeqanngilaq.
ake-qa-nngi-laq
cost-have-NEG-3SG
It's free.[8]

Atuagaq tamaat atuartariaqanngilaq.
atuagaq tamaat atuar-tariaqa-nngi-laq
book whole read-have.to-NEG-3SG
One doesn't have to read the whole book.

Ataataqanngilatit.
ataata-qa-nngi-latit
father-have-NEG-2SG
You don't have a father.

Argentinamut håndboldimik ajugaaneq puiorneqassanngilaq.
argentina-mut håndboldi-mik ajugaaneq puior-neqa-ssa-nngi-laq.
argentina-ALL handball-INS victory forget-PASS-FUT-NEG-3SG
The handball victory over Argentina will not be forgotten about.

Angerlarsimaffimmi ikiortit torersaajumanngillat.
angerlarsimaffim-mi ikiorti-t torersaa-juma-nngi-llat
home-LOC assistant-PL clean-want-NEG-3PL
Home care assistants don't want to clean.

7.11.1.1.2 TRANSITIVE

The following table contains the negative transitive indicative suffixes.

Subject	Negative transitive indicative suffixes					
	Object					
	1SG	1PL	2SG	2PL	3SG	3PL
1SG	–	–	-nngilakkit	-nngilassi	-nngilara	-nngilakka
2SG	-nngilarma	-nngilatsigut	–	–	-nngilat	-nngilatit
3SG	-nngilaanga	-nngilaatigut	-nngilaatit	-nngilaasi	-nngilaa	-nngilai
1PL	–	–	-nngilatsigit	-nngilassi	-nngilarput	-nngilavut
2PL	-nngilassinga	-nngilatsigut	–	–	-nngilarsi	-nngilasi
3PL	-nngilaannga	-nngilaatigut	-nngilaatsit	-nngilaasi	-nngilaat	

---

8 Literally: there is no cost.

Points to note:

- The negative transitive indicative endings are the same as their affirmative counterparts, e.g. negative 2SG>1SG -**nngi**<u>arma</u> vs. affirmative 2SG>1SG +(p/v)<u>arma</u>.
- These endings can be added predictably to verbs of all stem types.

The use of the negative transitive indicative suffixes is illustrated in the following examples.

Qitsuk <u>takusinnaanngilara</u>.
qitsuk taku-sinnaa-nngi-lara
cat see-be.able-NEG-1SG>3SG
I can't see the cat.

Matu parnaaqqammat <u>isersinnaanngilasi</u>.
matu parnaa-qqa-mmat iser-sinnaa-nngi-lasi
door lock-be.in.a.state.of-CAUS.3SG enter-be.able-NEG-2PL>3SG
You can't come in because the door is locked.

Atisasi <u>qimanngilavut</u>.
atisa-si qima-nngi-lavut
clothing-PL.2PL forget-NEG.1PL>3PL
We haven't forgotten your clothes.

Navaranap atuakkat <u>nassanngilai</u>.
navarana-p atuakka-t nassa-nngi-lai
navarana-REL book-PL bring-NEG-3SG>3PL
Navarana didn't bring the books.

Naalakkersuisut akileraarutit <u>qaffassanngilai</u>.
naalakkersuisu-t akileraaruti-t qaffa-ssa-nngi-lai
greenlandic.government-PL tax-PL raise-FUT-NEG-3SG>3PL
The Greenlandic government is not going to raise taxes.

| 7.11.1.2 | Interrogative |

| 7.11.1.2.1 | INTRANSITIVE |

The following table illustrates the negative intransitive interrogative suffixes.

7 Verbs

Negative intransitive interrogative suffixes	
1SG	-nngilanga?
2SG	-nngilatit?
3SG	-nngila?
1PL	-nngilugut?
2PL	-nngilasi?
3PL	-nngillat?

Point to note:

- The negative intransitive interrogative suffixes are all the same as the negative intransitive indicative suffixes except for the 3SG form.

The examples here illustrate the use of the negative intransitive interrogative suffixes.

Kaffisunngilatit?
kaffi-su-nngi-latit
coffee-consume-NEG-INT.2SG
Didn't you drink coffee?

Erruiguma ajunngila?
errui-guma aju-nngi-la
do.the.dishes-CAUS.1SG be.bad-NEG-INT.3SG
Is okay if I do the dishes?

Qiianngilasi?
qiia-nngi-lasi
be.cold-NEG-INT.2PL
Were you not cold?

Meeqqat suli sinilinngillat?
meeqqa-t suli sinili-nngi-llat
child-PL still fall.asleep-NEG-INT.3PL
Have the children still not fallen asleep?

7.11.1.2.2 TRANSITIVE

The following table illustrates the negative transitive interrogative suffixes.

Subject	Object					
	1SG	1PL	2SG	2PL	3SG	3PL
1SG	–	–	-nngilakkit?	-nngilassi?	-nngilara?	-nngilakka?
2SG	-nngilinga?	-nngilisigut?	–	–	-nngiliuk?	-nngiligit?
3SG	-nngilaanga?	-nngilaatigut?	-nngilaatit?	-nngilaasi?	-nngilaa?	-nngilai?
1PL	–	–	-nngilatsigit?	-nngilassi?	-nngilarput?	-nngilavut?
2PL	-nngilisinga?	-nngilisigut?	–	–	-nngilisiuk?	-nngilisigit?
3PL	-nngilaannga?	-nngilaatigut?	-nngilaatsit?	-nngilaasi?	-nngilaat?	

Point to note:

- The forms shaded in grey differ from their indicative counterparts. The remaining forms are the same as their indicative counterparts.

The negative transitive interrogative suffixes are illustrated in the following examples.

Nassiutinngiliuk?
nassiuti-nngi-liuk
send-NEG-INT.2SG>3SG
Did you not send it?

Biilit takunngilisigit?
biili-t taku-nngi-lisigit
car-PL see-NEG-INT.2PL>3PL
Did you not see the car?

Ilinniartitsisut tamaani ajorinngiligit?
ilinniartitsisu-t tamaani ajori-nngi-ligit
teacher-PL here dislike-NEG-INT.2SG>3PL
Do you like the teachers here?[9]

7.11.1.3 Imperative

7.11.1.3.1 INTRANSITIVE

The following table shows the negative intransitive imperative suffixes.

Negative intransitive imperative suffixes	
2SG	+nak
1PL	+nata
2PL	+nasi

The use of the intransitive negative imperative suffixes is illustrated next. Note that the first-person plural form is not used often, except with children and official messages.

Nerivallaarnak!
neri-vallaar-nak
eat-too.much-NEG.IMP.2SG
Don't eat too much!

Illup iluani arpannak.
illu-p iluani arpan-nak
house-REL inside run-NEG.IMP.2SG
Don't run inside the house.

Aliasunnata!
aliasun-nata
be.sad-NEG.IMP.1PL
Let us not be sad!

Imerpallaarnata!
imer-pallaar-nata
drink-too.much-NEG.IMP.1PL
Let's not drink too much!

9 Literally: do you not dislike the teachers here?

Taakkunnarnata!
taakkunnar-nata
go.there-NEG.IMP.1PL
Let's not go there!

Meeqqat, qianasi!
meeqqa-t qia-nasi
child-PL cry-NEG.IMP.2PL
Children, don't cry!

Nipituumik oqalunnasi!
nipituumik oqalun-nasi
loudly speak-NEG.IMP.2PL
Don't speak loudly!

7.11.1.3.2 TRANSITIVE

The following table shows the negative transitive imperative suffixes.

Subject	Negative transitive imperative suffixes			
	Object			
	1SG	1PL	3SG	3PL
2SG	+nanga	+natigut	+nagu	+nagit
1PL	–	–	+natigu	+natigit
2PL	+nasinga	+natigut	+nasiuk	+nasigit

Point to note:

- In r-stem verbs with a plural subject, as well as the 2SG>1PL, the **n-** may sometimes be omitted from the beginning of the suffix, e.g. **ikior(n) asiuk** 'don't help him'.

The use of the negative transitive imperative suffixes is illustrated in the following examples.

Matu matunagu!
matu matu-nagu
door close-NEG.IMP.2SG>3SG
Don't close the door!

7 Verbs

Qimmit anisinnagit!
qimmi-t ani-sin-nagit
dog-PL out-let-NEG.IMP.2SG>3PL
Don't let the dogs out!

Filmi nakunasiuk!
filmi taku-nasiuk
film see-NEG.IMP.2PL>3SG
Don't watch the film!

Aningaasat tigunatigit!
aningaasa-t tigu-natigit
money-PL take-NEG.IMP.1PL>3PL
Let's not take the money!

7.11.1.4 Optative

7.11.1.4.1 INTRANSITIVE

The following table shows the negative intransitive optative suffixes.

	Negative intransitive optative suffixes
3SG	-nngikkili
3PL	-nngikkilit

The use of the negative intransitive optative suffixes is illustrated in the following examples. These forms are largely restricted to archaic contexts such as the Bible.

Nunarsuarmi sorsunneqanngikkili.
nunarsuar-mi sorsunne-qa-nngikkili
earth-LOC war-have-NEG.OPT.3SG
Let there not be war on Earth.

Inuit tamarmik ajunngikkilit.
inu-it tamarmik aju-nngikkilit
person-PL all be.bad-NEG.OPT.3PL
Let all people be well.

7.11.1.4.2 TRANSITIVE

The following table shows the negative transitive optative suffixes.

Negative transitive optative suffixes		
Subject	Object	
	3SG	3PL
3SG	**-nngikkiliuk**	**-nngikkiligit**

Point to note:

- The transitive optative is quite rare and is limited to this small number of forms.

The following examples illustrate the use of the negative transitive optative. As in the case of the intransitive, it is largely restricted to archaic contexts.

Kunngip inuiaqatigiit naqisimanngikkiligit.
kunngi-p inuiaqatigii-t naqisimaneqa-nngikkiligit
king-REL citizen-PL oppress-NEG.OPT.3SG>3PL
Let the king not oppress the people.

Iffiaq nerinngikkiliuk.
iffiaq neri-nngikkiliuk
bread eat-NEG.OPT.3SG>3SG
Let him/her not eat the bread.

7.11.1.5 Causative

7.11.1.5.1 INTRANSITIVE

The following table shows the negative intransitive causative suffixes.

Negative intransitive causative suffixes	
1SG	**-nnginnama**
2SG	**-nnginnavit**
3SG	**-nngimmat**
4SG	**-nnginnami**
1PL	**-nnginnatta**
2PL	**-nnginnassi**
3PL	**-nngimmata**
4PL	**-nnginnamik**

7 Verbs

The following illustrates the use of the negative intransitive causative suffixes.

Nerinnginnama kaappunga.
neri-nnginnama kaap-punga
eat-NEG.CAUS.1SG be.hungry-1SG
I'm hungry because I didn't eat.

Aninnginnassi niaqorluppusi.
ani-nnginnassi niaqorlup-pusi
go.out-NEG.CAUS.2PL have.a.headache-2PL
You guys have a headache because you didn't go out.

Sininnginnami isumaluppoq.
sini-nnginnami isumalup-poq
sleep-NEG.CAUS.4SG be.in.a.bad.mood-3SG
S/he is in a bad mood because s/he didn't sleep.

7.11.1.5.2 TRANSITIVE

The following table shows the negative transitive causative suffixes.

Subject	Negative transitive causative suffixes — Object							
	1SG	1PL	2SG	2PL	3SG	3PL	4SG	4PL
1SG	–	–	-nnginnakkit	-nnginnassi	-nnginnakku	-nnginnakkit	-nnginnanni	-nnginnatsik
2SG	-nnginnamma	-nnginnatisigut	–	–	-nnginnakku	-nnginnakkit	-nnginnanni	-nnginnatsik
3SG	-nnginnanga	-nnginnatigut	-nnginnatit	-nnginnasi	-nnginnagu	-nnginnagit	-nnginnani	-nnginnatik
4SG	-nnginnaminga	-nnginnamisigut	-nnginnamisit	-nnginnamisi	-nnginnamiuk	-nnginnamigit	–	–
1PL	–	–	-nnginnatsigit	-nnginnassi	-nnginnatsigu	-nnginnatsigit	-nnginnatsinni	-nnginnatsik
2PL	-nnginnassinga	-nnginnatsigut	–	–	-nnginnassiuk	-nnginnassigit	-nnginnassinni	-nnginnatsik
3PL	-nnginnannga	-nnginnamitigut	-nnginnatsit	-nnginnasi	-nnginnassuk	-nnginnatigit	-nnginnanni	-nnginnatik
4PL	-nnginnaminnga	-nnginnamisigut	-nnginnamitsit	-nnginnamisi	-nnginnamikku	-nnaginnamikkit	–	–

The following examples illustrate the use of the negative transitive causative suffixes.

Aliasuppunga takunnginnakkit.
aliasup-punga taku-nnginnakkit
be.sad-1SG see-NEG.CAUS.1SG>2SG
I am sad because I didn't see you.

Illuga akigisinnaannginnakku aningaasanik ajornartorsiorpunga. Negation
illu-ga akigi-sinnaa-nnginnakku aningaasa-nik ajornartorsior-punga
house-1SG sell-be.able-NEG.CAUS.1SG>3SG economic-INS.PL have.problems-1SG
I had economic problems because I couldn't sell my house.

Qimalerpakkit asannginnamma.
qima-ler-pakkit asa-nnginnamma
leave-FUT-1SG>2SG love-NEG.CAUS.2SG>1SG
I'm going to leave you because you don't love me.

Isersinnaanngilanga matuersaat tunniutinnginnakku.
iser-sinnaa-nngi-langa matuersaat tunniu-ti-nnginnakku
enter-be.able-NEG.1SG key(s) give-VAL-NEG.CAUS.2SG>3SG
I couldn't go in because you didn't give me the key.

7.11.1.6 Conditional

7.11.1.6.1 INTRANSITIVE

The following table shows the negative intransitive conditional suffixes.

	Negative intransitive conditional suffixes
1SG	-nngikkuma
2SG	-nngikkuit
3SG	-nngippat
4SG	-nngikkuni
1PL	-nngikkutta
2PL	-nngikkussi
3PL	-nngippata
4PL	-nngikkunik

The following examples illustrate the use of negative intransitive conditional suffixes. Note that the negative conditional forms are used mostly in warnings and life advice.

Sininngikkuit ullaakkut artorsassaatit.
sini-nngikkuit ullaakkut artorsa-ssa-atit
sleep-NEG.COND.2SG in.the.morning struggle-FUT-2SG
If you don't sleep you'll struggle in the morning.

Nerinngikkussi allinavianngilasi.
neri-nngikkussi alli-navianngilasi
eat-NEG.COND.2SG grow-absolutely.NEG.2SG
If you don't eat you certainly won't grow.

Fjernsynerpallaanngikkuit suliaqarluarsinnaavutit.
fjernsyner-pallaa-nngikkuit suliaqar-luar-sinnaa-vutit
tv.watch-too.much-NEG.COND.2SG>3SG work-well-be.able-2SG
If you don't watch too much TV, you can achieve more.

Kigutigissanngikkuit aassapput.
kigutigissa-nngikkuit aa-ssa-pput
brush.teeth-NEG.COND.2SG melt-FUT-3PL
If you don't brush your teeth, they will rot.[10]

Negative conditional clauses can also be translated by English constructions beginning with 'unless'. Negative conditionals with this type of meaning can be used in a wider range of contexts than warnings and life advice, as shown in the following example. Context will generally distinguish a negative conditional with the sense of 'unless' from other negative conditional constructions.

Ataata sulinngikkuni piniassaaq.
ataata suli-nngikkuni pinia-ssaaq
father work-NEG.COND.4SG hunt-FUT.3SG
Unless father is working, he'll be hunting.

7.11.1.6.2 TRANSITIVE

The negative transitive conditional suffixes are illustrated in the following table.

Subject	Object							
	1SG	1PL	2SG	2PL	3SG	3PL	4SG	4PL
1SG	–	–	+nngikkukkit	+nngikkussi	+nngikkukku	+nngikkukkit	+nngikkunni	+nngikkutsik
2SG	+nngikkumma	+nngikkutsigut	–	–	+nngikkukku	+nngikkukkit	+nngikkunni	+nngikkutsik
3SG	+nngippanga	+nngippatigut	+nngippatit	+nngippasi	+nngippagu	+nngippagit	+nngippani	+nngippatik
4SG	+nngikkuninga	+nngikkunisigut	+nngikkunisit	+nngikkunisi	+nngikkuniuk	+nngikkunigit	–	–
1PL	–	–	+nngikkutsigit	+nngikkussi	+nngikkutsigu	+nngikkutsigit	+nngikkutsinni	+nngikkutsik
2PL	+nngikkussinga	+nngikkutsigut	–	–	+nngikkussiuk	+nngikkussigit	+nngikkutsinni	+nngikkutsik
3PL	+nngippannga	+nngippatigut	+nngippatsit	+nngippasi	+nngippassuk	+nngippatigit	+nngippanni	+nngippatik
4PL	+nngikkunninnga	+nngikkunisigut	+nngikkunitsit	+nngikkunisi	+nngikkunikku	+nngikkunikkit	–	–

---

10 Literally: melt.

The use of the negative transitive conditional suffixes is shown in the following examples.

Suliassaq <u>naammassinngikkuniuk</u> angusinavianngilaq.
suliassaq naammassi-nngikkuniuk angusi-navianngi-laq
assignment finish-NEG.COND.4SG>3SG pass-absolutely.NEG-3SG
If s/he doesn't finish the assignment, s/he definitely won't pass.

<u>Akilinngippannga</u> allaffigissavakka.
akili-nngippannga allaffigi-ssa-vakka
pay-NEG.COND.3PL>1SG write-FUT-1SG>3PL
If they don't pay me, I'll write to them.

7.11.1.7 Contemporative

7.11.1.7.1 INTRANSITIVE

The following table shows the negative intransitive contemporative suffixes.

Negative intransitive contemporative suffixes	
1SG	+nanga
2SG	+nak
4SG	+nani
1PL	+nata
2PL	+nasi
4PL	+natik

Points to note:

- In r-stem verbs, the initial **n-** may be omitted in the 4SG and all the plural forms. (A similar phenomenon occurs in the negative transitive imperative; see 7.11.1.3.2.)
- These suffixes are the same as the negative intransitive imperative suffixes (see 7.11.1.3.1).

The use of the negative intransitive contemporative is illustrated in the following examples.

Nerinanga innarpunga.
neri-nanga innar-punga
eat-NEG.CONT.1SG go.to.bed-1SG
I went to bed without eating.

Oqorsarnanga aneerpunga.
oqorsar-nanga aneer-punga
have.warm.clothes.on-NEG.CONT.1SG go.out-1SG
I went out without having warm clothes on.

Kaasipap tuaviornani ingerlagami illu tikippaa.
kaasipa-p tuavior-nani ingerla-gami illu tikip-paa
kaasipat-REL hurry-NEG.CONT.4SG walk-CAUS.4SG house arrive-3SG>3SG
Kaasipat walks without hurrying and arrives at the house.

Nissuma qilusoornatik attassinnaasimavaat.
nissu-ma qilusoor-natik attas-sinnaa-sima-vaat
leg-1SG have.cramp-NEG.CONT.4PL keep.going-be.able-PAST-3PL>3SG
My legs could keep it (i.e. the motion, the running) going without cramping.

7.11.1.7.2 TRANSITIVE

The following table shows the negative transitive contemporative suffixes.

Subject	Negative transitive contemporative suffixes							
	Object							
	1SG	1PL	2SG	2PL	3SG	3PL	4SG	4PL
4SG/PL	+nanga	+nata	+nak	+nasi	+nagu	+nagit	+nani	+natik

Point to note:

- In r-stem verbs, the initial **n-** may be omitted with the 4SG object and with the 1PL, 2PL, and 4PL objects. (A similar phenomenon occurs in the negative transitive imperative and in the negative intransitive contemporative; see 7.11.1.3.2 and 7.11.1.7.1 respectively).

The use of the negative transitive contemporative suffixes is illustrated in the following examples.

Ataataga <u>inuulluaqqunagu</u> anivunga.
ataata-ga inuulluaqqu-nagu ani-vunga
father-1SG say.goodbye.to-NEG.CONT.4SG/PL>3SG go.out-1SG
I went out without saying goodbye to my father.

Pisiniarfik qimapparput cola <u>akilernagu</u>.
pisiniarfik qimappar-put cola akiler-nagu
shop leave-3PL coke pay-NEG.CONT.4SG/PL>3SG
We left the shop without paying for the Coke.

Meeqqat angajoqqaatik <u>ilaginagit</u> angerlarsimapput.
meeqqa-t angajoqqaa-tik ilagi-nagit angerlarsima-pput
child-PL parent-PL.3PL be.with-NEG.CONT.4SG/PL>3PL be.at.home-3PL
The children are at home without being with their parents.

Telefoni ilivaa <u>paasitinnata</u> susoqarsimasoq.
telefoni ili-vaa paasitin-nata susoqar-sima-soq
telephone hang.up-3SG>3SG inform-NEG.CONT.4SG/PL>1PL tell-PAST-IP
S/he hung up the phone without telling us what happened.

7.11.1.8 Participial

7.11.1.8.1 INTRANSITIVE

The negative intransitive participial suffixes are shown in the following table.

Negative intransitive participial suffixes	
Subject	Vowel-stem
1SG	**-nngitsunga**
2SG	**-nngitsutit**
3SG	**-nngitsoq**
1PL	**-nngitsugut**
2PL	**-nngitsusi**
3PL	**-nngitsut**

The following example illustrates the use of the negative intransitive participial suffixes.

Tusarpara <u>nerinngitsusi</u>.
tusar-para neri-nngi-tsusi
hear-1SG>3SG eat-NEG-2PL
I heard that you haven't eaten.

7.11.1.8.2 TRANSITIVE

The negative transitive participial suffixes are shown in the following table.

Subject	Object							
	1SG	1PL	2SG	2PL	3SG	3PL	4SG	4PL
1SG	–	–	-nngikkikkit	-nngikkissi	-nngikkiga	-nngikkikka	-nngikkinni	-nngikkitsik
2SG	-nngikkimma	-nngikkitsigut	–	–	-nngikkit	-nngikkitit	-nngikkinni	-nngikkitsik
3SG	-nngikkaanga	-nngikkaatigut	-nngikkaatit	-nngikkaasi	-nngikkaa	-nngikkai	-nngikkaani	-nngikkaatik
1PL	–	–	-nngikkitsigit	-nngikkissi	-nngikkipput	-nngikkivut	-nngikkitsinni	-nngikkitsik
2PL	-nngikkissinga	-nngikkitsigut	–	–	-nngikkissi	-nngikkisi	-nngikkissinni	-nngikkitsik
3PL	-nngikkaannga	-nngikkaatigut	-nngikkaatsit	-nngikkaasi	-nngikkaat	-nngikkaat	-nngikkaanni	-nngikkaatik

The use of the negative transitive participial suffixes is illustrated in the following examples.

<u>Asanngikkit</u> isumaqarpunga.
asa-nngikkit isumaqar-punga
love-NEG.PART.2SG>3SG think-1SG
I think that you don't love him/her.

Anaanaga oqarpoq Najap nanoq <u>takunngikkaa</u>.
anaana-ga oqar-poq naja-p nanoq taku-nngikkaa
mother-1SG speak-3SG naja-REL polar.bear see-NEG.PART.3SG>3SG
My mother said that Naja hadn't seen a polar bear.

7.11.2 Negative suffixes with more specific meanings

In addition to the negative suffixes in the eight West Greenlandic moods detailed in the preceding section, there are also other suffixes that convey more specific types of negative meanings.

Negation

Suffix	Meaning	Example
+junnaarpoq, +gunnaarpoq, -kkunnaarpoq, -runnaarpoq, -unnaarpoq	no longer	**qitippoq** to dance > **qitikkunnaarpoq** no longer dances
-juippoq, -uippoq	never	**napparpoq** to be sick > **nappajuippoq** s/he is never sick
-ippoq, -appoq	has none; there is none; not; un-	**nuannerpoq** to be pleasant > **nuanniippoq** to be unpleasant **siku** ice > **sikuippoq** there is no ice
-nngikkallarpoq	not yet	**piareerpoq** to be ready > **piariinngikkallarpoq** s/he is not ready yet
-nngilerpoq	not for a long time, but should	**atuarpoq** to go to school > **atuanngilerpoq** s/he hasn't been at school for a long time, but should have been
-nngilluinnarpoq	not at all	**sulivoq** to work > **sulinngilluinnarpoq** s/he isn't working at all
-nngisaannarpoq	never	**puisinniarpoq** to go seal-hunting > **puisinnianngisaannarpunga** I never go seal-hunting
-nngitsoorpoq	not (after all, contrary to expectation)	**aggerpoq** to come > **agginngitsoorpoq** s/he didn't come after all
+naveerpoq	never again, to be unable to any more	**aallarpoq** to travel > **aallarnaveerpoq** s/he can't travel any more
+naveersaarpoq	to try not to	**sulivoq** to work > **sulinaveersaarpugut** we're trying not to work
+navianngilaq	absolutely not	**takuaa** to see it > **takunavianngilara** I absolutely didn't see it

Points to note:

- The suffix **+junnaarpoq** has a number of variants. The variant **+junnaarpoq** is used with vowel stems except those ending in -i-, the variants **+gunnaarpoq** and **-kkunnaarpoq** are used with consonant stems, the variant **-runnaarpoq** is used with r stems, and **-unnaarpoq** is used with verbal stems ending in -i-.
- The variant **-juippoq** is used with most stem types. The variant **-uippoq** is used with stems ending in -i-.
- The suffix **-ippoq**, **-appoq** can be attached to both nominal and verbal stems. When attached to nominal stems, it means 'there is no' or 'has none'. When attached to verbal stems, it means 'is not' or changes the meaning of the verbal stem to its opposite. In this latter respect it can be compared to the English suffix 'un-'.
- The variant **-ippoq** is used with most stem types. The variant **-appoq** is used with stems ending in -i or with historical -i (e.g. **aput** 'snow' > **aputi-** 'snow' [inflectional stem] > **aputaappoq** 'there is no snow') as well as with stems ending in -a or -a plus a consonant.

The following examples illustrate the use of these negative suffixes.

Misilinngisaannarpara.
misili-nngisaannar-para
try-never-1sg>3sg
I've never tried it.

Anguteeraq napparsimagami sulinngikkallarpoq.
anguteeraq napparsima-gami suli-nngikkallar-poq
anguteeraq be.sick-CAUS.4sg work-not.yet-3sg
Because Anguteeraq is sick, he is not working yet.

Aanaa tutsiutinngilerpoq.
aanaa tutsiuti-nngiler-poq
grandmother get.in.touch-not.for.a.long.time-3sg
Granny hasn't been in touch for a long time (although she should be).

Ajunngilluinnarpoq.
aju-nngilluinnar-poq
be.bad-not.at.all-3sg
It's very, very good.

Qimmeq illumut isinngisaannarpoq.
qimmeq illu-mut isi-nnisaannar-poq
dog house-ALL enter-never-3SG
The dog never enters the house.

Timmisartoq tikinngitsoorpoq.
timmisartoq tiki-nngitsoor-poq
aeroplane arrive-not.after.all-3SG
The plane did not arrive after all.

Meeraq sallunaveerpoq.
meeraq sallu-naveer-poq
child lie-never.again-3SG
The child will never lie again.

Illu igalaaqanngitsoq iluarnavianngilaq.
illu igalaa-qa-nngi-tsoq iluar-navianngi-laq
house window-have-NEG-IP be.liveable-absolutely.not-3SG
A house without windows is definitely not liveable.

7.11.3 Negative intransitive participle

West Greenlandic has a negative intransitive participle, **-nngitsoq**, which is used to convey the meaning of 'one who/which isn't X'. It is the negative equivalent of the intransitive participle (discussed in section 8.1), which ends in +**toq**/+**soq**, and has the meaning 'one who/which is X'. The formation and use of the negative participle is illustrated in the following table.

Verb	Intransitive participle	Negative participle
umeqarpoq to have a beard	**umeqartoq** bearded, one who has a beard	**umeqanngitsoq** beardless, one who doesn't have a beard
ammavoq to be open	**ammasoq** open, something that is open	**ammanngitsoq** unopened, closed, something that is not open
naammassivoq to finish	**naammassisoq** finished, something that is finished	**naammassinngitsoq** unfinished, something that is unfinished

Point to note:

- The **-nngitsoq** ending can be attached to all verbal stem types.

The use of the negative intransitive participle is illustrated in the following examples.

banki <u>aningaasaqanngitsoq</u>
banki aningaasa-qa-nngi-tsoq
bank money-have-NEG-IP
a cash-free bank

utoqqaq <u>kiguteqanngitsoq</u>
utoqqaq kigute-qa-nngi-tsoq
elderly.person tooth-have-NEG-IP
a toothless elderly person

The negative participle suffix can be preceded by a passive suffix (see section 7.9) and be inflected in the plural and in different cases like other participles (see section 8), e.g.:

atuagaq <u>atuarneqanngitsoq</u>
atuagaq atuar-neqa-nngi-tsoq
book read-PASS-NEG-IP
an unread book (or: a book that hasn't been read)

mamakujuttut <u>mamanngitsut</u>
mamakujuttu-t mama-nngi-tsu-t
sweet-PL taste.good-NEG-IP-PL
sweets that taste bad

Bankimi <u>aningaasaqanngitsumi</u> inoqaqaaq.
banki-mi aningaasa-qa-nngi-tsu-mi ino-qa-qaaq.
bank money-have-NEG-IP-LOC person-have-a.lot.3SG
There are a lot of people in the cash-free bank.

7.11.4 Negative indefinite pronouns and adverbs

The Greenlandic equivalent of an English sentence with a negative indefinite pronoun avoids the use of a pronoun at all, instead using a passive negative sentence without an agent. (See section 7.9 for explanation of passive verbs.) The following example illustrates this tendency:

Qulliit ikinneqarsimanngillat.
qulii-t ikin-neqar-sima-nngi-llat
light-PL switch.on-PASS-PAST-NEG-3PL
No one has turned on the lights.[11]

There is no West Greenlandic equivalent of the English negative indefinite pronoun 'nowhere'. The corresponding meaning is expressed by means of the indefinite form **sumiluunniit** 'anywhere' with a negative verb (see section 4.6 for discussion of negative indefinite pronouns). This applies to both intransitive and transitive sentences, as in the first and second examples respectively.

Kalaallit Nunaanni sumiluunniit banaanit naasinnaanngillat.
kalaalli-t nuna-anni sumiluunniit banaani-t naa-sinnaa-nngi-llat
greenlander-PL-LOC.3PL anywhere banana-PL grow-be.able-NEG-3PL
Bananas can't grow anywhere in Greenland.

Sumiluunniit nassaarisinnaanngilara.
sumiluunniit nassaari-sinnaa-nngi-lara
anywhere find-be.able-NEG-1SG>3SG
I can't find it anywhere.

7.11.5 Periphrastic negative constructions

Periphrastic negative constructions are verbal constructions with a negative meaning that consist of more than one part. In West Greenlandic, periphrastic verbal constructions can be used of instead of suffixes to indicate certain specific negative meanings (negative habituals and negative capability). These negative constructions consist of a lexical verb (i.e. a verb that doesn't conjugate or change its shape otherwise) in conjunction with a conjugated verb that has a particular negative sense. In all these constructions the lexical verb has the abstract participle suffix +neq (see section 8.3). These periphrastic negative constructions are listed in the following table.

---

11 Literally: the lights haven't been turned on.

Negative construction	Example
+neq ajorpoq usually doesn't	**biilerneq ajorpunga** I don't usually drive
+neq naluvoq doesn't know how to	**biilerneq naluvoq** s/he doesn't know how to drive
+neq artorpaa can't (i.e. can't manage to; is incapable of)	**kivinneq artorpaa** s/he can't manage to lift it (i.e. it's too hard)
+neq saperpoq can't (for any reason)	**biilerneq saperput** they can't drive (i.e. it's not possible for them to drive right now)

Points to note:

- The verb **ajorpoq** literally means 'to be bad' but is used in the periphrastic construction in the sense of 'not to do'. In the following examples, we have glossed it as be.bad according to its literal meaning.
- The verbs in the remaining constructions have transparent meanings, i.e. **naluvoq** 'to be unknowing', **artorpaa** 'to be unable to manage to do it', and **saperpoq** 'to be unable'.

These periphrastic constructions are illustrated in the following examples.

Marie sukkulerneq ajorpoq.
marie sukkuler-neq ajor-poq
marie sugar-AP be.bad-3SG
Marie doesn't use sugar.

Whiskisorneq ajorpunga.
whiski-sor-neq ajor-punga
whiskey-consume-AP be.bad-1SG
I don't usually drink whisky.

Piffissaqarpiarneq ajorpunga.
piffissa-qar-piar-neq ajor-punga
time-have-really-AP be.bad-1SG
I don't usually really have time.

Imerniartarfiit inunnut pinngitsaaliillutik <u>imigassartoqqusineq ajorput</u>.
imerniartarfi-it inun-nut pinngitsaaliillutik imigassar-toq-qusi-neq ajor-put
bar-PL person-ALL.PL by.force alcohol-consume-cause-AP be.bad-3PL
It's not usually the bars that force people to drink alcohol.

<u>Atorneq ajoratsigit</u> tuniniarpagut.
ator-neq ajor-atsigit tuni-niar-pagut
use-AP be.bad-CAUS.1PL>3PL sell-plan-1PL
We're planning to sell them because we don't use them.

Kaasipap illua tikikkamikku <u>iserneq sapilerput</u> qimmii ersigigamikkit.
kaasipa-p illu-a tikik-kamikku iser-neq sapiler-put qimmi-i ersigi-gamikkit
kaasipa-REL house-3SG arrive-CAUS.4PL>3SG enter-AP be.unable-3PL dog-PL.3SG be.afraid-CAUS.4PL>3PL
When they arrived at Kaasipat's house, they couldn't go in because they were afraid of his dogs.

Negation

Chapter 8
Participles

8.1 Intransitive participle

The West Greenlandic intransitive participle is a suffix that transforms verbs into nouns. Its meaning is 'someone who, something that'. In many cases it corresponds to the English agentive suffix -er, which can change verbs into nouns, e.g. 'to fish' > 'a fisher'; 'to write' > 'a writer'. It can also function like an English relative clause, participle, or adjective. The intransitive participle has three variants, as illustrated in the following table.

Intransitive participle suffix	Verb	Intransitive participle
+toq used after consonant-stems and r-stems	**sinippoq** to sleep	**sinittoq** the one who sleeps, the sleeping one, sleeping
+soq used with vowel stems	**anivoq** to go out	**anisoq** the one who goes out
+soq used with certain stems	**aggerpoq** to approach	**aggersoq** the one who approaches, approaching
+tsoq used with stems ending in **-t-**	**akikippoq** to be cheap	**akikitsoq** the one which is cheap, the cheap one, cheap

Points to note:

- Some verbs historically ended in an -i that has disappeared and therefore take the intransitive participle suffix **+soq** even though their stem does not end in a vowel in the modern language, e.g. **aggerpoq** 'to arrive' > intransitive participle **aggersoq**; **atuarpoq** 'to reads; to go to school' > intransitive participle **atuarsoq**. (See also section 2.5.1.)

- Some consonant-stem verbs have -t as the final consonant of their stem, but this is not usually visible as it assimilates into the person suffixes. Such verbs may take -ts instead of -t in the intransitive participle, e.g. **akikippoq** 'to be cheap' > intransitive participle **akikitsoq**. It is difficult to predict which verbs follow this pattern, so they must be learned individually.

Intransitive participle

The following examples illustrate the use of the intransitive participle. Note that the intransitive participle is marked by the abbreviation IP in the glossing.

qitsuk sinittoq
qitsuk sinit-toq
cat sleep-IP
a/the sleeping cat

meeraq qiasoq
meeraq qia-soq
child cry-IP
a/the crying child

Tuttu sikumi pangalittoq takuara.
tuttu siku-mi pangalit-toq taku-ara
reindeer ice-LOC run-IP see-1SG>3SG
I saw a reindeer running on the ice.

The intransitive participle inflects as a weak-stem noun ending in q (see 3.2.1). The following examples illustrate some inflected intransitive participles.

Qimmit anisut takuigit?
qimmi-t ani-su-t taku-igit?
dog-PL go.out-IP-PL see-INT.2SG>3PL
Did you see the dogs that went out?

Oqaluttuaq angummik eqalunngortumik atuarpara.
oqaluttuaq angum-mik eqalu-nngor-tu-mik atuar-para
tale man-INS salmon-become-IP-INS read-1SG>3SG
I read a tale about a man who became a salmon.

Milukaaq meeqqamut qiasumut tunniuppara.
milukaaq meeqqa-mut qia-su-mut tunni-up-para
lollipop child-ALL cry-IP-ALL give-VAL-1SG>3SG
I gave a lollipop to the crying child.

8
Participles

A considerable number of intransitive participles have become lexicalised in West Greenlandic, meaning that they have taken on a fixed meaning and are used as simple nouns. These lexicalised intransitive participles can be found in the dictionary (as opposed to intransitive participles which have not been lexicalised, in which case only the verbal stem will be listed in the dictionary and the meaning can be worked out from that). Examples of lexicalised participles are shown here.

Verb	Lexicalised intransitive participle
aalisarpoq to fish	**aalisartoq** fisherman
piniarpoq to hunt	**piniartoq** hunter
ilinniarpoq to study	**ilinniartoq** student
ilaavoq to be on-board	**ilaasoq** passenger
atuarpoq to read; to go to school	**atuartoq** pupil
iffiorpoq to bake	**iffiortoq** baker
atuivoq to use	**atuisoq** user

The following examples illustrate lexicalised intransitive participles.

<u>Aalisartoq</u> ikiorneqarsimavoq kingornalu piareeqqissimalluni.
aalisartoq ikior-neqar-sima-voq kingorna-lu piaree-qqis-sima-lluni
fisherman help-PASS-PAST-3SG then-and be.ready-again-PAST-CONT.3SG
The fisherman was helped, and then he was ready again.

Internetti sukkaneq Tele-Postimi <u>atuisut</u> akilerusussinnaavaat.
internetti sukka-neq tele-posti-mi atuisu-t akile-rusus-sinnaa-vaat
internet be.quick-AP tele-posti-LOC users-PL pay-be.willing-be.able-3PL>3SG
Tele Posti users are willing to pay for fast internet.

The intransitive participle may be suffixed to the passive suffix +neqarpoq (see section 7.9) to create a passive participle (+neqartoq). The interpretation can be either present or past and either progressive or completed, depending on the context. The use of +neqartoq is illustrated in the following examples. Note that West Greenlandic also has a separate passive participle with a similar function; see section 8.2.

Iffiaq <u>nerineqartoq</u> mamarpoq.
iffiaq neri-neqar-toq mamar-poq
bread eat-PASS-IP taste.good-3SG
The bread that was/is eaten tastes good.

Biilit <u>atorneqartut</u> sungaartuupput.
biili-t ator-neqar-tu-t sungaartu-u-pput
car-PL use-PASS-IP-PL yellow-be-3PL
The car being used is yellow.

Naatitat <u>sianneqartut</u> tipigipput.
naatita-t sian-neqar-tu-t tipigi-pput
vegetable-PL fry-pass-IP-PL smell.good-3PL
The fried vegetables smell good.

Intransitive participle

The intransitive participle can also be combined with the future suffix -ssavoq/-ssaaq (see section 7.3.3.1) and the verb -avoq 'to be' to create an alternative future construction +tussaavoq (and its predictable variants +sussaavoq and -tsussaavoq). This construction has a meaning similar to the English future progressive tense, e.g. 'I will be working in the garden tomorrow'. The following examples illustrate this use.

Aqagu <u>asaasussaavunga</u>.
aqagu asaa-su-ssa-a-vunga
tomorrow clean.the.floor-IP-FUT-be-1SG
I'll be cleaning (the floor) tomorrow.

Decemberimi <u>festertussaavoq</u>.
decemberi-mi fester-tu-ssa-a-voq
december-LOC have.a.party-IP-FUT-be-3SG
S/he will be having a party in December.

Aqqakkut aasaru <u>meerartaartussaapput</u>.
aqqa-kkut aasaru meerartaar-tu-ssa-a-pput
aqqa-COLL this.summer have.a.child-IP-FUT-be-3PL
Aqqa and the family will be having a child this summer.

The intransitive participle can also be combined with the verb -qarpoq 'to have', resulting in the form +toqarpoq (and its predictable variants +soqarpoq and +tsoqarpoq). This construction has the meaning of 'there is someone/something doing X' or 'there are people doing X', as in the following examples. (Note that the meaning of the intransitive participle in this construction can be either singular or plural.)

Igaffimmi <u>nerisoqarpoq</u>.
igaffim-mi neri-so-qar-poq
kitchen-LOC eat-IP-have-3SG
There is someone eating in the kitchen.

8 Participles

Quimiittoqarpoq.
qui-mi-it-to-qar-poq
shed-LOC-be-IP-have-3SG
There is someone in the shed.

The intransitive participle in this construction might be lexicalised, as in the following example, which features the lexicalised intransitive participle **asaasoq** 'cleaner'.

Pisiniarfimmi <u>asaasoqarpoq</u>.
pisiniarfim-mi asaaso-qar-poq
shop-LOC cleaner-have-3SG
There are cleaners in the shop.

The negative version of the construction is illustrated in the following example.

Uffartoqanngilaq.
uffar-to-qa-nngi-laq
shower-IP-have-NEG-3SG
There's no one showering.

Finally, the intransitive participle is often used in conjunction with +(r)suaq 'big, very' plus the verb -uvoq 'to be', resulting in the construction +torsuuvoq 'to be very' (or its predictable variants +sorsuuvoq and +tsorsuuvoq), e.g.:

Niviarsiaraq <u>naalattorsuuvoq</u>.
niviarsiaraq naalat-tor-su-u-voq
girl behave.well-IP-very-be-3SG
The girl is behaving very well.

Biilit <u>ajortorsuupput</u>.
biili-t ajor-tor-su-u-pput
car-PL be.bad-IP-very-be-3PL
It's a very bad car.

8.2 Passive participle

In addition to an intransitive participle, West Greenlandic has a passive participle, whose meaning is equivalent to the English passive participle, e.g. 'seen', 'invited', 'known'. It is formed by adding the suffix -gaq, +/-saq, -taq, or -aq to a transitive verb (e.g. takuaa 'to see it') or to an intransitive verb with an incorporated object (e.g. **pisivoq** 'to buy something'). (See section 14.2.2 for discussion of incorporated objects.) Passive participles are illustrated in the following table. Note that the passive participle is marked by the abbreviation PP in the glossing.

Passive participle

Passive participle suffix	Verb	Passive participle
+/-saq	**nerivaa** to eat it	**nerisaq** eaten, which was eaten
	takuaa to see it	**takusaq** seen, which was seen
	tunniuppaa to hand it over to someone	**tunniussaq** handed over, which was handed over
	nunguppaa to use it up	**nungutaq** used up, which was used up
-gaq	**atorpaa** to use it	**atugaq** used, which was used
	ornippaa to approach it	**ornigaq** approached, which was approached
-taq	**nassarpaa** to bring it along	**nassataq** brought along, which was brought along
	qimappaa to leave it	**qimataq** left, which was left
-aq	**sanavaa** to process it	**sanaaq** processed, which was processed

Points to note:

- Vowel-stem verbs, verbs whose stems end in historical -i-, and the ending -uppaa usually take +/-saq.
- Some vowel-stem verbs may take -aq. It is best to learn these individually.
- Most r-stem verbs take -gaq, but some take -taq. It can be difficult to predict which verb takes which suffix, so it is best to learn them on an individual basis.
- Consonant-stem verbs may take either -gaq or -taq. It can be difficult to predict which verb takes which suffix, so it is best to learn them on an individual basis.

- Consonant-stem verbs ending in **-t** (which is difficult to see in the modern language because of assimilation into the mood suffixes) can take +/-**saq**. Again, these forms are best learnt individually as it can be difficult to predict which ones behave in this way.

The following examples illustrate the use of passive participles. Note that passive participles can be inflected for case and number like other nominal forms.

> **Nuna takusaq kusanaqaaq.**
> nuna taku-saq kusana-qaaq
> land see-PP be.beautiful-very.3SG
> The land that was seen was very beautiful.

> **Inuit ornitat ungasipput.**
> inu-it orni-ta-t ungasi-pput
> people-PL go.to-PP-PL be.far.away-3PL
> The people we are going to are far away.

Passive participles may be incorporated into a verbal suffix, such as **-qarpoq** 'to have' and **-avoq** 'to be', e.g.:

> **Takusaqarpunga.**
> taku-sa-qar-punga
> see-PP-have-1SG
> I've seen something.

> **Nungusaavoq.**
> nungu-sa-a-voq
> use.up-PP-3SG
> It was used up.

A passive participle may appear with a possessive suffix indicating the agent of the passive action. If there is an explicit nominal agent present in the phrase, it will be marked by the relative case. This type of construction is illustrated in the following examples.

> **sanaara**
> sana-a-ra
> make-PP-1SG
> made by me

meeqqap <u>aserugaa</u>
meeqqa-p aseru-ga-a
child-REL break-PP-3SG
broken by the child

Passive participle

As with intransitive participles, many passive participle forms have been lexicalised and are used as nouns. In some cases these nouns have the meaning of 'someone or something who has been ... ed', while in other cases they denote basic nominal concepts that correspond to simple nouns in English, such as 'book', 'luggage', etc. Some common passive participles used as nouns are shown in the following tables.

Verb	Lexicalised intransitive participle
atuarpaa to read it	**atuagaq** book[1]
nassarpaa to bring it along	**nassatat** luggage[2]
ornippaa to visit him/her	**ornigaq** destination[3]
igippaa to throw it away	**igitat** rubbish[4]
pisivoq to buy something	**pisiaq** purchase[5]
sanavaa to process it	**sanaaq** product[6]
ativaa to put it on	**atisaq** item of clothing[7]
sulivoq to work	**suliaq** work

1 Literally: something that has been read.
2 Literally: things that have been brought along.
3 Literally: place that is visited.
4 Literally: things that are thrown away.
5 Literally: something that has been bought.
6 Literally: something that has been processed.
7 Literally: something that is put on; usually appears in the plural as **atisat** 'clothes'.

Points to note:

- Sometimes the same verb may take two different versions of the passive participle suffix, but each one has a different meaning, with one having a participial function and the other serving as a noun. For example, **ornippaa** 'to visit him/her' has the passive participle forms **ornigaq** 'visited, which is visited' and **ornitaq** 'destination'.
- Sometimes the lexicalised nouns are used only in the plural, e.g. **nassatat** 'luggage', **igitat** 'rubbish'.

8 Participles

- Intransitive verbs ending in **-livoq** may be used to form nominalised passive participles, e.g. **sulivoq** 'to work' > **suliaq** 'work'.

The following examples illustrate the use of passive participles that serve as nouns.

<u>Misigisaq</u> pikkunarpoq.
misigisaq pikkunar-poq
feeling be.strong-3sg
The feeling is strong.

<u>Atisai</u> qernertuupput.
atisa-i qerner-tu-u-pput
clothes-PL.3SG be.black-IP-be-3PL
Her clothes are black.

Al Gore Nuummut <u>qaaqqusaavoq</u>.
al gore nuum-mut qaaqqusa-a-voq
al gore nuuk-ALL invited.guest-be-3SG
Al Gore is an invited guest to Nuuk.

In many instances, lexicalised passive participle forms appear in conjunction with the nominal future suffix **-ssaq** (see section 7.3.3.2). Some common such forms are shown in the following table.

Verb	Lexicalised passive participle with future suffix
akilerpaa to pay it	**akiligaq + ssaq > akiligassat** money[1]
errorpaa to wash it	**errortaq + ssaq > errortassat** laundry[2]
nerivaa to eat it	**nerisaq + ssaq > nerisassat** food[3]
sanavaa to process it	**sanaaq + ssaq > sanaassaq** raw material[4]

1 Literally: things to be paid in the future.
2 Literally: things to be washed in the future.
3 Literally: things to be eaten in the future.
4 Literally: thing to be processed in the future.

Point to note:

- Many of these nouns appear only in the plural.

8.3 Abstract participle

The West Greenlandic abstract participle is equivalent to the English gerund (also known as verbal noun) ending in -ing, e.g. 'smoking is bad', 'driving is hard for me', etc. The abstract participle is formed by addition of the suffix **+neq** to a verbal stem. It is most typically attached to intransitive verbs, as shown in the following table. Note that the abstract participle is abbreviated as AP in the glossing.

Stem type	Verb	Abstract participle
Vowel-stem	**nerivoq** to eat	**nerineq** eating
	igavoq to cook	**iganeq** cooking
Consonant-stem	**qitippoq** to dance	**qitinneq** dancing
	allappoq to write	**allanneq** writing
R-stem	**atuarpoq** to read	**atuarneq** reading
	biilerpoq to drive (a car)	**biilerneq** driving

Point to note:

- The abstract participle suffix **+neq** inflects like an extra-strong q-stem noun (see 3.2.6).

The following examples illustrate the use of the abstract participle in various cases.

Pujortarneq inerteqqutaavoq.
pujortar-neq inerteqqutaa-voq
smoke-AP be.forbidden-3SG
Smoking is forbidden.

Arpanneq nuannaraara.
arpan-neq nuannara-ara
run-AP enjoy-1SG>3SG
I enjoy running.

Puisitorneq nuannaraarput.
puisi-tor-neq nuanna-raarput
seal-consume-AP like-VAL.1PL>3SG
We like eating seal.

8 Participles

Miki <u>arsarnermut</u> pikkorippoq.
miki arsar-ner-mut pikkorip-poq
miki play.ball-AP-ALL be.good.at-3SG
Miki is good at playing football.

Ilinniartut <u>oqallinnermut</u> sungiusarput.
ilinniartu-t oqallin-ner-mut sungiusar-put
student-PL debate-AP-ALL practise-3PL
The students are practising debating.

The abstract participle can take its own modifiers, as in the following example.

nuannersumik <u>qitinneq</u>
nuanner-su-mik qitin-neq
be.joyful-IP-INS dance-AP
joyful dancing

The abstract participle may take possessive suffixes like any noun, as in the following example.

<u>Iganera</u> pitsanngorpoq.
iga-ne-ra pitsanngor-poq
cook-AP-1SG improve-3SG
My cooking is improving.

When the abstract participle suffix is attached to a transitive verb, the abstract participle takes a possessive suffix. If there is a noun in the construction, it is marked by the relative case (as the possessor of the abstract participle). The following table illustrates this type of construction.

Object + verb	Abstract participle construction
filmi takuaa filmi taku-aa film see-3SG>3SG s/he sees the film	**filmip takunera** filmi-p taku-ner-a film-REL see-AP-3SG seeing the film
nuna ornippaa nuna ornip-paa country visit-3SG>3SG s/he visits the country	**nunap orninnera** nuna-p ornin-ner-a country-REL visit-AP-3SG visiting the country

If there is no noun in the construction, the possessive suffix on the abstract participle indicates the object. (The subject is not indicated in the participle and would instead appear elsewhere in the clause.) The following example illustrates this type of construction.

Abstract participle

Object + verb	Abstract participle construction
asavai	**asanerat**
asa-vai	asa-ner-at
love-3SG>3PL	love-AP-3PL
s/he loves them	loving them

An indefinite object appearing in conjunction with an abstract participle is marked by the instrumental case, e.g.:

nipilersuutinik tusarnaarneq
nipilersuuti-nik tusarnaar-neq
music-INS.PL listen-AP
listening to music

The abstract participle is commonly used in temporal clauses with the meaning 'while, when'. In such instances, the subject of the relative clause is marked by the relative case, and the abstract participle appears in the locative with a possessive suffix. This type of construction is illustrated in the following examples.

Anaanap nerinerani meeraq sinilerpoq.
anaana-p neri-ner-ani meeraq sini-ler-poq
mother-REL eat-AP-LOC.3SG child sleep-start-3SG
The child fell asleep while the mother was eating.

Qimmip qilunnerani qitsuk qimaavoq.
qimmi-p qilun-ner-ani qitsuk qimaa-voq
dog-REL bark-AP-LOC.3SG cat run.away-3SG
The cat ran away while the dog was barking.

Seqinnernerani meeqqat silami pinnguarput.
seqinner-ner-ani meeqqa-t sila-mi pinnguar-put
shine-AP-LOC.3SG child-PL outside-LOC play-3PL
The children are playing outside while the sun is shining.

Bussit ingerlaneranni angerlarpugut.
bussi-t ingerla-ner-anni angerlar-pugut
bus-PL run-AP-LOC.3PL go.home-1PL
We're going home while the buses are (still) running.

Some abstract participles with possessive suffixes could be regarded as postpositions, as in the following example. (See section 10 for discussion of postpositions.) As in the constructions introduced previously, the noun associated with the abstract participle appears in the relative case.

Qaammatip ingerlanerani piariissaaq.
qaammati-p ingerla-ner-ani piarii-ssaaq
month-REL go-AP-LOC.3SG be.ready-FUT.3SG
It will be ready over the course of the month.

Abstract participles may be marked by the instrumental suffix +**mik** or by the suffix +**mut** in order to form a causal clause with the meaning 'because of X', e.g.:

Kaannermik eqqarsarsinnaanngilanga.
kaan-ner-mik eqqarsar-sinnaa-nngi-langa
be.hungry-AP-INS think-be.able-NEG-1SG
I'm so hungry that I can't think.

Meeraq pikkorinnermik tulluussimaarpoq.
meeraq pikkorin-ner-mik tulluussimaar-poq
child be.good.at-AP-INS be.proud-3SG
The child is proud (of him/herself) because s/he is so good.

Qasunermut eqiasuppunga.
qasu-ner-mut eqiasup-punga
be.tired-AP-ALL not.feel.like.it-1SG
I don't feel like it because I'm tired.

Tuaviornermut mobiilini qimattoorpaa.
tuavior-ner-mut mobiili-ni qimat-toor-paa
rush-AP-ALL mobile.phone-4SG leave-unfortunately-3SG>3SG
S/he unfortunately left his/her mobile phone because s/he was rushing.

There are many lexicalised abstract participles that function as basic nouns, without necessarily having an abstract meaning. Some commonly used lexicalised abstract participles are illustrated in the following table.

Verb	Lexicalised abstract participle
kukkuvoq to make a mistake	**kukkuneq** mistake
marlunngorpoq to become two	**marlunngorneq** Tuesday
niuerpoq to trade	**niuerneq** trade
arpappoq to run	**arpanneq** run, running event
aalisarpoq to fish	**aalisarneq** fishery
pulaarpoq to visit	**pulaarneq** visit
soraarpoq to finish, to say farewell	**soraarneq** retiree

Abstract participle

The following examples illustrate the use of lexicalised abstract participles.

Kalaallit Nunaata Kinallu akornanni <u>niuerneq</u>
kalaalli-t nuna-ata kina-l-lu akornan-ni niuer-neq
greenlander-PL land-REL.3PL china-REL-and between-3PL trade
trade between Greenland and China

siallersumi 42 kilometerinut <u>arpanneq</u>
siallersu-mi 42 kilometeri-nut arpanneq
rain-LOC 42 kilometer-ALL.PL run
a 42-kilometre run in the rain

Biskoppi <u>soraarneq</u>, 87-nik ukiorqarluni maajip pingajuani toquvoq.
bishop soraarneq 87-nik ukioq-qar-luni maaji-p pingaju-ani toqu-voq
bishop retiree 87-INS.PL year-have-CONT.4SG may-REL third-PL.LOC.3SG die-3SG
The retired bishop died on 3 May at the age of 87.

Chapter 9

Adverbs

West Greenlandic does not have a single method of forming adverbs (in contrast to English, in which adverbs are typically formed by means of the suffix -ly). However, many West Greenlandic adverbs are actually nouns with case suffixes. The instrumental case suffix -**mik** (see section 3.3.6) is frequently used to form adverbs, e.g. **sivisuumik** 'for a long time'. Similarly, the equative case (see section 3.3.8) can be used in the formation of adverbs, e.g. **tuluttut** 'in English'. Other adverbs have no specific ending but rather are invariable independent words, for example: **assut** 'a lot'. Adverbial meaning is also often conveyed by means of suffixes that can be attached to a stem, e.g. -**lluarpoq** 'to do something well'. The various types of adverb categorised by semantic type are discussed in the following subsections.

9.1 Manner

Adverbs of manner describe the way in which an action occurs (e.g. quickly, slowly, nicely, etc.). Many West Greenlandic adverbs of manner are comprised of an intransitive participle +**toq**/+**soq**/+**tsoq**; see section 8.1) followed by the instrumental suffix +**mik** (see section 3.3.6). The following is a list of some of the more commonly used adverbs of manner.

Adverb of manner	English translation
akikitsumik	cheaply
alianartumik	sadly
arriitsumik	slowly
ersinartumik	in a horrible way
iluartumik	well
immikkut	separately
kigaatsumik	slowly
kusanartumik	nicely, politely

DOI: 10.4324/9781315160863-9

		Manner
nipituumik	loudly	
nuannersumik	pleasantly, in a fun way	
qanoq	in one way or another	
sallaatsumik	softly, weakly	
sivisuumik	for a long time	
sukkasuumik	quickly	
tuaviortumik	quickly	

The use of this type of adverb of manner is illustrated in the following examples. Note that the adverb typically appears immediately before the verb.

Sermersuaq arriitsumik aakkiartorpoq.
sermersuaq arriitsumik aakkiartor-poq
inland.ice slowly melt-3SG
The inland ice is melting slowly.

Maani umiatsiat akikitsumik attartorneqarsinnaasut!
maani umiatsia-t akiki-tsu-mik attartor-neqar-sinnaa-su-t
here boat-PL cheap-IP-INS rent-PASS-be.able-IP-PL
Boats can be rented cheaply here!

Ataasinngormat sivisuumik sulivunga.
ataasinngormat sivisuu-mik suli-vunga
on.monday long.time-ALL work-1SG
I worked for a long time on Monday.

Immikkut najugaqarput.
immikkut najugaqar-put
separately live-3PL
They live separately.

Politiit tuaviortumik ingerlapput.
politii-t tuavior-tu-mik ingerlaar-put
police-PL quick-IP-INS go.together-PL
The police are going quickly.

Erinarsortoq nipituumik appippoq.
erinarsortoq nipi-tu-u-mik appip-poq
singer loud-IP-INS start.to.sing-3SG
The singer starts to sing out loudly.

9 Adverbs

There are also suffixes that can convey an adverbial meaning. Some of these are shown in the following table.

Adverb suffix	English translation
-allappoq, -jallappoq	suddenly; a bit
-ffaarippoq	perfectly; very well
-gallarpoq	for now, temporarily
-galuttuinnarpoq, -kkaluttuinnarpoq, -raluttuinnarpoq	more and more
-innarpoq	only, just
-jartuaarpoq	more and more
-javoq, -avoq	easily
-jorarpai, -orarpai	one after the other
-jortorpai, -ortorpai	one after the other
-kaapput	in a group, many at once
-lertorpoq	quickly
-llaqqippoq	well, skilfully
-lluarpoq	well
-misaarpoq	lazily
+nerluppoq	badly
-pallappoq	quickly
-piluppoq, -piloorpoq	aggressively
-qatigiipput	together
+ussorpai	one after the other

Points to note:

- The suffixes appearing in the table in intransitive form can usually also be attached to transitive verbs, in which case they will take transitive endings (e.g. **nerivoq** 'to eat' > **nerilertorpoq** 'to eat quickly' vs. **nerivaa** 'to eat it' > **nerilertorpaa** 'to eat it quickly').
- Suffixes with a meaning involving more than one subject or object (e.g. 'together', 'one after the other') can only appear in the plural.
- Some suffixes can only be used transitively, e.g. **+ussorpai** 'one after the other'.

The use of these adverbial suffixes is illustrated in the following examples.

Pitsaaffaarippoq.
pitsaa-ffaarip-poq
be.nice-perfectly-3sg
S/he/it is perfectly nice.

Ataata pisaqarluarpoq.
ataata pisa-luar-poq
father catch-well-3SG
Dad had a good catch.[1]

Arpamisaarpunga.
arpa-misaar-punga
run-lazily-1SG
I was running lazily.

Naasut tigoorarpai.
naasu-t tigo-orar-pai
flower-PL collect-sequentially-3SG>3PL
S/he collected flowers one after the other.

Assilissat nivinngajorarpai.
assilissa-t nivinnga-jorar-pai
picture-PL hang.up-sequentially-3SG>3PL
S/he hung up pictures one after the other.

Meeqqat juullip inuanit mamakujunnik tuniorarneqarlutik ...
meeqqa-t juulli-p inu-anit mamakujun-nik tuni-orar-neqar-lutik
child-PL christmas-REL man-ABL.3SG sweet-INS.PL give-sequentially-PASS-CONT.3PL
Children, one after the other, were given sweets by Santa Claus ...

A number of adverbs of manner are based on contemporative verbal forms (see section 7.2.2.3), e.g.:

Adverb	English translation
akikinaarlugu	cheaply
toqqaannarlugu	directly
arajutsisillugu	behind someone's back
naammagalugu	patiently

The following example illustrates the use of this type of adverb.

Fjernsyni akikinaarlugu pisiariuk!
fjernsyni akikilaarlugu pisiari-uk
tv cheaply buy-IMP.2SG>3SG
Buy the TV cheaply!

---

1 Literally: Dad caught well.

9 Adverbs

9.2 Time

Adverbs of time describe when an action takes or took place (e.g. tomorrow, yesterday, now, recently). Like adverbs of manner (see 9.1), some West Greenlandic adverbs of time are independent words. Many of these independent adverbs are marked by case (e.g. **ilaannikkut** 'sometimes, occasionally'), possessive suffixes (e.g. **aqaguani** 'the following day'), or other suffixes (e.g. **ilaannigooq** 'once upon a time'), while others are indeclinable forms (e.g. **suli** 'still'). The following is a list of some of the more commonly used independent adverbs of time.

Adverb of time	English translation
aasit	now again, as usual
aatsaat	only now, only then
aqagu	tomorrow
aqaguagu	the day after tomorrow
aqaguani	the following day
erniinnaq	soon
ilaannigooq	once upon a time
ilaannikkut	sometimes, occasionally
ippassaq	yesterday
kingullermik	last (time)
maanna, maannakkut, massakkut	now
qanga	before, in the olden times
qaqugu	some day (in the future)
siornatigut	before, previously
suli	still
qanittumi	not long ago
ullaakkut	in the morning
ullumikkut	currently
ullut tamaasa	every day
unnugu	this evening, tonight
unnukkut	in the evening

Point to note:

- The form **qanittumi** can also be used as an adverb of place meaning 'close by' (see 9.3).

The use of the adverbs of time is illustrated in the following examples.

Time

Massakkut sumi najugaqarpit?
massakkut sumi najugaqar-pit
now where live-INT.2SG
Where are you living now?

Unnugu sutussaagut?
unnugu su-tu-ssaagut
tonight what-consume-FUT.INT.1SG
What shall we eat tonight?

Erniinnaq isissaaq.
erniinnaq isi-ssa-voq
soon come.in-FUT-3SG
S/he will be home soon.

Suli annernarpoq.
suli annernar-poq
still hurt-3SG
It still hurts.

Kingullermik kina erruiva?
kingullermik kina errui-va
last.time who do.dishes-INT.3SG
Who did the dishes last time?

Sila **siornatigut** taamak allanngorartiginngilaq.
sila siornatigut taamak allanngorar-tigi-nngi-laq
weather before in.this.way vary-VAL-NEG-3SG
The weather didn't use to vary in this way before.

Ilaannigooq anguteqarpoq inuusuttumik Allunnguamik atilimmik.
ilaannigooq angute-qar-poq inuusuttu-mik allunngua-mik ati-lim-mik
once.upon.a.time man-have-3SG young.man-INS allunngua-INS name-having-INS
Once upon a time there was a young man named Allunnguaq.

West Greenlandic has two different sets of adverbial expressions referring to the day of the week when something happens, as in English 'on Sunday', 'on Tuesday', etc. One set refers to a day in the past, while the other refers to a day in the future. These two sets are shown in the following table.

9 Adverbs

Day of the week	Past adverb	Future adverb
ataasinngorneq Monday	**ataasinngormat** on Monday (in the past)	**ataasinngorpat** on Monday (in the future)
marlunngorneq Tuesday	**marlunngormat** on Tuesday (in the past)	**marlunngorpat** on Tuesday (in the future)
pingasunngorneq Wednesday	**pingasunngormat** on Wednesday (in the past)	**pingasunngorpat** on Wednesday (in the future)
sisamanngorneq Thursday	**sisamanngormat** on Thursday (in the past)	**sisamanngorpat** on Thursday (in the future)
tallimanngorneq Friday	**tallimanngormat** on Friday (in the past)	**tallimanngorpat** on Friday (in the future)
arfininngorneq Saturday	**arfininngormat** on Saturday (in the past)	**afrininngorpat** on Saturday (in the future)
sapaat Sunday	**sapaatiummat** on Sunday (in the past)	**sapaatiuppat** on Sunday (in the future)

Points to note:

- The days of the week (except Sunday) are all composed of a numeral (e.g. **ataaseq** 'one') plus the verbal suffix -**nngorpoq** 'to become' plus the abstract participle suffix +**neq** (see 8.3).
- The forms ending in -**mat**, which refer to past days, are all 3SG intransitive causative verbal forms (see 7.2.2.2.1).
- The forms ending in -**pat**, which refer to future days, are all 3SG intransitive conditional verbal forms (see 7.2.2.2.2).
- The forms for 'on Sunday' are composed of the verb -**uvoq** 'to be' instead of -**nngorpoq** 'to become'.

The following examples illustrate the use of these expressions.

Sapaatiummat naalagiarpunga.
sapaati-u-mmat naalagiar-punga
sunday-be-CAUS.3SG go.to.church-1SG
I went to church on Sunday.

Marlunngorpat kaffillissavugut.
marlunngor-pat kaffilli-ssa-vugut
tuesday-COND.3SG hold.a.kaffimik-FUT-1PL
We're having a kaffimik on Tuesday.

There are also verbal suffixes which convey the meaning of an adverb of time. Some of the most common of these are shown in the following table. See section 7.11.2 for negative adverbial suffixes with a temporal meaning.

Adverb suffix	English translation
-jaarpoq, -aarpoq	early
+juannaarpoq, -tuannaarpoq, uannaarpoq	always
+juarpoq, -tuarpoq, -uarpoq	the whole time, always
-kulavoq	often
-llatuarpoq	finally
-ngajappoq	soon, almost
-qattaarpoq	again and again
+qqaarpoq	for the first time
-qqammerpoq	just (did it)
-qqippoq	again; further
-riikatappoq	already; a long time ago

Points to note:

- When a suffix has two variants, the variant beginning with -j is used with most stem types, and the variant beginning with a vowel is used after -i and -r.
- When a suffix has three variants, the variant beginning with -u is used after -i, the variant with -t is used after consonants and -r, and the -j variant is used with vowels other than i-.

The use of these suffixes is illustrated in the following examples.

Danmarkimi atuarnini oqaluttuariuarpaa.
danmarki-mi atuarner-ni oqaluttuari-uar-paa
denmark-LOC studies-4SG tell-always-3SG>3SG
S/he is always telling (people) about his/her studies in Denmark.

9 Adverbs

Meeqqat innariikatapput.
meeqqa-t inna-riikata-pput
child-PL go.to.bed-already-3PL
The children have already gone to bed.

Meeqqat itijaarput.
meeqqa-t iti-jaar-put
child-PL wake.up-early-3PL
The children woke up early.

Festimit angerlajaarpunga.
festi-mit angerla-jaar-punga
party-ABL go.home-early-1SG
I went home early from the party.

Sialleqqammerpoq.
sialleq-qammer-poq
rain-just-3SG
It has just rained.

Qimmit qiluttaqattaarput.
qimmi-t qilut-ta-qattaar-put
dog-PL bark-HAB-again.and.again-3PL
The dogs usually bark again and again.

Aningaasaqarnermut Siunnersuisoqatigiit isumasioqatigeeqq issapput.
aningaasaqarner-mut siunnersuisoqatigi-it isumasioqatigee-qqi-ssa-pput
economy-ALL council-PL have.a.seminar-again-FUT-3PL
The Economic Council is going to have a seminar again.

Ataata ernerlu rubininik tunisaqaqqaarput.
ataata erner-lu rubini-nik tunisa-qa-qqaar-put
father son-and ruby-INS.PL sale-have-for.the.first.time-3PL
Father and son have had a ruby sale for the first time.

9.3 Place and direction

Adverbs of place give information about where an action takes place, while adverbs of direction denote the direction towards which or from which a subject is moving. The following are some of the more common West Greenlandic adverbs of place and direction.

Place and direction

Adverb of place	English translation
ikani	there, over there
maani	here
qanittumi	close by
(sumi) tamaani	everywhere
sumiluunniit	somewhere
ungasissumi	far away
uani	near here

Points to note:

- These adverbs typically end in the locative singular suffix **-mi** or its plural counterpart **-ni**. See section 3.3.4 for discussion of the locative case.
- See section 4.2 for discussion of demonstrative pronouns, whose inflected forms can be used to convey the equivalent of an English adverb of place with a preposition (e.g. 'from over there', 'to here').
- The form **qanittumi** can also be used as an adverb of time meaning 'not long ago' (see 9.2).

	Adverbs of direction	
In	From	To
ataani below	**ataanit** from below	**ammut** (to) below, downwards
avannaani in the north	**avannaanit**, **avannga** from the north	**avannamut**, **avunga** to the north
kangiani in the east	**kangianit** from the east	**kangimut** to the east
kitaani in the west	**kitaanit** from the west	**kimmut** to the west
kujataani in the south	**kujataanit** from the south	**kujammut** to the south
qulaani above	**qulaanit** from above	**qummut** (to) above
saamimmi on the left	**saamimmit** from the left	**saamimmut** to the left
talerpimmi on the right	**talerpimmit** from the right	**talerpimmut** to the right

Point to note:

- There is a variant form **pavanga** meaning 'from the east' and variant forms **pavunga** and **tappavunga** meaning 'to the east'.

The following examples illustrate the use of adverbs of place and direction.

saamimmiit talerpimmut
saamim-miit talerpim-mut
left-ABL right-ALL
from left to right

Maaniippugut.
maani-ip-pugut
here-be-1PL
We are here.

Nattoralik kimmut timmivoq.
nattoralik kim-mut timmi-voq
eagle west-ALL fly-3SG
The eagle flies westwards.

Kalaallit Nunaanni sumiluunniit apisarpa?
kalaalli-t nuna-anni sumiluunniit api-sar-pa
greenlander-PL land-LOC.3PL everywhere snow-HAB-INT.3SG
Does it snow everywhere in Greenland?

Qanittumi ikani ungasissumi takuara.
qanittumi ikani ungasissumi taku-ara
not.long.ago over.there far.away see-1SG>3SG
Not long ago I saw him far away over there.

9.4 Degree, measure, and quantity

West Greenlandic adverbs of degree, measure, and quantity may end in the instrumental case suffix -**mik** (see section 3.3.6) but may also end in other suffixes or none. The following are some of the more common West Greenlandic adverbs in this category.

Adverb of degree/measure/quantity	English translation
aamma	more
amerlanersaat	most of them
amerlasuut	many
arlallit	many
assorsuaq	very much
assut	a lot, very
ikitsut	few
imannguaq	a little
immannguaannaq	only a little
ingammik	especially, particularly
minnerusumik	less
missaannik	approximately
naammattumik	enough
taamaallaat	the only, the sole

Degree, measure, and quantity

The following examples illustrate the usage of adverbs of degree, measure, and quantity.

Kreditkortit <u>amerlanersaat</u> akuerisarpavut.
kreditkorti-t amerlanersaat akueri-sar-pavut
credit.card-PL most accept-HAB-1PL>3PL
We accept most international credit cards.

Atuartitsineq <u>assut</u> soqutiginarpoq.
atuartitsi-neq assut soqutiginar-poq
study-AP very be.interesting-3SG
Studying is very interesting.

Meeqqat <u>ikitsut</u> namminneq mobiileqarput.
meeqqa-t ikitsut namminneq mobiile-qar-put
child-PL few own mobile-have-3PL
Few children have their own mobile phone.

9 Adverbs

Immannguaq kalaallisut oqaluttarpoq.
immannguaq kalaallisut oqalut-tar-poq
a.little greenlandic speak-HAB-3SG
S/he speaks a little bit of Greenlandic.

Sila assut nuannerpoq.
sila assut nuanner-poq
weather very be.nice-3SG
The weather is very nice.

Taamaallaat Naja kalaallisut oqalussinnaavoq.
taamaallaat naja kalaallisut oqalus-sinnaa-voq
only naja greenlandic speak-be.able-3SG
Only Naja can speak Greenlandic.

Qaannat amerlasuut aserorsimapput.
qaanna-t amerlasuut aseror-sima-pput
kayak-PL many go.to.pieces-PAST-3PL
Many kayaks are broken.

Nuummi 17.000-t missaannik inoqarpoq.
nuum-mi 17.000-t missaannik ino-qar-poq
nuuk-LOC 17,000-PL approximately person-have-3SG
Nuuk has approximately 17,000 inhabitants.

Ingammik toqqit aamma nammattakkat pisinianit pisiarineqarsimapput.
ingammik toqqi-t aama nammattakka-t pisinia-nit pisiari-neqar-sima-pput
especially tent-PL and backpack-PL customer-ABL.PL buy-PASS-PAST-3PL
Especially tents and backpacks have been bought by customers.

There are also suffixes that function as adverbs of degree, measure, or quantity. Some of the most common such suffixes are listed in the following table. Many of these suffixes are added to verbal stems, but some are added to nominal stems and form new nouns, while others are added to nominal stems and form verbs. The latter two types of suffixes are indicated in the table.

Degree, measure, and quantity

Adverb suffix	English translation
-ffarrippoq	to be very (something positive)
-innaq, -annaq (added to nouns)	only
-innarpoq, -annarpoq, -ginnarpoq	only
-isappoq, -asappoq, -visappoq (added to nouns)	(there is) very little
-kannerpoq	almost
+kiartorpoq	more and more
-kippoq	little, few
-kutsoorpoq	a lot
-laarpoq	a little bit
+lluinnarpoq	completely
+navianngilaq	absolutely not
+nerpaavoq	the most
+nerujussuuvoq	extremely
+ngaarpoq	a lot
-ngaatsiarpoq	really, quite a lot
-ngajappoq	almost
-pajaarpoq	partly
-qaaq (see following table)	to be very
-qinnaarpoq	totally
-qqarpoq	barely
-qqippoq	completely
-qqissaarpoq	totally, precisely
-rujuppoq	a little
-rujussuaq (added to nouns)	very much
-usarpoq	more or less
+vallaarpoq, +allaarpoq, +pallaarpoq	too much
-vippoq, -ippoq	totally, completely

Points to note:

- The variant **-annaq** is used with nouns ending in -a and -q. The variant **-innaq** is used with all other types of nouns.

- The variant **-isappoq** is used with vowel- and most consonant-stem nouns. The variant **-asappoq** is used with q-stem nouns and with nouns that historically ended in -i (e.g. **aput** 'snow' > **aputaasappoq** 'there is very little snow'). The variant **-visappoq** is used after -aa-.
- The variant **-ginnarpoq** is used with some r-stem verbs. The variant **-innarpoq** is used with consonant-stem verbs and after -i-. The variant **-annarpoq** is used with vowels other than -i- and with some r-stem verbs.
- The variant **+vallaarpoq** is used after -i-. The variant **+pallaarpoq** is used with r-stem and consonant-stem verbs. The variant **+allaarpoq** is used after vowels other than -i-.
- The variant **-vippoq** is used with most stem types, whereas **-ippoq** is used after -u-.

The verbal suffix -**qaaq** 'to be very, to be a lot' is slightly irregular in certain moods (like the future tense suffix -ssaaq; see section 7.3.3.1). The following table shows the conjugation of the intransitive indicative for this suffix.

Intransitive indicative of -**qaaq**	
Subject	All stem types
1SG	**-qaanga**
2SG	**-qaatit**
3SG	**-qaaq**
1PL	**-qaagut**
2PL	**-qaasi**
3PL	**-qaat**

Points to note:

- The interrogative indicative forms are the same as the intransitive ones except for the 2SG -qaat and the 3SG -qaa.
- The conjugation of the transitive indicative forms is similar to that of the negative transitive indicative forms (see 7.11.1.1.2).
- The other moods are regular except that some have only one **a** before the mood suffix, e.g. intransitive contemporative 1SG -**qalunga**; negative intransitive contemporative 1SG -**qinanga**.

The use of these adverbial suffixes is illustrated in the following examples.

> Degree, measure, and quantity

Atuartitsineq soqutiginaqaaq.
atuartitsi-neq soqutigina-qaaq
study-AP be.interesting-very.3SG
Studying is very interesting.

Naja ikiuinermut pikkoriffaarippoq.
naja ikiui-ner-mut pikkori-ffaarip-poq
naja help-AP-ALL be.good.at-very-3SG
Naja is very good at helping (people).

Kalaallisut oqalulaartarpoq.
kalaallisut oqalu-laar-tar-poq
greenlandic speak-a.little-HAB-3SG
S/he speaks a little bit of Greenlandic.

Puisit niaquinnaat immamit nuisasut takuai.
puisi-t niaqu-inna-at imma-mit nuisa-su-t takuai
seal-PL head-only-PL.3PL sea-ABL stick.out-IP-PL see-3SG>3PL
He only saw the seals' heads sticking out of the sea.

Misissuinerit nutaat takutippaat imeq bakteriaqarpallaarunnaarsimasoq.
misissuiner-it nutaa-t takutip-paat imeq bakteria-qar-pallaa-runnaar-sima-soq
test-PL new-PL water show-3PL>3PL bacteria-have-too.much-no.longer-PAST-IP
The new tests show that the water no longer has too much bacteria.

Mianersoqqissaarluni qanillattulerpai.
mianerso-qqissaar-luni qanillattu-ler-pai
be.careful-totally-CONT.4SG get.close-start-3SG>3PL
He started to get closer to them, being totally careful.

Kigutinut nakorsamut misissortinneq ajornangaatsiarpoq.
kiguti-nut nakorsa-mut misissortinneq ajorna-ngaatsiar-poq
tooth-ALL.PL dentist-ALL getting.examined be.difficult-quite.a.lot-3SG
It's quite difficult to get seen by[2] a dentist.

Immap naasuisa sermeq aatsikkiartortarpaat.
imma-p naasu-isa sermeq aatsi-kkiartor-tar-paat
water-REL plant-PL.REL.3SG ice melt-more.and.more-HAB-3PL>3SG
The algae make the ice melt more and more.

---

2 Literally: to.

9.5 Modal

Modal adverbs indicate possibility, likelihood and necessity, and also the speaker's attitude to what is being said. The following are some of the more common modal adverbs in West Greenlandic.

Modal adverb	English translation
ajoraluartumik	unfortunately
allatut ajornartumik	necessarily
ersarissumik	clearly
ilumut	actually
immaqa	maybe
kakkaak	indeed
malunnartumik	obviously
neriuginartumik	hopefully
qujanartumik	fortunately
qularnanngitsumik	probably, surely, undoubtedly
taamaaratarsinnaavoq	probably

The following examples illustrate the use of modal adverbs.

Ajoraluartumik qupperneq nassaassaanngilaq.
ajoraluartumik qupperneq nassaa-ssa-aa-nngi-laq
unfortunately page find-FUT-be-NEG-3SG
Unfortunately, the page is not found.

Immaqa Islandimiuupput.
immaqa islandi-miu-u-pput
maybe iceland-resident-be-3PL
Maybe they're Icelanders.

Neriuginartumik ukiaru pikkorissassaanga.
neriuginartumik ukiaru pikkorissa-ssaanga
hopefully next.autumn take.course-FUT.1SG
Hopefully I'll be taking the course next autumn.

Similar meanings can be expressed with suffixes. The following table contains some of the more common modal adverb suffixes in Greenlandic.

Adverb suffix	English translation
+jun(n)arpoq, -gun(n)arpoq, -kkun(n)arpoq, -run(n)arpoq	probably, most likely
-rluinnarpoq	absolutely
-nnguatsiarpoq	probably
+toorpoq, +soorpoq	unfortunately; unintentionally

Points to note:

- The variant -**jun(n)arpoq** is used with verbal stems ending in -**u**-, the variant -**gun(n)arpoq** is used with verbal stems ending in -**a**- and -**i**-, the variant -**kkun(nar)poq** is used with consonant-stem verbs, and -**rumavoq** is used with r-stem verbs.
- The variant +**toorpoq** is used with r-stem and consonant-stem verbs. The variant +**soorpoq** is used with vowel-stem verbs and verbal stems that historically ended in -i-, such as **aggerpoq** 'to come'.

The use of the modal adverb suffixes is illustrated in the following examples.

Meeraq inequnarluinnarpoq.
meeraq inequnar-luinnar-poq
child be.cute-absolutely-3SG
The child is totally cute.

Kukakkut puisikkunarput.
kuka-kkut puisi-kkunar-put
kuka-COLL catch.seal-probably-3PL
Kuka and the others probably caught a seal.

Qimmeq silami sinikkunarpoq.
qimmeq sila-mi sini-kkunar-poq
dog outside-LOC sleep-most.likely-3SG
The dog is most likely sleeping outside.

9.6 Interrogative

The following is a list of the more common West Greenlandic interrogative adverbs. These adverbs do not change their form. In contrast to many other West Greenlandic adverbs, the interrogatives cannot be verbalised.

9 Adverbs

Interrogative adverb	English translation
qanoq	how?
qanga	when? (in the past)
qaqugu	when? (in the future)
sooq	why?
naak, **sumi**	where?

The following examples illustrate the use of these interrogative adverbs.

Qimmeq qanoq isikkoqarpa?
qimmeq qanoq isikko-qar-pa
dog how look-have-INT.3SG
How does the dog look?

Qanga tikikkassi?
qanga tikik-kassi
when arrive-CAUS.2PL
When did you guys arrive?

Qaqugu atualissagamik?
qaqugu atua-li-ssa-gamik
when school-start-FUT-CAUS.4PL
When are they starting school?

Sooq qimmeq qiluppa?
sooq qimmeq qilup-pa
why dog bark-INT.3SG
Why is the dog barking?

Naak alersikka?
naak alersi-kka
where sock-PL.1SG
Where are my socks?

Chapter 10

Postpositions

West Greenlandic has a set of nominal stems that can be placed after a noun to convey meanings to do with location (e.g. 'under', 'over', 'behind'), movement (e.g. 'towards', 'from', 'out', 'in'), time (e.g. 'before', 'after', 'during'), and others. These postpositional stems function in much the same way as postpositions (which come after the noun) in languages like Finnish and Japanese, or as prepositions (which come before the noun) in languages like English and Danish.

There are two main types of postpositions, one derived from nouns and the other derived from verbs. Postpositions derived from nouns govern the relative case in a preceding noun, while the postpositions themselves take a possessive suffix in the relevant case (typically the locative, allative, or ablative, which indicate movement and location; see 3.4). For example, the postpositional phrase **nerriviup ataani** 'under the table', consists of the noun **nerrivik** 'table' in the relative case, followed by the postposition **ataani** 'under him/her/it', which is based on the nominal stem **ata-** 'under'.

Postpositions derived from verbs are preceded by a noun in the absolutive case, while the postpositions themselves often take contemporative mood suffixes. These forms can be confusing for learners at first, because they can be mistaken for contemporative verbal forms, for example, **ilanngullugu** 'including' from the verb **ilannguppoq** 'to include' and **sinerlugu** 'along' from the verb **sinerpaa**, **sinersivoq** 'to move along'. Less frequently, prepositions derived from verbs may take other mood suffixes such as the conditional and the causative.

The various types of postpositions are discussed in the following subsections.

10.1 Place and direction

Postpositions of place and direction correspond to English prepositions with meanings such as 'in', 'on', 'under', 'behind', etc. Most of these are noun-derived. The following phrases exemplify the use of this type of postposition in conjunction with nouns. The noun appears in the relative case and the postposition takes a 3SG possessive suffix in the relevant case.

nerriviup ataani
nerriviu-p ata-ani
table-REL underside-LOC.3SG
under the table

nerriviup ataanit
nerriviu-p ata-anit
table-REL underside-ABL.3SG
from under the table

illup iluanut
illu-p ilu-ani
house-REL inside-ALL.3SG
into the house

Instead of following a noun, this type of postposition may be used with a possessive suffix referring to a pronoun. The following table illustrates an example noun-derived postpositional stem, **sani-** 'next to', with locative possessive suffixes. Other noun-derived postpositional stems inflect in the same way as this one.

	sani- next to	
Person SG		PL
1	**saninni** next to me	**sanitsinni** next to us
2	**saninni** next to you	**sanissinni** next to you
3	**saniani** next to him/her/it	**sanianni** next to them
4	**sanimini** next to him/her/itself	**saniminni** next to themselves

Points to note:

- In order to express direction towards, e.g. 'to next to me', the locative possessive suffixes shown in the table are replaced with the allative possessive suffixes (see 3.4.3).
- In order to express direction away from, e.g. 'from next to me', the locative possessive suffixes shown in the table are replaced with the ablative possessive suffixes (see 3.4.5).

The following examples illustrate the use of some of these postpositional stems with possessive suffixes.

tununni
tunu-nni
back-LOC.1SG
behind me

akunnitsinni
akunni-tsinni
among-LOC.1PL
among us

eqqassinnit
eqqa-ssinnit
near-ABL.2PL
from near you guys

Place and direction

The following are some of the most common noun-derived West Greenlandic postpositional stems relating to place and direction.

Postpositional stem	English translation
aki-	opposite, on the other side of
akunni-	between, among
ata-	under
ava-	outside
eqqa-	near, around, next to
ilu-	inside of
qaa-	on top of
quli-, qu-	above
saa-	in front of
sani-	next to
sila-	outside of
tungi-	towards
tunu-	behind
unga-	on the other side of

Points to note:

- Some of these forms are based on nouns (e.g. **ilu-** 'inside of' is based on the independent noun **iloq** 'inside'), while others exist only as stems.

- If a stem ends in -i-, it usually changes to -a- when a suffix beginning in -a- is attached (e.g. **tungi-** 'towards' > **tungaanut** 'towards it').

The following examples illustrate the use of these postpositional stems.

Akitsinni issiaveqarpoq.
aki-tsinni issiave-qar-poq
opposite-LOC.1PL chair-have-3SG
There is a chair opposite us.

Qimmip **saniani** saanikoqarpoq.
qimmi-p sani-ani saaniko-qar-poq
dog-REL next.to-LOC.3SG bone-have-3SG
There is a bone next to the dog.

Meeqqeriviup **eqqaani** meeqqat pinnguarput.
meeqqerivi-up eqqa-ani meeqqa-t pinnguar-put
kindergarten-REL near-LOC.3SG child-PL play-3PL
The children are playing near the kindergarten.

Illoqarfiup **tungaanut** angalavugut.
illoqarfi-up tunga-anut angala-vugut
town-REL towards-ALL.3SG travel-1PL
We are travelling towards the town.

Kalaaliaraq Brugsenip **eqqaaniippoq**.
kalaaliaraq brugseni-p eqqa-ani-ip-poq
kalaaliaraq brugsen-REL near-LOC.3SG-be-3SG
Kalaaliaraq market is next to the Brugseni supermarket.

Sisimiut **eqqaani** pingasunik nunaqarfeqarpoq.
sisimiut eqqa-ani pingasu-nik nunaqarfe-qar-poq
sisimiut near-LOC.3SG three-INS.PL village-have-3SG
There are three villages near Sisimiut.

Akisuallaanngilaq illoqarfiup **iluani**.
akisu-alla-nngilaq illoqarfiu-p ilu-ani
expensive-too-NEG.3SG town-REL inside-LOC.3SG
It's not too expensive in town.

Food Festivalernermit assit allaaserisap **ataani** takukkit!
food festivalerner-mit assi-t allaaserisa-p ataani taku-kkit
food festival-ABL photo-PL article-REL under see-IMP.2PL>3PL
See photos from the Food Festival under the article!

A few postpositions of place and direction are based on verbs, for example, **sinerlugu** 'along', as in the following example. Note that the postposition is preceded by a noun in the absolutive case.

> **Kalaallit Nunaata kitaata sineriaa <u>sinerlugu</u> sioraqarfippassuaqarpoq.**
> kalaalli-t nuna-ata kita-ata sineri-a sinerlugu siora-qar-fip-passua-qar-poq
> greenlander-PL land-REL.3PL west-REL.3SG coast-3SG along sand-have-location-much-have-3SG
> There are many places with sand along the west coast of Greenland.

10.2 Time

Some of the most common West Greenlandic noun-based postpositions relating to time are listed in the following table.

Postposition	English translation
ingerlanerani	during, over the course of
kingorna	after
naallugu (SG), **naallugit** (PL)	all, the whole, until the end of
nalaani	during, in the time of
siornatigut	ago
tulliani	next
tungaanut	until

Points to note:

- These postpositions do not usually change their form because they are typically found in conjunction with nouns rather than pronouns.
- Most of these postpositions are composed of a nominal stem with a possessive suffix in the locative case. Others may take a different possessive case suffix, such as **tungaanut** 'until', which is in the allative.
- The postpositions **ingerlanerani** and **nalaani** are preceded by a noun in the relative case.
- The postpositions **kingorna** and **siornatigut** are preceded by a noun in the absolutive case.

10 Postpositions

The following examples illustrate the use of these noun-derived postpositions of time.

qaammatip tulliani
qaammati-p tulliani
month-REL next
next month

ukiup 2019 ingerlanerani
ukiu-p 2019 ingerlanerani
year-REL 2019 during
during the year 2019

Ullut tallimat ingerlanerini peqataasut nutaanik ilisarisima saqalerput.
ullu-t tallima-t ingerlanerini peqataasu-t nutaa-nik ilisarisimasa-qa-ler-put
day-PL five-PL in.the.course.of participant-PL new-INS.PL acquaintance-have-start-3PL
Over the course of the five days, the participants have started to make[1] new acquaintances.

Ulloq naallugu ulapippugut.
ulloq naallugu ulapip-pugut
day all be.busy-1PL
We are very busy all day.

Pingasuniit tallimat tungaanut timmersorpugut.
pingasu-niit tallimat tungaanut timmersor-pugut
three-ABL.PL five until do.sport-1PL
From three to five o'clock we did sport.

Aasap ingerlanerani arsaattarfissaq piariissaaq.
aasa-p ingerlanerani arsaattarfi-ssaq piaree-ssaaq
summer-REL during football.pitch-FUT ready-FUT.3SG
The football pitch will be ready during the summer.

Nerinerup kingorna qittatissaagut.
neri-ner-up kingorna qittati-ssaagut
eat-AP-REL after dance-FUT.1PL
We'll dance after eating.

1 Literally: have.

Juullip <u>nalaani</u> meeqqat tipaatsupput.
juulli-p nalaani meeqqa-t tipaatsup-put
christmas-REL during child-PL be.happy-3PL
The children are happy during Christmas.

Ukiut qulit matuma <u>siornatigut</u> naapippara.
ukiu-t quli-t matuma siornatigut naapip-para
year-PL ten-PL this ago meet-1SG>3SG
I met him/her ten years ago.

There are several postpositions of time that are contemporative verb forms. Some of these postpositions are listed in the following table.

Postposition	English translation
ilutigalugu	simultaneously with
sioqqullugu	before, ahead of

Points to note:

- These forms are 3SG intransitive contemporative forms.
- The singular postpositions are replaced by 3PL forms when following a plural noun.

The following examples illustrate the use of these postpositions.

Sermersuup aakkiartornera <u>ilutigalugu</u> nunarsuarmi imaq qaffakkiartorpoq.
sermersu-up aak-kiartor-ner-a ilutigalugu nunarsuar-mi imaq qaffak-kiartor-poq
ice.cap-REL melt-more.and.more-AP-3SG simultaneously.with world-LOC ocean rise-more.and.more-3SG
Simultaneously with the ever-increasing melting of the ice cap, the world's ocean(s) are rising more and more.

Anaana ullut marluk <u>sioqqullugit</u> asaavoq.
anaana ullu-t marluk sioqqullugit asaa-voq
mother day-PL two ahead cleaning-3SG
Mother cleaned two days prior.

In certain cases a verb in another mood can function as a postposition. For example, the verb **qaangiuppoq** 'to be finished, to be over' can be used in the causative in the sense of 'ago', and in the conditional in the sense of 'in … time', as in 'in three days' time', e.g.:

ullut pingasut <u>qaangiuppata</u>
ullu-t pingasut qaangiup-pata
day-PL three be.over-COND.3PL
in three days' time

ukioq ataaseq <u>qaanngiummat</u>
ukioq ataaseq qaanngium-mat
year one be.over-CAUS.3PL
one year ago

Finally, the enclitic particle +li can function as a postposition meaning 'since' or 'ago', as in the following example. See section 12.2 for discussion of enclitic particles.

<u>Ukiarli</u> illuga piareerpoq.
ukiar-li illu-ga piareer-poq
autumn-since house-1SG be.ready-3SG
My house has been finished since autumn.

10.3 Other

Some West Greenlandic verb-derived postpositions have meanings that do not fit into the semantic categories of place, direction, or time. Some of the most common of these are listed in the following table.

Postposition	English translation
aqqutigalugu	via, by means of
ilanngullugu	including; in addition to
inorlugu (usually PL)	less than, under (with numbers)
malillugu	after, according to
marluutillugit	including both
naapertorlugu	according to, in accordance with
peqatigalugu	at the same time as, together with, during
pillugu	in relation to, concerning, with respect to
pissutigalugu	because of
sanilliullugu	compared to
sinnerlugu	more than, above (with numbers); instead of, on behalf of

Points to note:

- These forms are 3SG intransitive contemporative forms.
- The singular postpositions are replaced by 3PL forms when following a plural noun.
- The postposition **inorlugu** usually appears in the plural (as **inorlugit**), because it usually follows a plural noun.

The following examples illustrate the use of these postpositions.

politiit <u>naapertorlugit</u>
politi-it naapertorlugit
police-PL according.to
according to the police

Aataa <u>malillugu</u> ikani kangerlummi saarulleqarluarpoq.
aataa malillugu ikani kangerlum-mi saarulle-qar-luar-poq
grandfather according.to over.there fjord-LOC cod-have-a.lot-3SG
According to grandfather, there is a lot of cod in the fjord over there.

Naalakkersuisoq sulisuni <u>peqatigalugit</u> angalavoq.
naalakkersuisoq sulisu-ni peqatigalugit angala-voq
minister worker-PL.4SG together.with travel-3SG
The minister is travelling together with his staff.

Panikka <u>marluullutik</u> atuariartorput.
pani-kka marluullutik atuariartor-put
daugther-PL.1SG both go.to.school-3PL
Both my daughters are going to school.

Weekend <u>ilanngullugu</u> sulissaanga.
weekend ilanngullugu suli-ssaanga
weekend including work-FUT.1SG
I will be working including the weekend.

Ataatap kaffi, tii kaagillu <u>ilanngullugit</u> akilerpai.
ataata-p kaffi tii kaagil-lu ilanngullugit akiler-pai
father-REL coffee tea cake-PL-and in.addition.to pay-3SG>3PL
Father paid for coffee and tea in addition to cakes.

Anorersuarneq <u>pissutigalugu</u> timmisartut timmisanngillat.
anorersuar-neq pissutigalugu timmisartu-t timmisa-nngi-llat
be.stormy-AP because.of plane-PL fly-NEG-3PL
Planes are not flying because of storm weather.

10 Postpositions

2019-imut <u>sanilliullugu</u> aningaasat isertitat qaffassimapput.
2019-i-mut sanilliullugu aningaasa-t iserti-ta-t qaffas-sima-pput
2019-HV-ALL compared.to money-PL earn-PP-PL rise-PAST-3PL
Compared to 2019, the money earned has risen.

Kim Kielsen partii Siumut <u>sinnerlugu</u> qineqqusaarpoq.
kim kielsen partii siumut sinnerlugu qineqqusaar-poq
kim kielsen party siumut on.behalf.of run.for.election-3SG
Kim Kielsen is running for election on behalf of Siumut.

5 kiilut <u>sinnerlugit</u> paarmanik nuniassimavoq.
5 kiilu-t sinnerlugit paarma-nik nunias-sima-voq
5 kilo-PL over berry-INS.PL pick-PAST-3SG
S/he picked over 5 kilos of berries.

Coronavirus <u>pillugu</u> apeqqutissaqaruit, hotlinemut sianerit.
coronavirus pillugu apeqquti-ssa-qar-uit hotline-mut sianer-it
coronavirus about question-FUT-have-COND.2SG hotline-ALL phone-IMP.2SG
If you have questions about coronavirus, phone the hotline.

Nassiussat app <u>aqqutigalugu</u> aqunneqartarput.
nassiussa-t app aqqutigalugu aqun-neqar-tar-put
shipment-PL app via manage-PASS-HAB-3PL
Shipments are managed via an app.

Chapter 11

Conjunctions

West Greenlandic has two different types of conjunctions, coordinate and subordinate. Coordinate conjunctions link two independent clauses, while subordinate conjunctions introduce a subordinate clause. West Greenlandic conjunctions can be either independent words or enclitic particles (i.e. dependent forms that attach to the end of another word; see section 12.2). Each type of conjunction is discussed in the following subsections.

11.1 Coordinating

The following is a list of some of the most common West Greenlandic coordinating conjunctions. Note that some of these are in fact enclitic particles: these are suffixes that attach to the end of a word, not independent words themselves (see section 12.2 for discussion of enclitic particles).

Coordinating conjunction	English translation
aamma	and; also
kisianni	but
imaluunniit, +luunniit	or; even
+li	but
+lu	and; also
+lu ... +lu	both ... and
taava	so

Points to note:

- The conjunction **aamma** has two different meanings depending on its placement. When it is placed between two nouns, it means 'and', whereas when it is placed after a noun it means 'also'.

11 Conjunctions

- The enclitic particles in the table are marked by an initial +; they attach to a preceding noun like an additive suffix.

The use of the coordinating conjunctions is illustrated in the following examples.

Svalbardimi aamma nunatsinni assut nanoqarpoq.
svalbardi-mi aamma nuna-tsinni assut nano-qar-poq
svalbard-LOC and land-LOC.1PL many polar.bear-have-3SG
Svalbard and Greenland[1] have many polar bears.

Meeqqat sinipput, anaana aamma sinippoq.
meeqqa-t sinip-put anaana aamma sinip-poq
child-PL sleep-3PL mother also sleep-3SG
The children are sleeping; the mother also is sleeping.

Tuuma, Ari Piitarlu neripput, Asali nerinngilaq.
tuuma ari piitar-lu neri-pput asa-li neri-nngi-laq
tuuma ari piitar-and eat-3PL asa-but eat-NEG-3SG
Tuuma, Ari, and Piitaq are eating, but Asa is not eating.

Sutorusuppisi? Kaffi tiiluunniit?
su-to-rusup-pisi kaffi tii-luunniit
what-consume-want-INT.2PL coffee tea-or
What would you like to have? Coffee or tea?

Tiilu kafffilu mamaraakka.
tii-lu kaffi-lu mamar-aakka
tea-and coffee-and find.tasty-VAL.1SG>3PL
I like both tea and coffee.

11.2 Subordinating

Subordinating conjunctions are not a typical feature of West Greenlandic in the way that they are in, for example, Indo-European languages. Subordinate clauses are usually conveyed either by a verbal mood or another suffix. See section 14.5 on complex sentences for discussion of the various ways of constructing subordinate clauses in West Greenlandic.

1 Literally: our land.

Chapter 12
Particles

12.1 Discourse particles and interjections

Discourse particles and interjections are words that are used to facilitate communication and signal participation in the conversation by indicating sentiments such as surprise, agreement, disagreement, hesitation, uncertainty, and understanding, such as English 'oh', 'um', 'well', 'yeah', 'you know', etc. Some of the most common West Greenlandic discourse particles and interjections are shown in the following table.

Discourse particle/ interjection	English translation
aah	oh (expresses dissatisfaction)
aap	yes
aat?	for real? really?
ajja, hajja	oh no
alaa	that was close
asuki	dunno, I don't know
haar, haarmi	look at this
ha?	what? pardon me?
imaatt	ooh
kakkaak	OMG
naagga	no (polite)
naamik	no
naamivik	definitely not
nå	well
qaa	come on
qaami	OK
qujanaq	thank you
qujanarsuaq	thanks a lot

DOI: 10.4324/9781315160863-12

12 Particles

Discourse particle/ interjection	English translation
suu	yes (colloquial)
sussa	forget about it, never mind
ta	shh
torrak	well done, clever you, that's good
tuavi	hurry

The following examples illustrate the use of the discourse particles and interjections.

– Ataata tikippa? – Asuki.
ataata tikip-pa asuki
father arrive-INT.3SG dunno
– Has father arrived? – Dunno.

Radio ikimmat ataata oqarpoq 'ta!' meeqqat nipaarsaaq quniarlugit.
radio ikim-mat ataata oqar-poq ta meeqqa-t nipaarsaa-qqu-niar-lugit
radio turn.on-CAUS.3SG father say-3SG shh child-PL be.quiet-ask-intend.to-CONT.3PL
When the radio turned on father said 'shh!' to ask the children to be quiet.

Qujanaq ikiuukkavit.
qujanaq ikiuuk-kavit
thank.you help.out-CAUS.2SG
Thank you for helping out.

'Sussa aallarnata,' anaana oqarpoq.
sussa aallar-nata anaana oqar-poq
forget.about travel-NEG.IMP.1PL mother say-3SG
'Forget about us travelling,' mother said.

12.2 Enclitic particles

West Greenlandic has a number of enclitic particles, that is, particles that attach to the end of a word rather than existing as independent words. These particles have a distinct meaning even though they are not separate words. Many of the enclitic particles convey similar types of meanings to the interjections and discourse particles, i.e. nuances of hesitation, agreement, uncertainty, etc. However, some of them instead convey the meaning of an adverb (such as 'allegedly'), postposition (such as 'since'), or conjunction (such as 'and', 'but', 'or'). Some of the most common enclitic particles are listed in the following table.

Enclitic particles

Enclitic particle	English translation
-aasiit	as usual
-gooq, -rooq, -ngooq	they say, allegedly, I've heard
+li	but
+li	ago; since
+lu	and, also
-luunniit	or; (not) even
-lusooq	like
+mi	what about, how about; though, however
+mita, +mitaava	I wonder
-(t)taaq	also; either (in negative clauses)
+toq	I wonder
-una, -juna	it is ... who/which

Points to note:

- The variant **-gooq** is used following a vowel; the variant **-rooq** is used following -q-, and the variant **-ngooq** is used following a consonant.
- The variants **+mita** and **+mitaava** can be used interchangeably.
- The variant **-ttaaq** is used following vowels and consonants, while the variant **-taaq** is used following -r-.
- The particle **-una** is used for topicalisation, i.e. to create the equivalent of English sentences starting with 'It is/was X who ...', e.g. 'It was Piitaq who bought the present.' It is followed by a verb in the participial mood.
- The variant **-juna** can be used following -a- and -u-.

The following examples illustrate the use of the enclitic particles. Many of these particles are also illustrated elsewhere throughout this volume (e.g. you will find **-gooq/-rooq/-ngooq** under evidentials in section 7.6, and **+lu** under conjunctions in section 11.1).

12 Particles

Paaluuna raadiukkut oqaluttoq.
paalu-una raadiu-kkut oqalut-toq
paalu-it.is radio-PRO speak-PART.3SG
It is Paalu who is speaking on the radio.

Juullimi sumittoq tunilara.
juulli-mi sumit-toq tuni-lara
christmas-LOC what-wonder give-OPT.1SG>3SG
I wonder what I should give him/her at Christmas.

Lise sulisarpoq allakkiat nutserlugit qallunaatut kalaallisulluunniit.
lise suli-sar-poq allakkia-t nutser-lugit qallunaatut kalaallisul-luunniit
lise work-HAB-3SG document-PL translate-CONT.4SG>3PL danish greenlandic-or
Lise works translating Danish or Greenlandic documents.

Uangattaaq sukkulerneq ajorpunga.
uanga-ttaaq sukkuler-neq ajor-punga
i-also use.sugar-AP be.bad-1SG
I don't normally use sugar either.

Chapter 13
Suffixes

13.1 Suffix types

West Greenlandic has a large number of suffixes which play a major role in the language's grammar. Functions of adverbs range from the modification of nouns (e.g. by making them diminutive) to the indication of verbal information such as tense, aspect, and modality, among many other uses. The suffixes can be divided into the following four groups depending on whether they are attached to nouns or verbs and whether they themselves function nominally or verbally:

- Suffixes that are attached to nouns and make them into verbs, e.g. **kaffi** 'coffee' plus **+sorpoq** 'consume' > **kaffisorpoq** 'to drink coffee'
- Suffixes that are attached to nouns and make new nouns, e.g. **kangerluk** 'fjord' plus **+suaq** 'big' > **kangerlussuaq** 'big fjord'
- Suffixes that are attached to verbs and make them into nouns, e.g. **sinippoq** 'to sleep' plus **+fik** 'place' > **siniffik** 'bed'
- Suffixes that are attached to verbs and make new verbs or modify the meaning of verbs, e.g. **sulivoq** 'to work' plus **-lerpoq** 'to start' > **sulilerpoq** 'to start to work'

Suffixes have been discussed throughout the previous sections of this volume because they are often one of the most common – or the most common – ways of conveying basic aspects of West Greenlandic grammar. Details of specific suffixes can be found in these sections (e.g. suffixes expressing verbal tense and aspect are discussed in the sections on tense and aspect, etc.). The following subsection is devoted to the rules governing the order in which suffixes can appear in multi-suffix West Greenlandic words.

13.2 Order of suffixes

Greenlandic words may be composed of a root followed by multiple suffixes. An individual word may contain as many as a dozen suffixes, but high numbers of suffixes are relatively uncommon and are more likely to be seen in formal language such as the press and official documents. In everyday spoken language words typically have fewer suffixes (e.g. two to four), but it is not uncommon to see up to five or even six suffixes.

There is some flexibility regarding the order of the suffixes within a word, but certain tendencies can be observed. For example, aspectual suffixes such as **+tarpoq/+sarpoq** 'habitually, usually' typically appear before tense suffixes such as **-simavoq** (past tense marker) or **-ssaaq** (future tense marker). As a further example, nouns take suffixes (e.g. diminutive endings) first, followed by case endings in the singular or plural (either on their own or merged with possessive suffixes). These tendencies are illustrated in the following numbered lists. The lower the number in the list, the closer the associated suffix is to the beginning of the word. Note that many words will only contain a few of these possible suffix types. Note also that a nominal phrase may take a verbalising suffix and vice versa, which means that a single word may have components shown in both of the lists.

Nominal phrases	
1	Nominal stem
2	Derivative suffix (e.g. diminutive)
3	Other suffixes (e.g. tense or aspect suffix; see order in next list)
4	Case (singular or plural), with possessive suffix where relevant
5	Enclitic particle

Verbal phrases	
1	Verbal stem (or nominal stem plus verbalising suffix such as **-uvoq** 'to be')
2	Aspect suffix
3	Passive suffix
4	Tense suffix
5	Modal or adverb suffix
6	Negative suffix
7	Verbal mood marker with person suffix, or participial suffix
8	Enclitic particle

The following example illustrates a word with a relatively large number of suffixes, followed by a breakdown of their order.

Order of suffixes

West Greenlandic	**Kaffisortarsimagaluanngilangalu.**							
Breakdown	**kaffi**	**sor**	**tar**	**sima**	**galua**	**nngi**	**langa**	**lu**
Categories	incorporated object	verbal stem	aspect suffix	tense suffix	modal suffix	negation	person suffix	enclitic particle
Glossing	coffee	consume	HAB	PAST	if.only	NEG	1SG	and
English	And I would not otherwise have drunk coffee regularly.							

The following examples illustrate various types of words containing multiple suffixes to give you a clearer idea of how this ordering works in practice.

illussannguannilu
illu-ssa-nngu-anni-lu
house-FUT-small-LOC.1SG-and
and in my little future house

Anguterujussuanngorsimavutit.
angute-rujussua-nngor-sima-vutit
man-very.big-become-PAST-2SG
You have become a very big man.

Angalangaatsiassamaarpunga.
angala-ngaatsia-ssamaar-punga
travel-quite.a.lot-plan-1SG
I plan to travel quite a lot.

Ujarsinnaasimassagaluarpaat.
ujar-sinnaa-sima-ssa-galuar-paat
look.for-be.able-PAST-FUT-if.only-3PL>3SG
They could have been looking for him/her/it (but they weren't).

Inequnarluinnaqqissaarpoq.
inequnar-luinnaq-qissaar-poq
be.cute-really-completely-3SG
S/he is really *really* cute.

13 Suffixes

Neqitortarunnaarnikuuvungalu.
neqi-tor-ta-runnaar-nikuu-vunga-lu
meat-consume-HAB-no.longer-PAST-1SG-and
And I don't eat meat anymore.

Oqaasilerisunngorniassamaarpisi?
oqaasilerisu-nngor-nia-ssamaar-pisi?
linguist-become-want-plan-INT.2PL
Do you guys want to plan on becoming linguists?

Nuersaarusukkunnaarpunga.
nuersaa-rusu-kkunnaar-punga
knit-want-no.longer-1SG
I don't want to knit anymore.

Sinilluannguatsiaramiaasiit.
sinil-lua-nnguatsiar-ami-aasiit
sleep-well-probably-CAUS.4SG-as.usual
S/he probably slept well as usual.

Chapter 14

Phrases, clauses, and sentences

14.1 Basic word order

The basic word order in West Greenlandic is SOV (SUBJECT OBJECT VERB). This means that the first element of the sentence is typically the subject, followed by the object, with the verb at the end. This can be contrasted with English, in which the basic word order is SVO (SUBJECT VERB OBJECT). The basic West Greenlandic word order is illustrated next. Note that this basic SOV word order does not always apply because many West Greenlandic sentences consist of a single word which starts with an incorporated subject or object (see 14.2.).

Anaanama aviisi atuarpaa.
anaana-ma aviisi atuar-paa
mother-REL.1SG newspaper read-3SG>3SG
My mother is reading a newspaper.

Ivalu iipilimik nerivoq.
ivalu iipili-mik neri-voq
ivalu apple-INS eat-3SG
Ivalu is eating an apple.

Qitsuup imeq imerpaa.
qitsu-up imeq imer-paa
cat-REL water drink-3SG>3SG
The cat drank the water.

If the noun has a modifier, it follows the noun, as in the following example. See section 6.1 (attributive noun modifiers) and 14.2 (incorporation) for further details.

14 Phrases, clauses, and sentences

qitsuk qernertoq
qitsuk qerner-toq
cat be.black-IP
a black cat

Naja saarullinnik panertunik nerivoq.
naja saarullin-nik panertu-nik neri-voq
naja cod-INS.PL dried-INS.PL eat-3SG
Naja is eating dried cod.

Numerals, like modifiers, follow the noun, e.g.:

atuakkat qulit
atuakka-t quli-t
book-PL ten-PL
ten books

If a noun has an associated modifier and numeral, the modifier precedes the numeral, e.g.:

atuakkat nutaat qulit
atuakka-t nutaa-t quli-t
book-PL new-PL ten-PL
ten new books

If there is a demonstrative pronoun in a phrase with a modifier and/or numeral, the demonstrative comes last, e.g.:

atuakkat nutaat qulit taakku
atuakka-t nutaa-t quli-t taakku
book-PL new-PL ten-PL these
these ten new books

If there is an adverb or adverbial phrase in the sentence, it comes right before the verb, as in the following example. (Note that adverbial meaning can also be conveyed by verbal suffixes instead of by an independent adverb; see section 9.)

Ellen kusanartumik allattarpoq.
ellen kusanartumik allat-tar-poq
Ellen beautifully write-HAB-3SG
Ellen writes beautifully.

14.2 Incorporation

Incorporation is a term for the practice of combining nominal and verbal stems and suffixes to form single words that convey the content of what would be an entire phrase or sentence in a language such as English. Incorporation is a very prominent feature of West Greenlandic. Nouns serving as predicatives (explained in 14.2.1), objects, and adverbials can be merged into a verb in this manner. Each type of incorporation will be discussed in the following subsections.

14.2.1 Incorporated predicative

In West Greenlandic, a predicative (the equivalent of a word following the verb 'to be' in English, e.g. 'I am a doctor', 'he is a fisherman', 'they are nice') may be incorporated into the verbal suffix -**uvoq** 'to be'.

The predicative may be a noun, modifier, participle, or pronoun. If the predicative is a noun, modifier, or participle, it always appears in the singular form when incorporated to the verb. There are several different variants of the verb -**uvoq** depending on the ending of the nominal form to which it is attached. These variants are listed here.

	-**uvoq** to be	
Variant	Context	Example
-**uvoq**	after **i**, **u**, or **i/e/u/o** plus a weak consonant	**qernertoq** black > **qernertuuvoq** it is black **saarullik** cod > **saarulliuvoq** it is a cod
+**uvoq**	with strong q-stems, especially after +**neq**	**tanneq** the longest > **tanneruvoq** it is the longest
-**avoq**	after **a** or **a** plus a weak consonant	**anaana** mother > **anaanaavoq** she is a mother **arnaq** woman > **arnaavoq** she is a woman
-**juvoq**	after **aa** or **aa/uu** plus a weak consonant	**aanaa** grandmother > **aanaajuvoq** she is a grandmother **inuttuut** folksong > **inuttuujuvoq** it is a folksong

The suffix -**uvoq** (and its variants) has a complete paradigm in all persons, as shown in the following table.

Intransitive indicative of -**uvoq** to be (and variants)	
1SG	-**uvunga**
2SG	-**uvutit**
3SG	-**uvoq**
1PL	-**uvugut**
2PL	-**uvusi**
3PL	-**upput**

Point to note:

- Various mood and tense suffixes can be added to the base -**u**- and its variants, e.g. **aanaajuvoq** 'she is a grandmother' > **aanaajussaaq** 'she will be a grandmother', **aanaajusimavoq** 'she was a grandmother', etc.

The following examples illustrate how predicatives can be incorporated into -**uvoq**.

Sulisuuvunga.
sulisu-u-vunga
employee-be-1SG
I am an employee.

Atuartuuvutit.
atuartu-u-vutit
pupil-be-2SG
You are a pupil.

Kinaavit?
kina-a-vit
who-be-INT.2SG
Who are you?

Ilinniartuusimavunga.
ilinniartu-u-sima-vunga
student-be-PAST-1SG
I was a student.

An independent noun or proper name can be added as a separate subject in conjunction with an incorporated predicative, e.g.:

Ellen nutserisuulluarpoq.
ellen nutserisu-u-lluar-poq
ellen translator-be-good-3SG
Ellen is a good translator.

If an incorporated predicative is accompanied by a modifier, the modifier follows the incorporated predicative and appears in the absolute case, e.g.:

Anthon qimmiuvoq qernertoq.
anthon qimmi-u-voq qerner-toq
anthon dog-be-3SG black-IP
Anthon is a black dog.

If the predicative is plural, the plurality is indicated by the person suffix of the verb, not by the incorporated predicative.

Kalaaliuvugut.
kalaali-u-vugut
greenlander-be-1PL
We are Greenlanders.

Piniartuusimapput.
piniartu-u-sima-pput
hunter-be-PAST-3PL
They were hunters.

Predicatives may also be incorporated into the verbal suffix -**nngorpoq** 'to become', e.g.:

Ernera nakorsanngorpoq.
erne-ra nakorsa-nngor-poq
son-1SG doctor-become-3SG
My son became a doctor.

14.2.2 Incorporated direct object

The direct object of a verb can be incorporated into the verb in the same way that a predicative can. Objects can be incorporated into a much larger range of verbs than predicatives can. There are a number of verbal suffixes that commonly incorporate their objects. These are listed and exemplified in the following table.

Verbal suffix	Meaning	Example
-erniarpoq, **-arniarpoq,** **-verniarpoq**	to sell	**siku** ice > **sikuerniarpoq** to sell ice cream
-lerpaa	to equip with; to put on someone	**kamik** boot > **kamilerpaa** to put boots on him/her
-liarpoq	to travel to	**Kangerlussuaq** (village in Greenland) > **Kangerlussualiarpoq** to travel to Kangerlussuaq
-liorpoq	to make	**kaagi** cake > **kaagiliorpoq** to make a cake **su-** what > **suliorpit** what are you making?
+(p)poq	to catch (fish or prey)	**puisi** seal > **puisippoq** to catch seal
-qarpoq	to have	**ui** husband > **ueqarpoq** to have a husband
+siorpoq	to look for	**illu** house > **illusiorpoq** to look for a house
+sivoq	to buy, to receive, to acquire	**iffiaq** bread > **iffiarsivoq** to buy bread **pi-** something > **pisivoq** to buy something
+torpoq, **+sorpoq**	to consume	**tii** tea > **tiitorpoq** to drink tea
+/-uteqarpoq, **-ateqarpoq,** **-juteqarpoq**	to have something in one's possession	**immuk** milk > **immuuteqarpoq** to have some milk (in one's possession)
-nngortippaa	to make something into something, to appoint him/her as	**palasi** priest > **palasinngortippaa** to appoint him/her as a priest

Points to note:

- Incorporated objects are always based on the singular form of the noun. Therefore, only the context will distinguish a singular incorporated object from a plural one. For example, **kamilerpaa** 'to put boots on him/her' clearly refers to a pair (or multiple pairs) of boots even though it is based on the singular form **kamik** 'boot'.
- The indefinite form **pi-** 'something' cannot exist independently; it functions only as an incorporated object. See also section 4.6 (indefinite pronouns). The interrogative form **su-** 'what' can be incorporated in a similar way. See also section 4.3 (interrogative pronouns).
- The variant -**ateqarpoq** is used after **a**, or **a** plus a weak consonant. The variant +/-**uteqarpoq** is used after **i**, **u**, or **i/e/u/o** plus a weak consonant. The variant -**juteqarpoq** is used after **aa** or **aa/uu** plus a weak consonant.

The following examples illustrate various types of sentences featuring incorporated objects.

Kaffisortarpunga.
kaffi-sor-tar-punga
coffee-consume-HAB-1SG
I usually drink coffee.

Erneqarpunga.
erne-qar-punga
son-have-1SG
I have a son.

Immuuteqarpit?
immu-uteqar-pit
milk-have-INT.2SG
Do you have milk here?

Napparsimmaviliarpugut.
napparsimmavi-liar-pugut
hospital-travel.to-1PL
We are going to the hospital.

Angallateqarput.
angallate-qar-put
ship-have-3PL
They have a ship.

Ivalu koorpunik qarleqarpoq.
ivalu koorpu-nik qarle-qar-poq
ivalu jeans-INS.PL trouser-have-3SG
Ivalu is wearing jeans.[1]

Nukakkut inequnartumik meeraqarput.
nuka-kkut inequnartu-mik meera-qar-put
nuka-COLL cute-INS child-have-3PL
Nuka and her partner have a cute child.

Najap nakorsap oqaasii <u>kalaallisuunngortittarpai</u>.
naja-p nakorsa-p oqaas-ii kalaallisuu-nngortit-tar-pai
naja-REL doctor-REL word-PL.3SG greenlandic-make.into-HAB-3SG>3PL
Naja translates the doctor's words into Greenlandic.

Iisartakkat <u>arnanngortippaanga</u>.
iisartakka-t arna-nngortip-paanga
pill-PL woman-make.into-3PL>1SG
The pills are transforming me into a woman.

14.2.3 Incorporated noun in oblique cases

Nouns with oblique case suffixes can be incorporated into a verb. There are several verbal suffixes that are designed specifically to combine with a noun to convey the meaning of movement towards, away from, or other senses associated with the oblique cases. These verbal suffixes are actually verbalised forms of the oblique cases (see section 3.3 for discussion of these cases). The verbalised forms of the oblique cases are listed in the following table.

Verbalised suffix	English translation	Basic case suffix
-mukarpoq	to go to, towards	allative suffix **-mut**
-miippoq	to be located in	locative suffix **-mi**
-meerpoq	to come from; to be from originally	ablative suffix **-mi(i)t**
-moorpoq	to go in the direction of; to meet up	allative suffix **-mut**

---

1 Literally: jeans trousers.

			Incorporation
-minnganeerpoq	to be from originally	ablative suffix variant **-minngaanit**	
-kkoorpoq	to go via	prolative suffix **-kkut**	
-toorpoq, **-soorpoq**	to behave like; to do something like; to wear the clothes of; to have a lesson in a language	equative suffix **-tut**, **-sut**	

Points to note:

- When a plural noun is incorporated into one of the verbalised suffixes beginning with -m, the -m is replaced with -n (which marks the plural form of the corresponding noun cases), e.g. ini<u>m</u>iippoq 'it is in the room'; ini<u>n</u>iippoq 'it is in the rooms'.
- These verbalised suffixes are attached to nouns in the same way as the corresponding basic case suffixes (i.e. the form of the suffixed noun will depend on its stem type; see section 3.2).

The use of these verbalised suffixes is illustrated in the following examples.

Nuummiippunga.
nuum-miip-punga
nuuk-be.in-1SG
I'm in Nuuk.

Siullermeerluni Københavnimiippoq.
siullermeerluni københavni-miip-poq
for.the.first.time Copenhagen-be.in-3SG
S/he was in Copenhagen for the first time.

Qaqortumeerpunga.
qaqortu-meer-punga
qaqortoq-come.from-1SG
I come from Qaqortoq.

Londoniminngaaneerpugut.
londoni-minngaaneer-pugut
london-be.from-1PL
We are from London originally.

14 Phrases, clauses, and sentences

Biilit siumoorput.
biili-t siu-moor-put.
car-PL front-move.toward-3PL
The car drove forward.

Nuka pisiniarfimmukarpoq.
nuka pisiniarfim-mukar-poq
nuka shop-go.to-3SG
Nuka goes to the shop.

Ullumi aqqanermoorpugut.
ullumi aqqaner-moor-pugut
today eleven-meet.at-1PL
We met at 11 o'clock today.

Atuakkanik atorniartarfimmiippoq.
atuakka-nik atorniartarfim-miip-poq
book-INS.PL library-be.in-3SG
There are books in the library.

Aalisartoq sikukkoorniarpoq.
aalisartoq siku-kkoor-niar-poq
fisherman ice-go.via-intend-3SG
The fisherman intends to go over the ice.

Niviarsiaraq kalaallisoorpoq.
niviarsiaraq kalaalli-soor-poq
girl greenlander-behave.like-3SG
The girl is wearing the Greenlandic national costume.[2]

Rasmus aamma Lise kalaallisoortarput.
rasmus aamma lise kalaalli-soor-tar-put
rasmus and lise greenlandic-have.a.lesson.in-HAB-3PL
Rasmus and Lise take Greenlandic lessons.

Meeqqat tuluttoorput.
meeqqa-t tulut-toor-put
child-PL english-have.a.lesson.in-3PL
The children are having an English lesson.

2 Literally: behaving like a Greenlander.

Kalaallit pingasut filmfestivalimi Berlinimiittumi peqataapput.   Definiteness
kalaalli-t pingasu-t filmfestivali-mi berlini-miit-tu-mi peqataa-pput
greenlander-PL three-PL film.festival-LOC berlin-be.in-IP-LOC participate-3PL
Three Greenlanders are participating in the film festival, which is in Berlin.

14.3 Definiteness

West Greenlandic does not have definite articles (such as the English 'the' or French 'le', 'la'), or indefinite articles (such as the English 'a', 'an'). Instead, the definiteness of nouns can be expressed in other ways, which are outlined in this section.

One way of marking nouns for definiteness is by means of case. The instrumental case (singular -**mik**, plural -**nik**) can be used to mark a direct object as indefinite, with a meaning comparable to that of the English indefinite article or 'some' (see section 3.3.6). By contrast, the use of the absolutive case to mark a direct object typically indicates that the object is definite (see section 3.3.1). The following example illustrates the use of case to mark nouns as definite or indefinite.

Indefinite	Definite
Atuakkamik tunivara.	**Atuagaq tunivara.**
atuakka-mik tuni-vara	atuagaq tuni-vara
book-ins give-1SG>3SG	book give-1SG>3SG
I sold a/some book(s).	I sold the book.

The valency suffix -**uppaa** (discussed in section 7.10) can also be used with certain verbs to indicate a definite object, e.g.:

Indefinite	Definite
Ataatap Ivalu imermik tunivaa.	**Ataatap imeq Ivalumut tunniuppaa.**
ataata-p ivalu imer-mik tuni-vaa	ataata-p imeq ivalu-mut tunni-up-paa
father-REL ivalu water-ins give-3SG>3SG	father-REL water ivalu-ALL give-VAL-3SG>3SG
Father gives (some) water to Ivalu.	Father gives the water to Ivalu.

An incorporated object is always indefinite; see section 14.2.2.

14.4 Clause types

The various types of West Greenlandic clauses are detailed in the following subsections.

14.4.1 Copular

Copular clauses are clauses denoting states of being or becoming, as in the English clauses 'he is a doctor' and 'they have become tired'. Copular clauses are also known as equative clauses. Copular clauses in West Greenlandic are typically based around one of the following verbal suffixes. All of the suffixes meaning 'become' are synonyms and can be used interchangeably.

Suffix	English translation
+uvoq, -avoq, -juvoq	to be
-nngorpoq	to become
+sivoq	to become
+livoq	to become

Point to note:

- See section 14.2.1 for the rules governing the use of each variant of **+uvoq** 'to be'.

The following examples illustrate West Greenlandic copular clauses.

Aqqa sanasuuvoq.
aqqa sanasu-u-voq
aqqa builder-be-3sg
Aqqa is a carpenter/builder.

Aningaaq Qallunaat sakkutuuini sakkutuujuvoq.
aningaaq qallunaa-t sakkutuu-ini sakkutuu-ju-voq
aningaaq dane-PL army-LOC.3PL soldier-be-3SG
Aningaaq is a soldier in the Danish army.

Aasaq nuannersivoq.
aasaq nuanner-si-voq
summer be.pleasant-become-3SG
The summer is becoming pleasant.

Kissaataa maanna piviusunngorpoq.
kissaata-a maanna piviusu-nngor-poq
wish-3SG now reality-become-3SG
His/her wish is now becoming reality.

Illuminnut maanna angerlarsinnaanngorput.
illu-minnut maanna angerlar-sinnaa-nngor-put
house-ALL.PL now return-be.able-become-3PL
Now they have become able to return to their homes.

If there is a location (an adverb of place), then the verb -**miippoq** 'to be in' is used, e.g.:

Nuummiippoq.
nuum-miip-poq
nuuk-be.in-3SG
S/he is in Nuuk.

Nuissat qilammiipput.
nuissa-t qilam-miip-put
cloud-PL sky-be.in-3PL
The clouds are in the sky.

Silamiippunga.
sila-miip-punga
outside-be.in-1SG
I'm outside.

14.4.2 Intransitive

Intransitive clauses are clauses that do not contain a direct object. In West Greenlandic, verbs in intransitive clauses appear in a designated intransitive form. (West Greenlandic verbs have different intransitive and transitive suffixes; see section 7.2 for discussion and paradigms.) The subject of an intransitive verb appears in the absolutive case (see section 3.3.1). The following are examples of intransitive clauses.

14 Phrases, clauses, and sentences

Unnukkut sinippunga.
unnukkut sinip-punga
in.the.evening sleep-1SG
I sleep in the evening.

Qitsuk nunami nalavoq.
qitsuk nuna-mi nala-voq
cat ground-LOC lie-3SG
The cat is lying on the ground.

Anaanaga ajagalu ullumi Danmarkimut aallalerput.
anaana-ga aja-ga-lu ullumi danmarki-mut aalla-ler-put
mother-1SG aunt-1SG-and today denmark-ALL travel-going.to-3PL
My mother and my aunt (mother's sister) are going to travel to Denmark today.

Qulinut innalerpusi.
quli-nut inna-ler-pusi
ten-ALL.PL go.to.bed-going.to-2PL
You're going to go to bed at ten.

Niviaq Korneliussen atuakkiullaqqissuuvoq.
niviaq korneliussen atuakkiu-llaqqis-su-u-voq
niviaq korneliussen write.book-be.good.at-IP-be-3SG
Niviaq Korneliussen is a good writer.

Note that sometimes a Greenlandic intransitive clause might correspond to a transitive sentence in English. For example, the verbs -qarpoq 'to have' and -uteqarpoq 'to have in one's possession' are intransitive in Greenlandic, whereas the equivalent 'to have' is transitive in English. In Greenlandic, the direct object in such a clause is incorporated into the verb -**uteqarpoq**, as in the following example (see section 14.2.2 for discussion of object incorporation).

Naja qitsuuteqarpoq.
naja qitsu-uteqar-poq
naja cat-have-3SG
Naja has a cat.

Like -qarpoq, other verbs with incorporated objects are typically intransitive in Greenlandic, though the English equivalents are transitive, e.g.:

Kaffisorpugut.
kaffi-sor-pugut
coffee-consume-1SG
We're drinking coffee.

Likewise, an indefinite direct object is typically marked by the instrumental case (discussed in section 3.3.6) and appears in conjunction with an intransitive verb, e.g.:

Kaagimik nerivunga.
kaagi-mik neri-vunga
cake-INS eat-1SG
I'm eating cake.

14.4.3 Transitive

Transitive clauses are clauses that contain a direct object. In West Greenlandic, verbs in transitive clauses appear in a designated transitive form which encodes both the subject and the direct object. (See section 7 for more detailed discussion of transitive verbs.)

If the transitive verb has an explicit subject (in addition to the subject element of the transitive verb suffix), it appears in the relative case (see section 3.3.2). If the transitive verb has an explicit direct object (in addition to the object element of the transitive verb suffix), it appears in the absolutive case (see section 3.3.1). The following examples illustrate transitive clauses.

Nivip Anna pulaarpaa.
nivi-p anna pulaar-paa
nivi-REL anna visit-3SG>3SG
Nivi visited Anna.

Qimmeq nerisipparput.
qimmeq nerisip-parput
dog feed-1PL>3SG
We fed the dog.

Kuluup biilit benzinimik immerpai.
kulu-up biili-t benzini-mik immer-pai
kulu-REL car-PL petrol-INS fill-3SG>3PL
Kuluk filled the car with petrol.

Ilinniartsitsisup angajoqqaat atuarfimmut aggeqquai.
ilinniartsitsisu-p angajoqqaa-t atuarfim-mut agge-qqu-ai
teacher-REL parent-PL school-ALL come-invite-3SG>3PL
The teacher invited the parents to come to the school.

14.4.4 Half-transitive

This is a term commonly used in the Greenlandic grammatical tradition, with reference to intransitive verbs such as **nerivoq** 'to eat' or **igavoq** 'to cook' when they appear in conjunction with an indefinite direct object. If there is an explicit subject in the sentence (as opposed to just a verbal person suffix), it appears in the absolutive case. The indefinite direct object is marked with the instrumental suffix -**mik**. The following examples illustrate sentences with half-transitive verbs. See section 3.3.6 for discussion of the instrumental, and section 14.3 for discussion of definiteness.)

Neqimik igavugut.
neqi-mik iga-vugut
meat-INS cook-1PL
We're cooking meat.

Iipilimik nerivutit.
iipili-mik neri-vutit
apple-INS eat-2SG
You're eating an apple.

Nuka Elilu atuakkamik atuarput.
nuka eli-lu atuakka-mik atuar-put
nuka eli-and book-INS read-3PL
Nuka and Eli read a book.

14.4.5 Double transitive

This is a term often used in the Greenlandic grammatical tradition which has the same meaning as 'causative' in this volume, in the sense of 'to make or let someone do something'. See section 7.7 on causativity for discussion.

14.4.6 Existential

An existential clause is a clause giving information about something that exists. In English, existential clauses are expressed by means of the construction 'there is/there are', as in 'there's a car outside' or 'there are books in the school'. In West Greenlandic, existential clauses are expressed by means of the verbal suffix -**qarpoq** with an incorporated nominal object (see section 14.2.2 on incorporated objects). The verbal suffix -**qarpoq** can also mean 'to have', as in **Bente illoqarpoq** 'Bente has a house' (see section 14.4.7 for further discussion and examples of this verb with the meaning of 'to have'). The context generally determines whether a given construction means 'to have' or 'there is'. Note that throughout this volume, -**qarpoq** is glossed as 'have' regardless of its meaning in any given instance. The following are examples of existential clauses.

Kangerlummi illoqarpoq.
kangerlum-mi illo-qar-poq
fjord-LOC house-have-3SG
There is a house by the fjord.

Immami sikoqarpoq.
imma-mi siko-qar-poq
sea-LOC ice-have-3SG
There is ice in the sea.

Inimi sofaqarpoq.
ini-mi sofa-qar-poq
room-LOC sofa-have-3SG
There is a sofa in the room.

The verb in an existential clause always appears in the 3SG even if it refers to many things. Because incorporated objects are always based on singular forms, only the context will distinguish a singular referent from a plural one. This is illustrated in the following examples.

Aqqusinermi assut qimmeqarpoq.
aqqusiner-mi assut qimme-qar-poq
street-LOC a.lot dog-have-3SG
There are a lot of dogs in the street.

14 Phrases, clauses, and sentences

Nuummi inoqaqaaq.
nuum-mi ino-qa-qaaq
nuuk-LOC person-have-a.lot.3SG
There are a lot of people in Nuuk.

In negative existential clauses the verbal suffix -**qanngilaq** 'there isn't/there aren't' is used. As in the case of -**qarpoq** in affirmative existential clauses, this negative verb can have the meaning of 'not to have' as well as expressing lack of existence, with context distinguishing the two senses. Clauses with an explicit subject have the meaning of 'not to have', as in **Marie qimmeqanngilaq** 'Marie doesn't have a dog', whereas clauses without an explicit subject have a negative existential meaning. Such clauses are illustrated here.

Inimi sofaqanngilaq.
ini-mi sofa-qa-nngi-laq
room-LOC sofa-have-NEG-3SG
There isn't a sofa in the room.[3]

Illoqarfimmi inoqanngilaq.
illoqarfim-mi ino-qa-nngi-laq
town-LOC person-have-NEG-3SG
There aren't any people in the town.

Qaqqami aputeqanngilaq.
qaqqa-mi apute-qa-nngi-laq
mountain-LOC snow-have-NEG-3SG
There is no snow on the mountain.

Ullumi Narsami pisiniarfinni vindruaqanngilaq.
ullu-mi narsa-mi pisiniarfin-ni vindrua-qa-nngi-laq
today narsa-LOC shop-PL grape-have-NEG-3SG
Today there are no grapes in the shops in Narsaq.

The nominal stem **su-** 'what' can be used in conjunction with -**qanngilaq** to form the construction 'there isn't anything (literally 'there isn't what'), e.g.

Fjernsynikkut soqanngilaq.
fjernsyni-kkut so-qa-nngi-laq
television-PRO be.someone/something-NEG-3SG
There's nothing on TV.

---

3 Can also mean 's/he doesn't have a sofa in the room'.

14.4.7 Possessive

Possessive clauses correspond to English clauses with the verb 'to have', as in 'I have a book'. In West Greenlandic, possessive clauses can be formed by means of several different verbs which are used in slightly different contexts.

The first of these is the verbal suffix -qarpoq 'to have', used in conjunction with an incorporated object (see 14.2.2). The use of -qarpoq is illustrated in the following examples.

Nuka kajortumik qimmeqarpoq.
nuka kajortu-mik qimme-qar-poq
nuka brown-INS dog-have-3SG
Nuka has a brown dog.

Nutaamik computereqarpunga.
nutaa-mik computere-qar-punga
new-INS computer-have-1SG
I have a new computer.

The second verb used in possessive clauses is **peqarpoq** 'to have'. **Peqarpoq** has the same meaning as -qarpoq, but it appears in conjunction with an independent noun in the instrumental. The following sentences illustrate the use of **peqarpoq**. These can be compared with the sentences shown previously, which are identical except that they feature -qarpoq instead of **peqarpoq**.

Nuka kajortumik qimmimik peqarpoq.
nuka kajortu-mik qimmi-mik peqar-poq
nuka brown-INS dog-INS have-3SG
Nuka has a brown dog.

Computerimik nutaamik peqarpunga.
computeri-mik nutaa-mik peqar-punga
computer-INS new-INS have-1SG
I have a new computer.

There is another possessive verbal suffix, -ateqarpoq (or its variants +/-uteqarpoq and -juteqarpoq; see section 14.2.2 for explanation of when each variant is used).

For some speakers, this suffix is synonymous with -qarpoq and peqarpoq, simply meaning 'to have'.

For others, it is used somewhat differently from them, referring specifically to possessions that the subject owns (especially food and tools), or is in temporary possession of, as in the following examples:

Ilaqutariit Nielsenikkut illuuteqarput.
ilaqutari-it nielseni-kkut illu-uteqar-put
family-PL nielsen-COLL house-have-3PL
The Nielsen family owns a house.[4]

Naja pujortartarami cigaretsiuteqarpoq.
naja pujortar-tar-ami cigaretsi-uteqar-poq
naja smoke-HAB-CAUS.4SG cigarette-have-3SG
Naja has cigarettes because she smokes.

Iffiaateqarpugut.
iffia-ateqar-pugut
bread-have-1PL
We have bread.

Aanaa kaasarfimmini mamakujuttuuteqarpoq.
aanaa kaasarfim-mini mamakujuttu-uteqar-poq
grandma pocket-PL.LOC.4SG sweet-have-3SG
Grandma has sweets in her pockets.

In addition, certain derivational suffixes, such as -taq/-saq (discussed in section 8.2), tend to take -ateqarpoq (or +/-uteqarpoq and -juteqarpoq), e.g.:

Aningaasaateqarpit?
aningaasa-ateqar-pit
money-have-INT.2SG
Do you have any money?

Note that a nominal variant of this suffix, +/-ut (and the variants -at and -jut), can be attached to nouns to form a possessive construction similar to an English phrase such as 'a house which someone owns/has', 'an owned house'. It is commonly found in conjunction with nouns denoting animals (except dogs), equipment, and food.

---

4 That is a house that they may rent out and not live in.

Basic noun	Suffixed noun
illu house	**illuut** someone's house, an owned house, a house that someone owns/has
sava sheep	**savaat** someone's sheep, an owned sheep, a sheep that someone owns/has

The transitive verbal suffix +givaa/+rivaa, or its short variant +gaa/+raa 'to have as one's X' can be attached to nouns in order to form possessive clauses; for example, **erneq** 'son' plus +raa > **erneraa** 's/he has him as his/her son'. The conjugation of this suffix is shown in the following tables.

Transitive indicative suffix +**givaa**/+**rivaa**						
Subject	Object					
	1SG	1PL	2SG	2PL	3SG	3PL
1SG	–	–	+givakkit	+givassi	+givara	+givakka
2SG	+givarma	+givatsigut	–	–	+givat	+givatit
3SG	+givaanga	+givaatigut	+givaatit	+givaasi	+givaa	+givai
1PL	–	–	+givatsigit	+givassi	+givarput	+givavut
2PL	+givassinga	+givatsigut	–	–	+givarsi	+givasi
3PL	+givaannga	+givaatigut	+givaatsit	+givassi	+givaat	

Transitive indicative suffix +**gaa**/+**raa** (short variant of +**givaa**/+**rivaa**)						
Subject	Object					
	1SG	1PL	2SG	2PL	3SG	3PL
1SG	–	–	+gaakkit	+gaassi	+gaara	+gaakka
2SG	+gaarma	+gaatsigut	–	–	+gaat	+gaatit
3SG	+gaanga	+gaatigut	+gaatit	+gaasi	+gaa	+gai
1PL	–	–	+gaatsigit	+gassi	+gaarput	+gaavut
2PL	+gaassinga	+gaatsigut	–	–	+gaarsi	+gaasi
3PL	+gaannga	+gaatigut	+gaatsit	+gaasi	+gaat	

Point to note:

- All of these suffixes (both the long and the short variants) can appear with +r instead of +g. The variant with +g is typically used with weak-stem nouns, while the variant with +r is typically used with strong-stem nouns.

The use of these suffixes is illustrated in the following examples.

Sanileraara.
sanile-raara
neighbour-have.as.1SG>3SG
He is my neighbour.[5]

Tiitorfigaat.
tiitorfi-gaat
cup-have.as.2SG>3SG
It is your cup.[6]

If there is an explicit subject in the clause, it is marked by the relative case. Similarly, if there is an explicit direct object, it is marked by the absolutive case. This is illustrated in the following example.

Lisep Aqqa erneraa.
lise-p aqqa erne-raa
lise-REL aqqa son-have.as.3SG>3SG
Aqqa is Lise's son.[7]

The suffix can also be used in the sense of 'to use something as', e.g.:

Sofa siniffigaarput.
sofa siniffi-gaarput
sofa bed-use.as.1PL>3SG
We use the sofa as a bed.

---

5 Literally: I have him as my neighbour.
6 Literally: you have it as your cup.
7 Literally: Lise has Aqqa as her son.

Finally, the same suffix can also be used in the sense of 'to regard someone or something as', e.g.:

Erfalasut kusagaakka.
erfalasu-t kusa-gaakka
flag-PL be.pretty-regard.as.1SG>3PL
I think the flags are pretty.[8]

14.4.8 Impersonal

Impersonal clauses are clauses without a subject, either explicit or implicit. In English, impersonal clauses usually start with the dummy subject 'it', as in 'it's snowing', 'it's not hard to learn Greenlandic', 'it's crowded in Nuuk'. In West Greenlandic, impersonal clauses are typically expressed by means of an indicative verb in the third-person singular without a subject, e.g.:

Siallerpoq.
sialler-poq
rain-3SG
It's raining.

Ilulissani apivoq.
ilulissa-ni api-voq
ilulissat-LOC.PL snow-3SG
It's snowing in Ilulissat.

Kalaallisut ilinniarneq nalunanngilaq.
kalaallisut ilinniar-neq naluna-nngi-laq
greenlandic learn-AP be.difficult-NEG-3SG
It's not difficult to learn Greenlandic.

Impersonal clauses can also refer to actions that are generally done by non-specific subjects. In English these can be conveyed by means of the impersonal pronoun 'one', or less formally by the pronouns 'you' and 'they', or sometimes by a passive, e.g. 'that isn't done'. In West Greenlandic, this type of clause is expressed by means of an indicative verb in the third-person plural without a subject. In many cases the habitual suffix **-tarpoq** 'usually' is also found in such verbs because they refer to actions that are done regularly.

8 Literally: I regard the flags as pretty.

Torersaassisarput.
torersaassi-sar-put
clean.up-HAB-3PL
One cleans up.⁹

Maani erruisarput.
maani errui-sar-put
here wash.up-HAB-3PL
Here we do the dishes.¹⁰

Sumi timersortarpat?
sumi timersor-tar-pat
where exercise-HAB-INT.3PL
Where do people go to exercise?

14.4.9 Interrogative

Interrogative clauses are clauses consisting of a question. There are two types of questions: closed (which can be answered only by 'yes' or 'no') and open (which start with a question word such as 'where' or 'who' and can be answered in a variety of ways). In West Greenlandic, verbs in interrogative clauses appear in a special interrogative paradigm, which has different suffixes from verbs in statements (see section 7.2.1.2 for the interrogative paradigm). (Note, however, that in some instances, such as the 1SG, the interrogative suffix is the same as the indicative.) Interrogative clauses also have a distinct intonation: they fall at the end, in contrast to statements, which have a rising intonation (see section 2.4). In contrast to languages such as English, in which interrogative clauses have a different word order to statements, West Greenlandic interrogative clauses have the same word order as statements. The following examples illustrate various types of West Greenlandic interrogative clauses.

Angerlalerpit?
angerla-ler-pit
go.home-about.to-INT.2SG
Are you about to go home?

---

9 Said to children.
10 With the implication, why don't you help out?

Aggissaanga?
aggi-ssaanga
come-FUT.INT.1SG
Shall I come?

Kikkut naapippigit?
ki-kkut naapip-pigit
who-COLL meet-INT.2PL>3PL
Who did you meet?

Skuukka sumiippat?
skuu-kka sumi-ip-pat
shoe-PL.1SG where-be-INT.3PL
Where are my shoes?

14.5 Complex sentences

Complex sentences are sentences consisting of a main clause and a subordinate clause. West Greenlandic complex sentences are detailed in the following sections.

14.5.1 Adverbial

Adverbial clauses are clauses that provide more information about the manner in which the main clause occurs (e.g. when, why, etc.). The meanings associated with adverbial clauses in English are often expressed with subordinate moods or verbal suffixes in West Greenlandic. For example, the causative, conditional, and contemporative moods are used to convey temporal clauses (i.e. clauses telling you when something happened/happens). The various types of adverbial clauses are discussed in the following subsections.

14.5.1.1 Causal

West Greenlandic causal clauses (equivalent to English clauses starting with 'because' or 'since') are typically formed by means of the causative mood (see section 7.2.2.1), as shown in the following examples.

Siallilermat qimmeq iserumavoq.
sialli-ler-mat qimmeq iser-uma-voq
rain-begin-CAUS.3SG dog go.in-want-3SG
Because it began to rain, the dog wanted to go inside.

Qasugama innarpunga.
qasu-gama innar-punga
be.tired-CAUS.1SG go.to.bed-1SG
I went to bed because I was tired.

Kaakkatta nerivugut.
kaak-katta neri-vugut
be.hungry-CAUS.1PL eat-1PL
We ate because we were hungry.

Silami aneerami qiiavoq.
silami aneer-ami qiia-voq
outside play.outside-CAUS.4SG be.cold-3SG
S/he is cold because s/he is playing outside.

14.5.1.2 Concessive

Concessive clauses are clauses which, in English, start with 'although' or 'even though'. In West Greenlandic, concessive clauses are formed by means of a verb in the contemporative mood (see section 7.2.2.3). The contemporative verb is often accompanied by +galuarpoq/-raluarpoq/-kkaluarpoq 'if only …', 'although', 'would have, but …', e.g.:

Kalaaliugaluarlunga kalaallisut oqalunneq ajorpunga.
kalaali-u-galuar-lunga kalaallisut oqalun-neq ajor-punga
greenlander-be-although-CONT.1SG greenlandic speak-AP be.bad-1SG
Even though I am a Greenlander, I don't speak Greenlandic.

Aadameeraq nerigaluarluni suli kaappoq.
aadameeraq neri-galuar-luni suli kaap-poq
aadameeraq eat-although-CONT.4SG still hungry-3SG
Even though Aadameeraq ate, he is still hungry.

Concessive constructions are also sometimes introduced by the subordinating conjunction **naak** 'although, even though', e.g.:

Naak sinilluaraluarlutik, qasupput.
naak sinil-lua-raluar-lutik qasu-pput
although sleep-well-although-CONT.4PL be.tired-3PL
They are tired even though they slept well.

The clauses can be reversed, e.g.:

Qasupput, naak sinilluaraluarlutik.
qasu-pput naak sinil-lua-raluar-lutik
be.tired-3PL although sleep-well-although-CONT.4PL
They are tired even though they slept well.

14.5.1.3 Conditional

See section 7.2.2.2 for a discussion of the ways of conveying conditional ('if ... then') clauses in West Greenlandic, and section 7.11.1.6 for a discussion of negative conditional clauses.

14.5.1.4 Purpose

Purpose clauses correspond to English clauses starting with the phrase 'in order to' or 'so that'. West Greenlandic purpose clauses are typically formed by means of the suffix **+niarpoq** 'in order to' (in other contexts: 'to intend to; to try to; to want to') in conjunction with a verb in the contemporative mood (see section 7.2.2.3) to convey the meaning of 'in order to', e.g.:

F̱jernsynerniarluni ingippoq.
fjernsyner-niar-luni ingip-poq
watch.tv-in.order.to-CONT.4SG sit.down-3SG
He sat down in order to watch TV.

Purpose clauses may also be formed by **+niarpoq** in conjunction with a verb in the causative mood (see section 7.2.2.1). This type of construction is actually a causal clause (see section 14.5.1.1) with a literal meaning of something like 'to do X because one wanted to achieve Y', but it can be regarded as the equivalent of an English purpose construction. This is illustrated in the following example.

Kalaallit nunaannut nuuppunga a̱a̱naga qanilliniassagakku.
kalaalli-t nuna-annut nuup-punga aana-ga qanilli-nia-ssa-gakku
greenlander-PL land-ALL.3PL move-1SG grandmother-1SG be.close-want-FUT-CAUS. 1SG

14
Phrases, clauses, and sentences

I moved to Greenland so that I could be close to my grandmother (literally: I moved to Greenland because I wanted to be close to my grandmother).

The suffix **-jumavoq** (or its variants **-kkumavoq**, **-rumavoq**, and **-umavoq** 'to want to'; see section 7.5 for explanation of when each variant is used) can be combined with the contemporative to convey purpose clauses in the same way as **+niarpoq**, e.g.:

Aputaajaajumalluta anivugut.
aputaajaa-juma-lluta ani-vugut
clear.snow-in.order.to-CONT.1PL go.out-1PL
We went out in order to clear snow.

The suffix **-riarpoq** (or its variants **-kkiarpoq** and **-giarpoq**) 'to go in order to do something (an activity or an event)' can also be attached to a verb in order to form a purpose clause. These suffixes are typically found only in conjunction with certain specific verbs, so it is best to learn each one individually, e.g. **qitippoq** 'to dance' > **qitikkiarpoq** 'to go out in order to dance, to go out dancing'; **nuniappoq** 'to pick berries' > **nuniagiarpoq** 'to go out in order to pick berries, to go out berry-picking'; **sisorarpoq** 'to ski' > **sisorariarpoq** 'to go out in order to ski, to go out skiing'.

14.5.1.5 Temporal

Temporal clauses give information about when something has happened or will happen. In English they are typically introduced by 'when', e.g. 'when I opened the door I heard laughter'.

In West Greenlandic, temporal clauses can be formed by means of a verb in the causative, conditional, or contemporative mood. The causative mood is typically used in past contexts, while the conditional is used in future contexts, and the contemporative can be used in either. In such instances, the causative, conditional, or contemporative verb may appear on its own or may be augmented by another suffix indicating a specific temporal nuance. These types of constructions are discussed in sections 7.2.2.1 (causative mood), 7.2.2.2 (conditional mood), and 7.2.2.3 (contemporative mood).

Temporal clauses can also be formed by means of the abstract participle **+neq** (see section 8.3) in the locative case. When translated into English, this type of construction literally means something like 'in X's doing Y'. Idiomatically, they correspond to English constructions with 'during' or 'while'. The following sentences illustrate this type of temporal clause.

Complex sentences

Mikisuuninni walkmaneqarpunga.
miki-su-u-ni-nni walkman-e-qar-punga
be.small-IP-be-AP-LOC.4SG walkman-HV-have-1SG
During my childhood, I had a Walkman.

Qassiarsummiinnissinni oqalufik alakkassavarsi.
qassiarsum-mi-in-ni-ssinni oqalufik alakka-ssa-varsi
qassiarsuk-LOC-be-AP-LOC.2PL church go.to-FUT-2PL>3SG
During your stay in Qassiarsuk, you should[11] go to the church.

Iisaakkut Danmarkimiinneranni illuat paarivara.
iisaa-kkut danmarki-mi-in-ner-anni illu-at paari-vara
iisaaq-COLL denmark-LOC-be-AP-LOC.3PL house-3PL take.care.of-1SG>3SG
While Isaaq and the others were in Denmark, I took care of their house.

Københavnimiinnermini ukiortaami ilassinninnermut peqataassaaq.
københavni-mi-in-ner-mini ukiortaa-mi ilassinninner-mut peqataa-ssaaq
copenhagen-LOC-be-AP-LOC.3SG new.year-LOC reception-ALL take.part-FUT.3SG
While he is in Copenhagen, he is going to take part in a New Year's reception.

This type of construction can be given a more specific temporal sense by means of a postposition such as **tungaanut** 'until' (see section 10), e.g.:

Sinilernissama tungaanut sulivunga.
sini-ler-ni-ssa-ma tungaanut suli-vunga
sleep-start-AP-FUT-REL.1SG until work-1SG
I worked until I fell asleep.

---

11 Literally: will.

14 Phrases, clauses, and sentences

The suffix +gaangat/-raangat/-kkaangat 'when, every time, whenever' can be used in conjunction with a verbal stem to form a temporal clause, e.g.:

Unnukkaangat ullorissat nuisarput.
unnu-kkaangat ullorissa-t nui-sar-put
become.evening-whenever star-PL appear-HAB-3PL
When the evening comes, the stars usually appear.

14.5.2 Relative

A relative clause is a subordinate clause that gives more information about a noun appearing in a main clause. In English, relative clauses are introduced by 'who', 'which', or 'that', for example, 'that's the man who knows Greenlandic'.

Relative clauses in West Greenlandic are typically composed of the intransitive participle +toq/+soq, which is suffixed to the verb denoting the action of the clause. The following examples illustrate Greenlandic sentences with a relative clause. See section 8.1 (on the intransitive participle) for further discussion and examples.

Anaanaga igaffimmi erruisoq ikiulaassavara.
anaana-ga igaffim-mi errui-soq ikiu-laa-ssa-vara
mother-1SG kitchen-LOC wash.up-IP help-a.little.bit-FUT-3SG>3SG
I'm just going to help my mother, who is washing up in the kitchen.

Suliassaq pissangananngittoq suliarivara.
suliassaq pissangana-nngit-toq suliari-vara
assignment excite-NEG-IP work.with-1SG>3SG
I am working on the assignment, which is not exciting.

The head noun of a relative clause (i.e. the noun introducing a relative clause) can be omitted, resulting in a relative construction with a meaning similar to the English 'the one who, the one that', e.g.:

Igaffimmi sulisoq qatanngutigivara.
igaffim-mi suli-soq qatannguti-givara
kitchen-LOC work-IP be.sibling-have.as.1SG>3SG
The one who works in the kitchen is my sibling.

If the relative element is the object of the relative clause, +toq/+soq is not used. Instead, the verb takes a passive participle suffix

(-aq/-gaq/-saq/-taq, etc.; see section 8.2), as in the following example. Note that in some cases the relative element of the Greenlandic sentence will correspond more closely to an English adjectival construction than to a relative one.

Complex sentences

neqi siataq
neqi sia-taq
meat fry-PP
meat that is fried[12]

In many cases, the passive participle takes a nominal possessive suffix (see section 3.4) to mark the subject of the relative clause, e.g.:

Atuagaq atuagara pissanganarpoq.
atuagaq atua-ga-ra pissanganar-poq
book read-PP-1SG excite-3SG
The book which I'm reading is exciting.[13]

Arsaattut isiginnaakkakka naammaannarput.
arsaattu-t isiginnaa-kka-kka naammaannar-put.
football.game-PL watch-PP-PL.1SG be.mediocre-3PL
The football game that I was watching was boring.

Ataatap annoraaq atugaa oqorpoq.
ataata-p annoraaq atu-ga-a oqor-poq
father-REL anorak wear-PP-1SG be.warm-3SG
The anorak which dad is wearing is warm.

Qitsuk nukkama asasaa ittoorpoq.
qitsuk nukka-ma asa-sa-a ittoor-poq
cat younger.sibling-REL.1SG love-PP-3SG be.shy-3SG
The cat that my younger sibling loves is shy.

Qimmeq paarisara kusanarpoq.
qimmeq paari-sa-ra kusanar-poq
dog take.care.of-PP-1SG be.nice-3SG
The dog that I'm taking care of is nice.

---

12 Or: fried meat.
13 Literally: my read book is exciting.

14.5.3 Complement

Complement clauses usually follow main clauses with verbs of cognition, perception, understanding, or desire, such as 'think', 'know', 'hope', 'discover', etc. In English complement clauses are introduced by 'that', e.g. 'he knows that he has to do it'. In West Greenlandic complement clauses are typically formed by means of the contemporative mood (if both clauses have the same subject; see 7.2.2.3) or participial mood (if both clauses have a different subject; see 7.2.2.4), e.g.:

Nunaqarfimmut tikikkamik paasivaa <u>uini allamik nuliarsimasoq</u>.
nunaqarfim-mut tikik-kamik paasi-vaa ui-ni alla-mik nuliar-sima-soq
town-ALL arrive-CAUS.4SG discover-3SG>3SG husband-4SG another-INS marry-PAST-PART.3SG
When she arrived in the town, she discovered that her husband had married another.

There is a special suffix, +gasugaa (which has several variants, such as +nasugaa, +sorigaa, +gasorigaa), meaning 'to believe that someone/something is ...'. The end of this suffix is actually a suffix of its own, +gaa/+raa, which can itself mean 'to regard someone/something as'; see section 14.4.7. This compound suffix often appears in contexts corresponding to English complement clauses, e.g.:

Qallunaajusoraakkit.
qallunaa-ju-sora-akkit
danish-be-believe-regard.1SG>2SG
I thought you were Danish.

Asagasugaanga.
asa-gasu-gaanga
love-believe-regard.3SG>1SG
S/he believes that s/he loves me.

List of essential suffixes

There are around 400–500 nominal and verbal suffixes in West Greenlandic. The following section contains a selection of some of the most widely used ones, listed in alphabetical order. Familiarity with these suffixes will be of great help in learning West Greenlandic. Note that this list does not include nominal case and possessive suffixes, verbal person and mood suffixes, or enclitic suffixes.

Suffix	Example
+allaarpoq, **+pallaarpoq**, **+vallaarpoq** too much	**sulivoq** to work > **sulivallaarpoq** to work too much
+aq, **+gaq**, **+saq**, **+taq** PASSIVE PARTICIPLE	**nerivaa** to eat it > **nerisaq** eaten
+figaa (or **+figivaa**) VALENCY, to do it, to do it to/for him/her	**oqarpoq** to say > **oqarfigaa** to say something to him or her
+fik place, object	**sinippoq** to sleep > **siniffik** bed
+gaa, **+raa** (or **+givaa**, **+rivaa**) to have as one's ...; to use it as; to regard it as	**erneq** son > **erneraa** s/he has him as his/her son (i.e. he is his/her son)
-galuarpoq, **-kkaluarpoq**, **-raluarpoq** if only, although, would but ...	**sulivoq** to work > **suligaluarpoq** would work, but...
+gunarpoq, **-kkunarpoq**, **-runarpoq** to seem to be	**siallerpoq** to rain > **siallerunarpoq** it seems to be raining
+juaannarpoq, **-tuaannarpoq**, **-uaannarpoq** always, all the time	**apivoq** to snow > **apiuaannarpoq** it snows all the time

List of essential suffixes

Suffix	Example
-kkut and company, and family, and crew	**Jensen** Jensen > **Jensenikkut** the Jensen family
-koq former; old; ruined	**suleqat** colleague > **suleqakoq** former colleague
-laarpoq a little bit	**issippoq** to be cold (of weather) > **issilaarpoq** it's a little bit cold
-lerpoq to begin; to be going to; to be about to	**atuarpoq** to study > **atualerpoq** to begin studying
-lik having X	**orpik** tree > **orpilik** tree-filled
-liorpoq, **-siorpoq** to make, to build	**kaagi** cake > **kaagiliorpoq** to make cake
+luarpoq, **-lluarpoq** to do well	**sinippoq** to sleep > **sinilluarpoq** to sleep well
+miippoq (with SG noun), **+niippoq** (with PL noun) to be in	**Nuuk** Nuuk > **Nuummiippoq** to be in Nuuk
+mukarpoq (with SG noun), **+nukarpoq** (with PL noun) to go to	**Nuuk** Nuuk > **Nuummukarpoq** to go to Nuuk
+neq ABSTRACT PARTICIPLE	**qitippoq** to dance > **qitinneq** dancing
+neqarpoq PASSIVE	**takuaa** to see it > **takuneqarpoq** to be seen
+neruvoq to be more; to be the most	**mikivoq** to be small > **mikineruvoq** to be smaller; to be the smallest
+niarpoq to intend to, to want to, to try to	**angalavoq** to travel > **angalaniarpoq** to intend to travel
+nikuuvoq PAST TENSE; used to	**biilerpoq** to drive > **biilernikuuvoq** drove
-nngilaq NEGATION	**imerpoq** to drink > **iminngilaq** s/he doesn't drink
-nngorpoq to become	**præsidenti** president > **præsidentinngorpoq** to become president

List of essential suffixes

-nnguaq little and cute	**qimmeq** dog > **qimmennguaq** cute little dog
-qaaq very, a lot	**ajorpoq** to be bad > **ajoqaaq** to be very bad, to be terrible
-qarpoq to have; to be there	**meeraq** child > **meeraqarpoq** to have a child/children; there is a child/there are children
+qatigiipput to do something with each other, to be equally something	**nerivoq** to eat > **neriqatigiipput** to eat together
-qquaa CAUSATIVE, to make, to ask, to invite	**iserpoq** to go/come in > **iseqquaa** to ask him/her to come in
-riarpoq, -kkiarpoq, -giarpoq to set out, to go somewhere	**arpappoq** to run > **arpakkiarpoq** to go out for a run
-reerpoq PERFECT TENSE; already	**makippoq** to get up > **makereerpoq** s/he has already got up
-rusuppoq, -kkusuppoq, -usuppoq to want to	**aalisarpoq** to fish > **aalisarusuppoq** to want to fish
+simavoq PAST TENSE; apparently it happened (not witnessed)	**aappanippoq** to get married > **aappanissimavoq** s/he got married
+sinnaavoq to be able	**atuarpoq** to read > **atuarsinnaavoq** to be able to read
+sivoq to buy	**iffiaq** bread > **iffiarsivoq** to buy bread
-ssaaq FUTURE TENSE	**inerpoq** to be ready > **inissaaq** s/he will be ready
-ssaq future (with nouns)	**ui** husband > **uissaq** future husband
+(r)suaq (SG), **+(r)suit** (PL) big	**nerrivik** table > **nerrivissuaq** big table

List of essential suffixes

Suffix	Example
+tariaqarpoq, +sariaqarpoq to have to	**sulivoq** to work > **sulisariaqarpoq** s/he has to work
+tarpoq, +sarpoq HABITUAL, usually	**aalisarpoq** to fish **aalisartarpoq** to fish regularly, to fish habitually, to fish usually
+toq, +soq INTRANSITIVE PARTICIPLE	**erinarsorpoq** to sing > **erinarsortoq** one who sings
+torpoq, +sorpoq to consume, to eat, to drink	**kaffi** coffee > **kaffisorpoq** to drink coffee **neqi** meat > **neqisorpoq** to eat meat
+/-uppaa, -appaa VALENCY, to do something with it, for him/her	**tikippoq** to arrive > **tikiuppaa** to arrive with it
-uvoq, -avoq, -juvoq to be	**peqqissaasoq** nurse > **peqqissaasuuvoq** to be a nurse

Suggested resources

The following resources are helpful for learners of West Greenlandic. Note that many of them are written in Danish.

Grammars of West Greenlandic

Bjørnum, Stig. 2012. *Grønlandsk grammatik*. Forlaget Atuagkat.
Fortescue, Michael. 1984. *West Greenlandic*. Croom Helm Descriptive Grammars.
Janussen, Estrid. 2001. *Håndbog i grønlandsk grammatik*. Ilinniusiorfik.
Lennert Olsen, Lise and Birgitte Hertling. 2011. *Grønlandsk tilhængsliste*. Ilinniusiorfik.
Nielsen, Flemming A.J. 2014. *Vest-Grønlandsk Grammatik*. www.groenlandskgrammatik.dk/
Sadock, Jerrold M. 2003. *A Grammar of Kalaallisut*. Languages of the World/Materials 162. Lincom Europe.

Textbooks of West Greenlandic

Brochmann, Helene. 2006. *Qanoq 1*. Ilinniusiorfik.
Hertling, Birgitte and Pia Rosing Heilmann. 2007. *Qaagit*. Ilinniusiorfik.
Meilvang, Bente. 2016. *Kalaallisut ilikkarit 1*. Ilikkarit.

Dictionaries of West Greenlandic

Berthelsen, Chr. et al. 2013. *Oqaatsit Kalaallisuumiit Qallunaatuumut/ Grønlandsk Dansk Ordbog*. Ilinniusiorfik.
Petersen, Robert et al. 2003. *Ordbogen: dansk–grønlandsk/qallunaatut–kalaallisut*. Ilinniusiorfik.

Graded readers of West Greenlandic

Berthelsen, Christian. 2012. *Kalaallisut sungiusaatit 28-t*. Ilinniusiorfik.

Suggested resources

Phrasebooks

Hertling, Birgitte. 2013. *Grønlandsk parlør*. Hertling.

Online resources for West Greenlandic

Comprehensive West Greenlandic–Danish–West Greenlandic dictionary (online version of Berthelsen et al. and Petersen et al.): www.ilinniusiorfik.gl/oqaatsit/daka
West Greenlandic newspaper – *Sermitsiaq*: http://sermitsiaq.ag/
Greenlandic Broadcasting Corporation – *Kalaallit Nunaata Radioa (KNR)*: http://knr.gl/kl
The Language Secretariat of Greenland – *Oqaasileriffik*: https://oqaasileriffik.gl/en/
The Greenlandic House in Copenhagen – *Kalaallit Illutaat*: www.sumut.dk/
Learn Greenlandic website by Per Langgård: https://learngreenlandic.com/
West Greenlandic morphological generator: https://oqaasileriffik.gl/sprogteknologi/lookdown/
Kleinschmidt orthography converter: https://tech.oqaasileriffik.gl/tools/kleinschmidt/
Greenlandic bookshop – *Atuagkat*: www.atuagkat.gl/

Resources on Eskimo-Aleut languages

Fortescue, Michael, Steven Jacobson, and Lawrence Kaplan. 2010. *Comparative Eskimo Dictionary with Aleut Cognates*. Alaska Native Language Center.
Holst, Jan Henrik. 2005. *Einführung in die eskimo-aleutischen Sprachen*. Helmut Buske Verlag.
Online textbook of Inuktitut: https://tusaalanga.ca/

Index

abbreviations xiii–xiv, 13–16
ablative 31, 52–54, 76–78, 111, 113, 134, 216, 308–310
absolutive 12, 15–16, 31, 48, 64–67, 124–125, 150–151, 216, 222, 281, 285, 305, 311, 313, 315, 316, 322
abstract participle 245, 257–261, 268, 328–329
additive suffix 12–13, 23, 292
adjective: see noun modification
adverbial clause 325–329
adverb 262–280; degree, measure, and quantity 272–277; direction: see place and direction; interrogative 279–280; manner 262–265; modal 278–279; negative 244; place and direction 270–272; time 266–270
agreement 109–110, 115, 132, 136
allative 50–51 , 71–73, 112–113, 308
alphabet 3, 10–11, 17
aspect 201–205; completed 201; habitual 201–204; inchoative 204–205
assimilation 23, 26, 44, 45, 254
attributive 119–129, 132

cardinal numerals 105–114
case 9, 31–32, 48–63; ablative 31, 52–54, 76–78, 111, 113, 134, 216, 308–310; absolutive 12, 15–16, 31, 48, 64–67, 124–125, 150–151, 216, 222, 281, 285, 305, 311, 313, 315, 316, 322; allative 50–51 , 71–73, 112–113, 308; equative 31–32, 63–64, 83–85; grammatical 31, 38, 40, 43, 44, 46, 47; incorporated 308–311; instrumental 31–32, 54–60, 78–81, 103, 108, 110–111, 125–126, 130, 134, 259–260, 262, 272, 311, 315, 316, 319; locative 10, 26, 31–32, 51–52, 73–76, 88, 111, 115, 259–260, 271, 282, 285, 308, 328–329; oblique 31, 40, 47, 79, 81, 84, 89, 97, 99, 222, 308–311; prolative 31–32, 38, 60–62, 81–83, 309; relative 16, 31–32, 33, 40, 41, 43, 44, 45, 49–50, 56, 68–70, 111, 112–113, 115, 117, 138, 150, 222, 254–255, 258, 259, 260, 281, 282, 285, 315–316, 322; with possessive suffixes 64–85
causal clause 260, 325–326
causative mood 143, 144–145, 166–172, 178, 190, 194–195, 233–235, 268, 287–288, 325–326, 327–328
causativity 210–214, 217, 316
clause; adverbial 325–329; complement 144, 180, 184, 332; conditional 327; double transitive 316; existential 317–318; half-transitive 316; impersonal 323–324; interrogative 324; intransitive 313–315; possessive 319–323; relative 330–331; transitive 315–316
collective suffix 85–86
comparative 53, 132–135
comparison 53, 132–141
complement clause 144, 180, 184, 332
completed aspect 201
complex sentence 292, 325–332
conditional; clause 327; mood 172–178, 235–237
conjunction 291–292; coordinating 291–292; subordinating 292
consonant 19–22, 23–25
consonant change 23–25
consonant-stem 28, 142
contemporative 178–184, 237–239
coordinating conjunction 291–292
copular clause 312–313

definiteness 55–56, 311–312
demonstrative 90–93
diphthong 19
direct object 31, 48–50, 56–57, 125, 143, 210, 219, 222–223, 305–308, 311
discourse particle 293–294
double transitive 316

enclitic particle 9, 24, 288, 291–292, 294–296

Index

equative 31–32, 63–64, 83–85
Eskimo-Aleut 1–3, 10
evidentiality 207–210
existential clause 317–318

fourth person 64, 143, 166, 172, 178, 179, 182, 185
future tense 175, 195–200

gender 9
glide 19, 27
glossing 13–16
grammatical case 31, 38, 40, 43, 44, 46, 47

habitual aspect 201–204
half-transitive clause 316
helping vowel 26–27

imperative mood 156–162, 230–232
impersonal clause 323–324
inchoative aspect 204–205
incorporation 10, 57, 303–311; direct object 125, 305–308; noun 10, 57, 125, 303–311; oblique case 308–311; predicative 303–305
indefiniteness 55–57, 311, 315
independent; mood 145–165; pronoun 87–88
indicative mood 16, 144, 145–151, 225–227
instrumental 31–32, 54–60, 78–81, 103, 108, 110–111, 125–126, 130, 134, 259–260, 262, 272, 311, 315, 316, 319
interjection 293–294
interrogative; clause 324; mood 151–156, 227–229; pronoun 93–96; sentence 324
intonation 22–23, 151, 324
intransitive; clause 313–315; verb 9, 16, 145

Kleinschmidt 5, 30
k-stem 28, 34–36, 46–47

locative 10, 26, 31–32, 51–52, 73–76, 88, 111, 115, 259–260, 271, 282, 285, 308, 328–329

metathesis 43–45
modality 205–207
modifier 119–132, 301–302; attributive 119–129, 132; comparative 53, 132–135; predicative 129–132; superlative 135–141
mood; causative 143, 144–145, 166–172, 178, 190, 194–195, 233–235, 268, 287–288, 325–326, 327–328; conditional 172–178, 235–237; contemporative 178–184, 237–239; imperative 156–162, 230–232; independent 145–165; indicative 16, 144, 145–151, 225–227; interrogative 151–156, 227–229; main 145–165; optative 162–165, 232–233; participial 184–189, 239–240; subordinate 165–190
morphophonological variation 23–29

negation 224–247
negative suffix 224–244
noun; case 9, 31–32, 48–63; gender 9; k-stem 28, 34–36, 46–47; number 31–32; q-stem 40–42; stem type 32–47; strong-stem 40–47; t-stem 28, 38–39; weak-stem 33–39
noun incorporation 10, 57, 125, 303–311
noun modification 119–141
number 31–32
numeral 105–118; cardinal 105–114; ordinal 114–118

object; direct 31, 48–50, 56–57, 125, 143, 210, 219, 222–223, 305–308, 311; indirect 50, 57, 222; suffixes 143
oblique case 31, 40, 47, 79, 81, 84, 89, 97, 99, 222, 308–311
optative 62–165, 232–233
order of suffixes 298–300
ordinal numeral 114–118
orthography 5, 17; Kleinschmidt's 30

participial 184–189, 239–240
participle 248–261; abstract 245–247, 257–261; intransitive 119–120, 122, 248–252; passive 218–219, 252–256
particle; discourse 293–294; enclitic 9, 24, 288, 291–292, 294–296
passive 215–219; participle 18–219, 252–256
passivity 215–219
past tense 169, 172, 190, 191–195
periphrastic construction 245–247
person 142; fourth 64, 143, 166, 172, 178, 179, 182, 185
personal pronoun 87–89
phonology 17–29
phrase 301–302
possessive; clause 319–323; phrase 49–50; suffix 64–85, 99, 101, 117, 124, 137–138, 254, 258, 259, 281–285
postposition 281–290; direction and place 281–290; other 288–290; time 285–288
predicative 129–132; incorporated 303–305
present tense 90
prolative 31–32, 38, 60–62, 81–83, 309

Index

pronoun 87–104; demonstrative 90–93; interrogative 93–96; other 100–104; personal 87–89; reciprocal 98–100; reflexive 96–98

q-stem 40–42

reciprocal; pronoun 98–100; verb 214–215
reciprocity 98–100, 214–215
reflexive; pronoun 96–98; verb 213–214
reflexivity 96–98, 213–214
relative; case 16, 31–32, 33, 40, 41, 43, 44, 45, 49–50, 56, 68–70, 111, 112–113, 115, 117, 138, 150, 222, 254–255, 258, 259, 260, 281, 282, 285, 315–316, 322; clause 330–331
r-stem 28, 142

sentence; complex 92, 325–332; interrogative 324
sound alternation: 23–29
stem type 28; nouns 32–47; verbs 142
stress 22
strong-stem 40–47
subject 48–49, 142
subordinate; clause 143, 292; mood 165–190
subordinating conjunction 292
suffixes; additive 12–13, 23, 292; case 48–63; collective 85–86; essential 333–336; negative 224–244; object 143; order of 298–300; possessive 64–85, 99, 101, 117, 124, 137–138, 254, 258, 259, 281–285; subject 142–143; truncative 12–13, 25

superlative 135–141
syllable 19, 22

tense; future 175, 195–200; past 169, 172, 190, 191–195; present 90
transitive; clause 315–316; double 316; half- 316; verb 9, 16, 143
truncative suffix 12–13, 25
t-stem 28, 38–39

valency 219–224
variation; morphophonological 23–29
verb; causative 143, 144–145, 166–172, 178, 190, 194–195, 233–235, 268, 287–288, 325–326, 327–328; conditional 172–178, 235–237; consonant-stem 28, 142; contemporative 178–184, 237–239; double transitive 316; half-transitive 316; imperative 156–162, 230–232; independent 145–165; indicative 16, 144, 145–151, 225–227; interrogative 151–156, 227–229; intransitive 9, 16, 145; negative 224–244; optative 162–165, 232–233; participial 184–189, 239–240; r-stem 28, 142; subordinate 165–190; transitive 9, 16, 143; vowel-stem 28, 33, 34–35, 142
vowel 17–19; helping 26–27
vowel change 25–26
vowel-stem 28, 33, 34–35, 142

weak-stem 33–39
word order 9, 301–302

Taylor & Francis eBooks

www.taylorfrancis.com

A single destination for eBooks from Taylor & Francis with increased functionality and an improved user experience to meet the needs of our customers.

90,000+ eBooks of award-winning academic content in Humanities, Social Science, Science, Technology, Engineering, and Medical written by a global network of editors and authors.

TAYLOR & FRANCIS EBOOKS OFFERS:

A streamlined experience for our library customers

A single point of discovery for all of our eBook content

Improved search and discovery of content at both book and chapter level

REQUEST A FREE TRIAL
support@taylorfrancis.com

Printed in Great Britain
by Amazon